Concise Desk Guide

to Real Estate

Practice and Procedure

Other Books by Jerome S. Gross

*Illustrated Encyclopedic Dictionary
of Real Estate Terms*

Encyclopedia of Real Estate Forms

Concise Desk Guide

to Real Estate

Practice and Procedure

JEROME S. GROSS

PRENTICE-HALL, INC.

ENGLEWOOD CLIFFS, N. J.

Prentice-Hall International, Inc., of *London*
Prentice-Hall of Australia, Pty. Ltd., *Sydney*
Prentice-Hall of Canada, Ltd., *Toronto*
Prentice-Hall of India, Private Ltd., *New Delhi*
Prentice-Hall of Japan, Inc., *Tokyo*

"This publication is designed to provide accurate and authoritative information with regard to the subject matter covered. It is sold with the
understanding that the publisher is not engaged in rendering legal, accounting, or other professional advice. If legal advice or other expert
assistance is required, the services of a competent professional person
should be sought."

*—From a Declaration of Principles jointly adopted by a
Committee of the American Bar Association and a Committee of Publishers and Associations.*

Library of Congress Cataloging in Publication Data

Gross, Jerome S
   Concise desk guide to real estate practice and
procedure.

   Includes index.
   1.   Real estate business--Handbooks, manuals, etc.
2.   Real estate business--United States--Handbooks,
manuals, etc.   I.   Title.
HD1375.G728   658'.91'33333   75-28326
ISBN 0-13-166934-6

Printed in the United States of America

To Jane Gross

WHAT THIS DESK GUIDE

WILL DO FOR YOU

Within the pages of this desk guide you will find not only a concise compendium of information on the most important aspects of real estate practices, but also clear guidelines and tested procedures for applying that information in the day-to-day activities of the real estate office. This book not only will tell you what it's all about, it will show you what to do with this information and how you should do it.

When I was breaking into the real estate field some 20 years ago, I could have used such a book. I needed the facts and techniques explained to me clearly not the soporific treatises on real estate theory offered at that time. There seemed to be little literature available that delved into the essential, work-a-day, details of conducting a profitable real estate business. Theory, yes, but the "meat and potatoes" of how to be a success in this field was barely touched upon.

I suppose the concept of this desk guide began to take shape even then. Over the years, I have kept an ever-expanding file of what I found to be the most useful and essential information on real estate practice and procedure. These notes were maintained strictly for my own edification, but when I began researching material for this book in earnest, they were there for my use. This book is, then, a distillation of my experience in real estate over the past two decades.

Clearly, only the fittest will survive and thrive in real estate. This diverse, never static, field demands that you have a firm grasp on much more than just the basics. Whether you are dealing with homeowners and sellers or with sophisticated investors, mortgage bankers and attorneys; with a vacant lot, a family residence or a multi-million dollar high-rise complex, a high degree of expertise is required. In order to be successful in any of these transactions, you must have a clear, working understanding of all the procedures and details involved. This work is designed to give you that understanding. It covers all of the most essential aspects of real estate practice. It is written in non-technical, concise and, I trust, easy-to-grasp language. It will provide all real estate personnel with a working knowledge of everything from A (Appraising) to Z (Zoning)—not just the facts, but how to apply them in your day-to-day dealings.

A chapter on "Condominiums and Cooperatives," for example, first tells you what these forms of ownership are all about, then shows you how these concepts are translated into by-laws, contracts, deeds and leases. Then it tells you in very concrete terms how to promote and sell a condominium unit. Other chapters follow this same pattern—facts and their applications. In addition, you will find a concise guide to real estate law, a complete glossary of the most important real estate terms, over 30 effective model letters and a final section containing the charts and financial tables you will need in your every-day dealings. I have endeavored to provide a ready-reference covering in an authoritative and brief way all the information you will find useful in the practice of real estate, whether you are in the office or out in the field. Finally, this book is backed by my many years of practical experience as an active Realtor.

Jerome S. Gross

Contents

3. CONDOMINIUMS AND COOPERATIVES *(cont.)*

4. EXCHANGING 83

5. INVESTING IN REAL ESTATE 97

6. INVESTMENT ALTERNATIVES—SYNDICATES AND REITS 111

7. LEASING 123

Concise Desk Guide

to Real Estate

Practice and Procedure

1

APPRAISALS

*The Modern Appraiser's Role . . . Forms of Value . . .
Highest and Best Use . . . Evaluating Vacant Land . . .
Cost Approach to Value . . . Market Comparison . . .
Capitalization of Income . . . Evaluation by
Correlation . . . Affidavit and Certificate of
Appraisal . . . Appraisal Report in Letter Form . . .
Appraisal Report (Another Form) . . . The Formal
Book-Bound Report . . . Basic Ethics . . . Appraisal
Fees . . . Appraisal Societies.*

THE MODERN APPRAISER'S ROLE

The appraiser's function is to estimate value. But before he can effectively do this he must have a thorough knowledge of the forces that create value in his community. Social changes such as growth and shifts in population; physical features, as the topography of the area and its natural resources; governmental restrictions, as zoning ordinances and building codes; and the economic trends, including building cycles. Is the area prospering? Will it continue, and if so for how long? Which neighborhoods will be favorably or adversely effected? These are the underlying aspects of the community he must be familiar with. An appraiser will, thus, be expected to knowledgeably estimate the direction future development will take.

Nothing is static in real estate. A good appraiser, always aware of this, must make a conscious effort to know his community's past, present and future before he can presume to estimate value properly. He should be aware of a neighborhood's amenities as well as its deficiencies. In short, he must be an informed, aware, real estate expert.

FORMS OF VALUE

Appraisals are made for numerous reasons. An appraiser must first determine the purpose of his report before he can proceed with estimating value.

Most appraisals are made to determine market or sales value. (What properties will bring on the open market under normal conditions.) However, appraisers also make evaluations for determining assessed value, loan value, insurance value, leasehold value, business value, liquidation value, litigation value (for fraud, damage, estate division, and condemnation), as well as for other special purposes. Once the reason for making the appraisal is determined he can proceed from a definite and logical base.

Highest and Best Use

When an appraiser calculates value he must take into account whether the property is being put to its highest and best use—that is, its most productive, logical use over a period of time. It means the utilization of property to bring the greatest present and future benefit (usually monetary) to the owner.

Evaluating Vacant Land

Evaluating unimproved land, as distinct from sites already built upon, can be arrived at by any one or combination of the following methods:

1. *Market Comparison*. This technique is the most frequently used. The appraiser carefully studies the sales in an area. If no recent sales were

made, or if they occurred too infrequently for him to form a valid conclusion, then one or more of the other methods must be applied.

2. *Anticipated Development Method.* Applied to undeveloped land, the cost to make needed improvements, such as roads, utilities, and sidewalks, is taken into account. Add to this other costs, as surveyor fees, sales commissions, advertising, taxes, and carrying charges. After including a profit for the promoter, a market price of each site can be estimated.

3. *Distribution of Value.* When an improved property's selling price is known, appraisers frequently are called upon to determine the distribution of values between land and the improvements. This situation occurs particularly with commercial real estate, where depreciation of the improvement is important for tax purposes. As land, on the other hand, is *not* a factor in gaining depreciation benefits, an owner needs to know the value of the land, as apart from the buildings. Here the appraiser has several ways of determining land value alone. Public records and tax bills generally show separate assessed valuations. He may also check vacant land sales in the area under study with comparable improved property sales. A pattern establishing land values of the improved properties will soon emerge. Though slight variations are bound to exist, logical conclusions invariably can be reached.

4. *Residual Value.* This is the assigning of a selling price to vacant land after a hypothetical improvement representing the land's highest and best use is projected for it. As an example, if a 10-story, 100 unit apartment house that will net the owner $25,000 is seen as bringing the highest yield to the property, by using the Capitalization of Income Method[1] the land value can be determined with a reasonably high degree of accuracy. This method is often used as a check against other techniques for establishing land values.

THE THREE METHODS OF MAKING APPRAISALS

It is accepted as good appraisal practice to evaluate improved real

---

[1]See page 20

property, when possible, by the three acknowledged appraisal methods—Cost Approach to Value, Market Comparison, Capitalization of Income—and then correlate these conclusions to arrive at a knowledgeable, single estimate of value.

1. *Cost Approach to Value.* This method is arrived at by first determining the reproduction (replacement) cost of the improvement in today's market, and deducting the accrued depreciation.[2] Then add the land value. In formula form, it is expressed as: Reproduction Cost − Depreciation + Land Value = Market Value. When done properly the technique of carefully determining the cost to duplicate a property gives the appraiser valuable conclusions that allow him to reach an accurate judgment of worth.

2. *Market Comparison.* This is the appraisal method of obtaining the recent selling prices of as many comparable properties as possible, and using them to arrive at a logical conclusion of the market price of the property under study. It is based on the realistic maxim that real estate is worth only what it will sell for on the open market. The problem confronting appraisers when using this method, however, is that real estate is not a standardized product such as an automobile of a certain year, make and model. No two properties are alike and many factors must be considered before a true basis of comparison can be reached. Nevertheless, the Market Comparison method is widely used by appraisers and assessors, and is given much credence when the information is accurately obtained.

3. *Capitalization of Income.* Because of the many variable factors, the most complex method of appraising is the Capitalization of Income approach, yet appraisers consider this method as the most important when investment real estate is under study. Value is determined by the net income a property is able to generate under typical management[3] (Gross Income − Expenses = Net Income). An appropriate capitalization rate is determined.[4] This may vary with the type of property, fluctuation of the real estate market, remaining life expectancy of the property, future of the community and immediate neighborhood, as well as a host of other factors. Once the capitalization rate (%) is fixed, multiply it by the net income to arrive at a fair market value.

---

[2]Depreciation, as used here, is the difference between the replacement cost and the market value of the property.

[3]Net income is before interest payments on mortgages and depreciation are deducted.

[4]The percentage of return or yield expected on cash invested.

Another method for finding value under this approach is by multiplying the gross income by an established multiplier. Real estate men have devised formulas for the various types of investment properties, but like all realty, it is an ever-changing figure based on risks, areas, condition and types of property. For example, old apartment houses in some cities are valued at 5 times the gross annual rentals, while newer ones as high as 9 times. Warehouses 8-11, office buildings 6-8, shopping centers 8-9, net leases 10-15, and stores 7-10. Experts agree, however, that this method, at best, is only an indication of value and should only be used as a rule-of-thumb.

EVALUATION BY CORRELATION

Most appraisers use the three recognized value approaches discussed above first as separate entities, then by correlating the conclusions into one single estimate of value. Sometimes, all three approaches cannot be used. (For example, the income approach obviously would not be applicable for house appraisals.) But when at least two independent approaches can be made and then correlated, the conclusions thus reached generally represent the appraiser's most accurate judgment of value.

MAKING THE APPRAISAL REPORT

Appraisal documents can vary from a one-page report on the appraiser's letterhead, to a formal ring- or book-bound, comprehensive study complete with maps, plats, elevation drawings, structural details, aerial and ground photos, etc. Some are made in the form of an affidavit or certificate, or the combination of these. Examples follow:

AFFIDAVIT AND CERTIFICATE OF APPRAISAL FORM

State of New York

County of Nassau

})ss:

Edward Brown being duly sworn, deposes and says:

1. I reside at 246 Grey Street, in the City of Hempstead, and State of New York. I have been duly licensed by the State of New York as a licensed real estate broker. I maintain an office for the transaction of business at 188 Blue Street, in the city of Hempstead, State of New York.

2. At the request of Henry R. Smith, I have made an investigation and analysis of the following described real property:

> Lots 10, and 11, block 17, Battersea Estates, plat book 14, page 72. More commonly known as 10185 Crandon Blvd., South Hempstead, New York

3. I am of the opinion that on the 1st day of June, 197- when I made a detailed inspection of the aforesaid premises, the market value of the land and improvements thereon was as follows: $80,000.
    $17,500 allocated as to land
    $62,500 allocated as to improvements

I CERTIFY that to the best of my knowledge and belief the evaluation contained in this Appraisal is correct.

4. I have no present or contemplated future interest in the property appraised, and the compensation for making this Appraisal is in no manner contingent upon the value reported.

5. The physical condition of the improvements described herein was based solely on visual inspection, and no liability is assumed for the soundness of structural members, since no engineering tests were made of the same.

IN WITNESS WHEREOF, I hereunto set my hand and seal on the day of   , 19   .

                                                        Edward Brown

Qualifications of Edward Brown

Senior Member, American Society of Appraisers
Member Appraisal Institute
Instructor In Real Estate, New York University
Licensed Real Estate Broker, Certificate No. 6467616

APPRAISAL REPORT

To Whom It May Concern:

I, Jerome S. Gross, do hereby state that upon the request of the Circuit

Court Of The Eleventh Judicial Circuit, Rockford County, New York, General Jurisdiction Division, Case No. 173 31 225 (Judge Peter R. Blake) I have made an inspection and analysis of the following described property:

> Lot 8, Block 11, Greenville Manors, Plat Book 58, Page 79, Rockford County, New York, more commonly known as a single family house at 3450 N.W. 183rd Street, Rock City, New York

and that I am of the opinion that on June 10, 197- when a detailed investigation of the premises was made, the *Market Value* of the land and improvements thereon was:

$$\$56,000$$

I further state that, to the best of my knowledge and belief, the evaluation contained in this appraisal is correct.

I have no present nor contemplated future interest in the property appraised, and compensation for making this appraisal is in no manner contingent upon the value reported.

The physical conditions of the improvements seemed sound throughout, but was based on visual inspection. No liability is assumed for the structural members since no engineering tests were made of same.

Respectfully submitted,

Jerome S. Gross
Realtor - Appraiser
Licensed Real Estate Broker
State of New York License No. 3446700-36-817076
Member, National Society of Fee Appraisers

THE FORMAL BOOK-BOUND REPORT

The full appraisal report has three distinct parts:

1. The introduction, containing the title page, table of contents, photographs, and a letter to the one ordering the report stating its purpose and the highpoints of the appraiser's conclusions (Letter of Transmittal). Also, a statement of the appraiser's qualifications.

APPRAISAL REPORT

PROPERTY LOCATION 10101 Silver Palm Rd., Miami, Florida
LEGAL DESCRIPTION Lot 7, Block 4, Broadview Estates, Plat Book 41, Page 16,
Dade County

Lot size 100_____ X 115_____ Construction: Existing X_____ Proposed _____
Living units 1_____ Construction CBS_____ (siding material) stucco_____ Stories 1_____ Age 15 yrs.
Rooms: LR 1___ DR 1___ K 1___ BR 3___ Closets 7___ Bath 2___Other Den

INTERIOR: Walls – Plaster X_____ Dry_____ Other_____
        Floors Terrazo & cement_____ Carpeting throughout-good quality
        Fireplace No_____
        Bathroom – Floor Terrazo_____ Wainscoting X_____ Fixtures 3 each
        Kitchen – Floor Tile_____ Appliances Gas range,dishwasher,refrig-freezer
        Air conditioning – Type Central rev.cycle_____ No. of Units one
        Water heater Gas_____ Heating central rev.cycle Fuel_____
ROOF: Type gable-tile Condition good_____ Gutters and downspouts good condition
WINDOWS: alum. jalousy AWNINGS: no_____ FENCE: 120' cyclone type
SWIMMING POOL: no_____ Screened yes_____ Roofed patio none
MISCELLANEOUS:

CONDITION: (a) Exterior excellent_____ Remaining useful life of building 40 years
       (b) Interior excellent_____ Recommended Repairs: none

GARAGE/CARPORT: none_____ Roof_____ No. of cars _____
    Size _____ Type of doors _____ Driveway _____
OTHER BUILDINGS: small tool house_____
UTILITIES: Sewer – X_____ Water X_____ Gas X_____ Electric X_____
    Well_____ Septic tank _____
STREET IMPROVEMENTS: Walks_____ Paving_____ C. & Gutter_____ Alley _____
ASSESSED VALUATION: $22,760._____ Homestead Exemption $5,000_____ Taxes $369.59
COMMENT: Neighborhood trend good residential. Most dwellings well kept
    Type structures Ranch_____ Condition Good_____ Age 15 years
    Any area detrimental influences: none apparent
    This property could rent for $400._____per month.
    The marketability of this property is very good_____ .
Perimeter drawing of building.

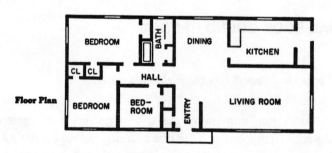

Floor Plan

Figure 1-1.

COMPUTATION – COST APPROACH: Show sq. ft./front foot value of land; sq. ft. rate of reproduction and
depreciable factors and percentages:

LIVING AREA – 2,368   sq. ft. @ $14.00   = $ 33,152
   LESS DEPRECIATION – @   18 % Estimate   =   6,000

IMPROVEMENTS – Value added: Nicely landscaped. Concrete walk, $ 27,152
2 paved driveways $700
120' cyclone type fence & metal tool shed on conc. slabs $200
Gas stove and hood fan, Refrig-freezer $250
Dish washer $ 75
Carpets throughout-good quality $600
Central a/c reverse cycle $1800
                                                                        $ 3,625

TOTAL VALUE ADDED BY IMPROVEMENTS – $30,777
LAND VALUE – $ 7,000
                                                             $37,777

            TOTAL VALUE BY COST APPROACH – $ 37,800

COMPARABLE PROPERTIES:

	Address	Date	Sale Price	Sq. Ft.	Lot Size	Adjusted Price
No. 1	18610 Sunshine Dr.	6/7	$30,000	1,574	80x110	$36,500
No. 2	18801 Frostproof Lane	5/7	$31,500	1,596	75x100	$36,750
No. 3	18831 Belview Terr.	5/7	$33,200	1,790	80x115	$38,200

            VALUE BY MARKET APPROACH – $ 38,000

Remarks as to adverse influences or other factors affecting the marketability of this property:

House may be overimproved for area. Owner has improved and
renovated entire interior. New cabinets in Kitchen.

CERTIFICATION: I hereby certify that my office has examined the property as described in this appraisal and
after personal reveiw, I believe that its reasonable present market value is $ 38,000
I also hereby certify that I have no interest, present or future, in the applicant borrower,
property or mortgage.

Date _____ Appraiser _____

Figure 1-1 (continued).

2. The formal statement describing and analysing the property, detailing the techniques and methods used to arrive at the appraiser's concluded value.

3. The addenda. All of the exhibits relating to the property such as comparable photographs, maps, plot plans, surveys and supporting statistical data.

The appraiser has much latitude in preparing his detailed report. There is no universally recognized form. However, his aim should be for clarity in presenting his conclusions. The report should take the reader step by step through the appraisal processes he used until his conclusions are shown to be arrived at through facts, knowledge and logic. A typical table of contents page of a formal book-bound appraisal is reproduced here to show the areas that might be covered in making such a report.

Typical

TABLE OF CONTENTS

of a Formal Appraisal Report

Page

BASIC ETHICS

Under the Code of Ethics adopted by the American Institute of Real Estate Appraisers (an affiliate of the National Association of Realtors), among other standards, it is unethical:

1. To accept a fee if it is contingent upon a predetermined or specified amount.

2. To accept compensation higher than a fair professional fee for the time, responsibility, work and expense involved.

3. For an appraisal report to be issued if the appraiser is acting in the capacity of a broker or manager, or if he has an ownership interest, unless such interest is fully disclosed.

4. For an appraiser to certify a valuation based on assumed income and expenses which he does not feel are able to be achieved under ordinary, competent management.

5. To omit a reasonably complete description of the property, date and amount of value, and a statement that the appraiser has no present or future interest in the property, or a full disclosure statement if such an interest exists.

APPRAISAL FEES

Appraisal fees should be based on time expended, responsibility involved and expenses incurred. Appraisal organizations do not set fees. However, individual fee appraisers invariably have fixed rates for their services. Aside from the VA and FHA appraisal fees below, which are set by the government and are subject to periodic change, those shown are merely suggested amounts.

VA House Appraisal	$50
FHA House Appraisal	$40
Conventional House Appraisal (Single page report)	$75
Conventional House Appraisal (Comprehensive report)	$150-$250
Vacant Land	$250 & up
Proposed Subdivision of Land	$750 & up
Acreage (Large Tracts)	$500 & up
Apartment House Large	$1,000 & up
Small	$300 & up
Office Building, Shopping Center Large	$1,000 & up
Small	$300 & up
Motel, Hotel Large	$3,500 & up
Small	$1,000 & up
Court Appearance (per day)	$250-$500

APPRAISAL SOCIETIES

Any real estate broker or salesman who desires to do appraisal work to supplement his income, or as a full time endeavor, would do well to join an active appraisal society. There are excellent local and regional groups that offer regular lecture and study programs. Some are independent, others are affiliated with one of the national societies.

The three leading national appraisal organizations, with a brief resume of their aims and functions are listed below.

1. American Institute of Real Estate Appraisers, 36 South Wabash Ave., Chicago, Illinois 60603. An affiliate of the National Association of Real Estate Boards, its members are highly trained, rigidly examined professional appraisers with many years of practical experience. Once they qualify, members are awarded the highly coveted designate of M.A.I. (Member Appraisal Institute).

2. American Society of Appraisers (A.S.A.), 1028 Connecticut Ave., N.W., Washington, D.C. 20006. An independent organization that appraises most forms of personal property, as well as real estate. One of its goals is to improve the standards of the appraisal practice. Members subscribe to a strict code of professional ethics.

3. Society of Real Estate Appraisers, 7 South Dearborn Street, Chicago, Illinois 60603. This society is international in scope. It is the oldest and largest independent appraisal society in North America. It has two classifications of members: a) Senior Real Estate Appraiser (S.R.E.A.), for members who specialize in commercial and industrial real property, and b) Senior Residential Appraiser (S.R.A.), whose members are qualified in evaluating all types of residences.

2

BROKERAGE

ERA OF SPECIALIZATION

Every real estate professional knows that brokerage today covers many specialized areas. It is a multi-faceted business encompassing selling, leasing, exchanging, subdividing, developing, managing, appraising, and financing of residential and commercial properties. In the commercial field alone, there are brokers who work exclusively with acreage, warehouses, apartments, mobile home parks, office buildings, stores, or shopping centers, to name just some types of properties.

Because of the varied scope and intricacies of each form of real estate, more and more brokers wisely choose to concentrate mainly in one direction. As a consequence, they become expert in their particular fields, and come to be well known for it.

As real estate is by nature a local business dealing in a unique

31

service, success depends upon knowledge, and the kind of service you can render. Brokers who perform well in their chosen areas of specialization are generally more successful. Even the larger real estate offices long ago discovered that they must departmentalize by putting managers and vice-presidents in charge of the various specialties. Each concentrates on one area of real estate. Result: A more competent and skilled service. It, therefore, behooves brokers who run average size, general real estate businesses to consider separating their staffs into distinct divisions of specialization. And in the case of the single practicioner or the small office having one or two salesmen, it may prove far more rewarding financially to become expert in one segment of real estate to the exclusion of all others.

A WORD ABOUT LOCATION

If you are contemplating relocating or opening a branch office, first survey your community with an eye toward locating in a promising growth area.

Naturally, offices specializing in residential sales would do well to be on or near a high traffic-count, main thoroughfare where you will be readily seen. The commercial and industrial broker can operate just as effectively in less prominent areas, on upper floors of office buildings, and off the main street. Customers rarely walk into a real estate office on impulse, but being accessible and offering ample parking are two important requisites. Avoid districts that have too many old buildings and where the area appears to be static or heading downhill. Rather, try to select a location in the path of growth and activity—where business is booming and the action is. Proper site selection can mean the difference between success and failure.

The office itself should be well-furnished and exude an air of prosperity and professionalism both inside and out.

JOINING REAL ESTATE ASSOCIATIONS

If you haven't already done so, every progressive real estate broker should become an active member of his local Board of Realtors. Joining, automatically carries with it membership in the affiliated state and national[1] associations. Attending regular local meetings and conventions affords the opportunity of knowing your fellow Realtors on a friendly, informal basis, which fosters cooperative sales. Most Boards of Realtors have computerized Multiple Listing services (giving you hundreds of cooperative listings you wouldn't otherwise have), continuing education and lecture programs, a reference library, standardized printed legal and office forms, plat book and photo services, a group hospitalization plan, participation in local and national institutional advertising programs, an ethical and arbitration committee, to name just some of the advantages and services. If you make one small cooperative deal a year through the multiple listing service, it will more than compensate for your membership dues. To become a member, one must subscribe to a strict code of ethics.[2] Once accepted, you are allowed to display the prestigious Realtor emblem.

RECRUITING SALESMEN

Hiring sales personnel must be a continuing program. Advertise for them daily through display and classified ads, window signs, word of mouth, by contacting teachers of real estate courses, inviting prospective salesmen to attend company held seminars, etc. Even put it out over the airwaves, if need be, but get the word around that you are hiring and training personnel; for like all sales-oriented businesses, a turnover of salesmen is the norm. The wise broker accepts this as a fact of life. Consequently, he knows that it is a constant recruiting job to replace the ones who couldn't make it, those who defect to a competitor, or who progress from salesman to broker and open for themselves. This is not to imply that an office should hire every applicant who comes along. On the contrary, brokers would do well to be selective. Thoroughly interviewing and testing each prospective salesman can save a lot of wasted time, money and grief later on.

What qualities should you look for in real estate salesmen? Consider the following:

---

[1] National Association of Realtors.

[2] See page 289, Realtor's Code of Ethics.

Aptitude. Does he appear to have the talent to make a good salesman? Look for qualities such as self-assurance, an outgoing personality and a genuine liking for people.

Attitude. Does he have a pleasant personality? Does he smile easily? Has he the quality of putting people at ease? Will he be compatible with others in the office? He should possess an affirmative, cooperative attitude.

Professionalism. Does he consider himself a full-time professional in real estate? Determine if he is planning to make this his life's work. If you get the impression that selling real estate might be just a passing fancy, think twice before putting him on.

Trainable. Is he so set in his ways that he would have trouble conforming to your training programs, policies and work schedules?

Appearance. Does he dress well? In your view, are his bearing and demeanor acceptable? Will he be a credit to your organization?

Common Sense. Has he that elusive quality of logic? Does he marshal his facts convincingly when getting a point across? Is what he says sensible and believable? Can he motivate clients to act?

Hard Work. Is he willing to put in a hard-working, eight-hour day, six days a week, including evenings if necessary?

Ethical Behavior. Do his views on business ethics and fairness conform to high standards? Is he an honorable person?

Optimistic. Can he bounce back in the face of adversity? Determine if his outlook on life in general and business in particular is a bright one.

Technical Knowledge. Is he knowledgeable about the mechanics of real estate? Ascertain if he is familar with preparing contracts, obtaining mortgages, escrowing funds, zoning regulations, real estate law, and the countless other important technical points that must be known to be a good real estate person. If not, does he express a willingness to learn?

HOW I.R.S. CLASSIFIES REAL ESTATE SALESMEN

The Internal Revenue Service looks upon the real estate salesman as an independent contractor,[3] and as such his withholding tax and social security payments are not deducted from his commissions.

---

[3]Most state licensing laws, however, recognize the broker as an "employer." He must vouch for the salesman's honesty, integrity and ethical behavior.

Every broker should enter into written agreements with his salesmen that outline the responsibilities of each to the other. Matters of mutual concern, such as office policies, personal conduct, commission division, expense accounts, advertising allowances, listing and selling procedures, as well as other points of common interest should be spelled out in detail.

To be certain that salesmen are classified as independent contractors in the agreement, properly worded contracts must be used.

EMPLOYMENT CONTRACT

The contract that was cited as a test case[1] relevant to this point stands as a good example of a broker-salesman agreement. With only slight modifications for clarity, it is otherwise reproduced here in full.

BROKER-SALESMAN AGREEMENT

This Agreement made this_____ day of _____ by and between _____ , Party of the First Part, herein after referred to as Broker, and _____, Party of the Second Part, hereinafter referred to as Salesman, for and in consideration of their mutual promises and agreements and for their mutual benefits, Witnesseth:

Whereas, said Broker is now, and has for many years, been engaged in business as a general real estate broker in the City of_____ , and is qualified to and does operate a general real estate business and is duly qualified and does procure the listings of real estate for sale, lease or rental and prospective purchasers, lessees and renters thereof and has and does enjoy the good will of, and reputation for fair dealing with the public, and,

Whereas, said broker maintains an office in said County, properly equipped with furnishings and other equipment necessary and incidental to the proper operation of said business, and staffed with employees, suitable to serving the public as a real estate broker, and,

Whereas, said salesman is now, and has been engaged in business as a real estate salesman, and has enjoyed and does enjoy a good reputation for fair and honest dealing with the public as such, and,

Whereas, it is deemed to be to the mutual advantage of said Broker

---

[1]*Dimmitt-Rickhoff-Bayer Real Estate Company, St. Louis vs. James P. Finnegan, Collector of Internal Revenue,* United States Court of Appeals for the Eighth Circuit—Number 13,987.

and said Salesman to form the association hereinafter agreed to under the terms and conditions hereinafter set out, Therefore:

1. LISTINGS. The Broker agrees to make available to the Salesman all current listings of the office and agrees to assist the Salesman in his work by advice, instruction, and full cooperation in every way possible.

2. OFFICE FACILITIES. The Broker agrees that the Salesman may share with other Salesmen all the facilities of the office now operated by said Broker in connection with the subject matter of this contract, which office is now maintained at _____ .

3. SALESMAN'S DILIGENCE. The Salesman agrees to work diligently and with his best efforts to sell, lease or rent any and all real estate listed with the Broker, to solicit additional listings and customers of said Broker, and otherwise promote the business of serving the public in real estate transactions to the end that each of the parties hereto may derive the greatest profit possible.

4. CONDUCT. The Salesman agrees to conduct his business and regulate his habits, so as to maintain and to increase the good will and reputation of the Broker, and the parties hereto agree to conform to and abide by all laws, rules and regulations, and codes of ethics that are binding upon or applicable to real estate brokers and real estate salesmen.

5. COMMISSIONS. The usual and customary commissions shall be charged for any service performed hereunder, and the Broker shall advise the Salesman of any special contract relating to any particular transaction which he undertakes to handle. When the Salesman shall perform any service hereunder, whereby a commission is earned, said commission shall, when collected, be divided between the Broker and Salesman, in which division the Salesman shall receive a proportionate share as set out below:

Basic Commission Division   _____ % to Salesman
                                  _____ % to Broker

When Salesman Sells own
Listing to Own Buyer   _____% to Salesman
                                  _____% to Broker

In the event of special arrangements with any client of the Broker or the Salesman, a special division or commission may apply, such rate of division to be agreed upon by the Broker and the Salesman. In the event that two or more Salesmen participate in such a service, or claim to have done so, the amount of the commission over that accruing to the Broker shall be divided between the participating salesmen according to agreement between them or by arbitration. In no case shall the Broker be personally liable to the Salesman for any commission, nor shall said Salesman be personally liable to said Broker for any commissions, but when the commission shall have been collected from the part or parties for whom the service was performed, said Broker in the event such commissions are paid to him, shall hold the same in trust for said Salesman and himself to be divided according to the terms of this agreement, and in the event such commissions are paid to said Salesman, said Salesman shall pay over to said Broker said Broker's proportionate share of such commission according to the terms of this agreement.

6. DISTRIBUTION OF COMMISSION. The division and distribution of the earned commissions as set out in paragraph five hereof, which may be paid to or collected by said Broker, shall take place as soon as practicable after collection of such commissions from the party or parties for whom the services may have been performed.

7. BROKER NOT LIABLE FOR SALESMAN'S EXPENDITURES. The Broker shall not be liable to the Salesman for any expense incurred by him, or for any of his acts, nor shall the Salesman be liable to the Broker for office help or expense, and the Salesman shall have no authority to bind the Broker by any promises or representation, unless specifically authorized in a particular transaction; but expenses for attorney's fees, costs, revenue stamps, title abstracts and the like which must, by reason of some necessity, be paid from the commission, shall be paid by the parties in the same proportion as provided for herein the division of the commissions. Suits for commissions shall, agreeable to the law, be maintained only in the name of the Broker, and the Salesman shall be construed to be a (sub) agent only with respect to the clients and customers for whom services shall be performed, and shall otherwise be deemed to be an independent contractor and not a servant, employee, or partner of the Broker.

8. TERMINATION. This contract and the association created hereby, may be terminated by either party hereto, at any time upon notice given to the other, but the rights of the parties to any commission which accrued prior to said notice, shall not be divested by the termination of this contract.

9. INDEPENDENT CONTRACTOR. The parties hereto specifically agree that Salesman is an Independent Contractor, and not an employee, or partner of the Broker. That the provisions of this contract shall be construed to be directing the end result of Salesman's efforts, and not the methods by which they are accomplished. Broker is directed to not withhold from commissions Income Tax, Social Security, Workmen's Com-

pensation or Unemployment Tax. In the event the courts shall decide, notwithstanding this provision, that such sums are due, or should Salesman be deemed to be an employee, Salesman shall be personally liable for all such taxes or sums that may be due thereby, and agrees to not be bound by the Workmen's Compensation Act. This provision shall be binding upon the heirs, executors, and administrators of the parties hereto.

10. USE OF MATERIAL BY SALESMAN AFTER TERMINA-TION. The Salesman shall not, after the termination of this contract, use to his own advantage, or the advantage of any other person or corporation, any information gained for or from the files or business of the Broker.

In Witness Whereof, the parties hereto have signed, or cause to be signed, these presents, this_____ day of_____, 19__.

By _____
                                    Party of the First Part

_____
                                    Party of the Second Part

TRAINING PROGRAM

Salesmen new to real estate first have to learn how to list[5] properties and then how to sell them. They must also learn office policy and procedure. Sometimes experienced salesmen joining an office have to "unlearn" bad habits acquired along the way. A good real estate office will have a well-organized training program for those coming into the organization. Meetings and lectures should be regularly scheduled. A suggested list of subject matter for such sales meetings might include:

1. The importance of having a positive mental attitude (P.M.A.)

2. The art of handling people tactfully and with understanding.

3. Acquiring technical knowledge. What books to read, lectures to go to, courses to take.

4. Techniques in selling and listing.

5. How to get signatures on a contract.

---

[5]See page 139, Listing Properties.

6. Professionalism and ethics.

7. Cooperating policy with other offices.

8. Body Language.

9. Motivation.

10. Maintaining sales quotas.

11. What hard work can accomplish.

12. Office forms, procedure and policy.

13. Advancement to management possibilities.

14. Company image.

15. How to structure income property deals.

16. How to write a contract.

17. How to write a lease.

18. The mortgage market.

19. Real Estate Law.

20. How to Make Real Estate Trades.

PREPARING BROCHURES, PROPERTY BRIEFS AND ANALYSIS REPORTS

For residential sales as well as commercial, properly prepared fact sheets and brochures to be given out to prospects, are invaluable sales aids. Such reports range from one-page briefs printed on office stationery to elaborate analysis reports that include photos, maps, profit and loss statements, rent rolls and comparable studies of properties in the immediate area. The latter, of course, apply to income properties primarily, such as apartments, office buildings, shopping centers, warehouses, business properties, etc., where conclusions as to cash flow, depreciation benefits, and structural details are of prime importance to the purchaser. A good analysis report should take the reader on a "mini-tour" of the property via pictures and words covering the following essentials: (1.) The *location* should be pinpointed by maps and photos, with features of the surrounding neighborhood taken into account. (2.) The *plot size* and its topography with noteworthy features of each highlighted. (3.) A detailed *description* of the improvements. How many buildings, the square footage, type of construction, general condition, age, how many units or offices, etc. (4.) The annual *income* and expenses figures itemized in complete details. Rent rolls and C.P.A. statements if possible will be extremely helpful. (5.) *Mortgage information* giving original amount and exact balance, interest rate, monthly payments, name of the lending institution or individual, length of the original mortgage and how many years remaining. Other facts such as prepayment penality data, should also be detailed. (6.) *Price*. (7.) *Terms*. How much cash is required? Will the owner take back a mortgage? (8.) Any additional comments of significance not included above. (9.) Name, address, phone number of the salesmen and the real estate office he is representing. (10.) A statement giving the source of information, plus a "disclaimer" to protect the broker against erroneous or inaccurate information supplied him. A brief paragraph such as follows will serve this purpose.

> "Any information given herewith is obtained from sources we consider reliable. However, we are not responsible for misstatement of facts, errors, omissions, prior sale, withdrawal from market, or change in price without notice."

ADVERTISING SLOGANS

Many brokerage firms have adopted slogans to help keep their names fresh in the public's mind. Finding a suitable one may take considerable study, thought and creativeness, for a good one must meet certain criteria to be effective. It ought to be succinct yet distinctive. In order for a motto to be completely effective it should also be a precise expression that doesn't waste words in making its point. And to be truly distinctive it must be cleverly different, possessing an attention-getting phrase that will linger in the reader's mind. A sampling of real estate promotional slogans currently in use throughout the United States and Canada illustrates a wide variety of ideas and subject matter:

> We are not #1—you are.
> Putting our client first puts us first.
> No. 1 with our clients.

First choice for results.

Where serving you comes first.

Seek it first at _____.

First in service and service first.

Service measured not by gold, but by the golden rule.

Golden rule service.

Do unto others as you would have them do unto you. Isn't that
what its all about?

Trust is everything.

With special trust and confidence.

Integrity: not just a word but our way of LIFE.

List with us then start packing.

If our sign is on your property, hurry home—you're moving.

It's the sold sign that counts.

We don't sit. We go get.

Many people save time in the end by coming here in the
beginning.

One call does it all.

We care about you.

One good real estate investment is worth a lifetime of labor.

Your needs are our deeds.

Your dream is our business.

Your home is our business.

Your satisfaction is our future.

A "house-sold" word in real estate.

The home of homes since 19__.

For a house that's a home.

The home folks.

The friendly ones.

For action with satisfaction.

Action not promises.

The action team.

We have lots to sell.

We specialize in your real estate needs.

The best investment in the world is to own a piece of the earth.

We sell the earth and everything on it.

A five-minute call could prove priceless.

Independent but exclusive.

A reputation is not merely earned but is a continual responsibility.

The office that knows its subject.

Service is responsible for our success.

Personalized not computerized.

Your listing deserves our personal attention.

Old fashioned integrity with modern techniques.

Old enough to be experienced. Young enough to be aggressive.

The quick way to make your front lawn someone else's.

Proven performance is our best asset.

Over 50 associates serving all your real estate needs.

See sold sign sooner.

Get sold on the sign.

The sign of quick action.

We don't sell you. We help you buy.

Things turn out better in the end when I'm in the middle.

Satisfying buyer and seller since 19__.

One name—one address since 19__.

The preferred agency for 32 years.

The name you're proud to recommend.

It pleases us to please you.

Service is our business. Satisfied customers our goal.

Real service in real estate.

For the finest in real estate service.

For all your tomorrows—make the right move today.

Resultful service.

Results make us a leader.

We are known by our good listings.

Give us a chance to serve you and we'll make another friend.

Personalized service our best asset.

Your personal, professional office.

For the kind of real estate service you deserve, call _____.

We can put a roof over your head.

We can take it from the ground up. Total real estate service.

We are successful because we get results.

Service and knowledge are our stock in trade.

We take the time to serve your best interests.

If you want it sold, get us told.

If we don't have what you want, we'll build it.

We sell most of our listings within 30 days.

Individualized treatment of each transaction.
Our speciality, your listing.
A new company with young ideas plus years of experience.
The company that gets results.
If we can't sell it, we'll buy it.
Diversified real estate concept.
Dedicated service for over 20 years.
A staff of specialists to serve your need.
A full service Realtor.
Selling real estate is our only business.
Selling Seattle since 19__.
We specialize in satisfied buyers and sellers.
Where listings quickly become sales.
Our enthusiastic staff is interested in serving you.
Knowing real estate is our business.
Select before you inspect.
The firm with the female touch.
It takes a woman to find the bargains.
Service by experts.
The all woman agency.
Consult us when leasing space—a room, a suite, a floor, a
    building.
Dedicated to the family—its needs, its environment and its
    dreams.
A happier home is one you own.
We know what a family's dreams are worth.
We make families happy.
The friendly agency.
Tell a friend.
You are never sold, you are served.
Property is wealth—ever increasing wealth.
The people who care.
Personal people company.
Helping people with a need.
People are our business.
The results people.
Specialist in the people business.
We love people.
People helping people.

For real estate you want or don't want, call _____.
For land sake, call day or night.
When you think real estate, think _____.
Our aim is to satisfy.
Homes for living.
Your real estate problem is our business.
Let us help you with your new address.
We can help you to or from any place in America.
Don't just wish for your dream home, see _____.
We try a little harder.
Meet the professionals.
Have property, will show.
We'd like to help you chase rainbows.
Over 800 sales yearly.
Professional actions in all our transactions.
Select from over 1,000 listings.
A home sold every day.
Big enough to know. Small enough to care.
Where *helping* is a habit.   .
A satisfied client is our only consideration.
For sales that make friends and service that keeps them.

The possibilities of incorporating one's name in a slogan are as infinite as there are names. Those that readily lend themselves for rhyming or that are naturally descriptive make especially catchy slogans. Witness the following:

Get rich quick. Call Rich Realty.
Stop shopping, call Topping.
Want action? Call Action.
Deal with Dennis.
For a golden opportunity—Golden Associates.
King Real Estate—where clients are kings.
When it's time for a change. Klock Realty.
It's a pleasure to do business with treasure. Treasure Realty.
Your key to value. Key Real Estate Co.
Justice for buyer and seller—Jack Justice, Realtor.
Our mission—to serve you better. Mission Realty.
You can bet on Betts.
Light your way to better living. Lamp-lighter Realty.

See Frey's guys.
Call Sal's gals.
Hall does it all. Hall Bros. Realty, Inc.
Lancer has the answer. Lancer Realty Co.
Get Lucky. Charles Lucky, Realtor.
Wm. F. Apple. We are happy apples.
Soaring to new heights. Airport Realty.
Sell your home with pride. Pride Real Estate, Inc.
The much more intelligent way. Muchmore Co.
For direction in real estate—Compass Realty.
Olshan the real estate man.
Claude Pace Co. The pacesetters.
Get a tiger working for you. Tiger Associates.
See Furst first.
Yell for Pennell.
Call in the Gale force—Gale Assoc., Inc.
Deal with a Duer. Duer, Inc.
Doolittle did it.
Make the Wright move thru Lewis E. Wright & Assoc.
George Goodness & Co. Service as good as the name.
The best listings in town display the sign with the crown. King
    Real Estate Co.
Results to crow about. Edward Crow Corp.
Our heart is in our work—DeHart Realty Co.
Realty is our middle name. Consolidated Realty Co.

After studying the foregoing varied slogans, you may be sufficiently inspired to fashion one of your own. Remember to keep it short and meaningful. If it accurately describes your service or your aims, consider using it throughout all your promotions. It could appear on letterheads, brochures, in telephone directory yellow pages, newspaper ads, billboards as well as other forms of advertising. A good slogan will make it easier to keep your name foremost in the minds of your community.

CLASSIFIED ADVERTISING

With the exception of salesmen's commissions, the single biggest item in the real estate broker's budget is advertising. By far the most common form is classified ads, but whether you use display ads or classified, they must be attention getting, crammed full of pertinent facts, and be provocative enough to cause the reader to act immediately.

In painting word pictures of a house or other property, for example, first strive to create an attention getting headline—one that tells the reader something and/or jogs him into looking further. For example:

NAUTICAL BUT NICE
Lakefront Home With Private Dock

S E X
Now that I have your attention,—

A LITTLE LAND
A LOT OF LIVING

STEAL THIS

LIKE THE GOOD LIFE?

ARTIST HIDEAWAY

PATTER OF SMALL FEET
5 bedroom house for large, happy family—

ONCE IN A LIFETIME

OWNER MOVED
Demands Action

TRY ME—MAKE OFFER

NOW HEAR THIS!
Waterfront Beauty

LEGAL PROBLEMS
REQUIRE OFFER NOW

DESPERATE OWNER MUST SELL

ILLNESS FORCES SALE

OWNER ANXIOUS

TASTE—CLASS—STYLE

A TOUCH OF CLASS

GREAT ASSUMPTION

PARTNER DISPUTE

NET $22,000—IRS PROOF

Begin the body of the ad by describing the exterior amenities, then take the reader on a verbal inspection of the grounds, through the front entrance into the living areas, bedrooms, kitchen, baths, and finally the attic, basement, and garage. Once the descriptive word tour is over, discuss the hard facts—the financing needed to obtain the house—price, mortgage, terms and cash. Conclude by making it inviting and easy to reach you. An ad typifying these points is illustrated below:

RARE FIND
Transferred Exec *must* sell

In picturesque Highland Lakes area on a slow rolling, naturally wooded acre. Bass caught right from your private dock. (160 ' shore front). Bird sanctuary setting, yet minutes from shopping and downtown. Circular drive leads to Colonial style, pillared front entrance, centerhall, large carpeted, sunken living room, 3 spacious beedrooms, walk-in closets, all electric kitchen, 2 baths, laundry, central a/c, pool and patio, double garage. This small estate is in mint condition. Asking $98,000. Owner will help finance. $20,000 cash needed. First time advertised! This is truly a rare find. Call now for inspection. Bright Realty, 646-7616.

Commercial ads need not be as descriptive, but instead should contain more of the "arithmetic" of the property. The ad should be literally laden with facts. In addition to the price and terms, the investor in, or user of, income property wants to know the cash flow, amortization, depreciation benefits, gross income. If these points meet his standards, only then is he interested in the bricks and mortar. Examples follow:

100% Location
PRIME OFFICE BUILDING

NET $25,000 YEARLY

$200,000 down buys this well known 35,000 sq. ft. (28,000 sq. ft. rentable) brick, 3 story, well-constructed building, with 1/3 acre adjoining parking lot. 12½% proven cash flow. Grossed $168,000 last year on average rental of $6 per sq. ft. Owner increasing rents to $7 as

leases come due. Over 95% occupied. 5 years old on main, downtown
street. One 7½%, 20-year mortgage. Priced to sell at $1,150,000. Call
INVESTOR REALTY, 234-5280.

The commercial ad may be succinct and bold, as in the all-headline
ads shown here.

SHOPPING CENTER
3 NATIONAL TENANTS
100% OCCUPIED
GROSSING $102,000
NETTING $79,000
NO MORTGAGE
PRICE $790,000
BRIGHT-LITE REALTY
645-7689

20 BREAD AND BUTTER
APARTMENTS
3 YEARS YOUNG
POOL—PATIO
GROSSING $45,000
NETTING $12,500
PRICE: 7½ × INCOME
PROFESSIONAL REALTY
834-8990

Make your ads at once interesting, provocative and to the point.
They should stir the reader into wanting to know more. Strive to make
your classified ads brief thumb-nail sketches designed to foster inquiries.
If they accomplish that, they have succeeded.

OPERATING BUDGET

Successful brokers know in advance how to allocate money to operate their offices. Their budgets are estimates of expenses based on expected revenues. Expressed in percentage form, the actual amounts allocated will be governed by the volume of sales made. Proper budgeting
and cost control have been the salvation of many real estate offices. The

table shown below is a suggested budget for the operation of a general real estate office.

	Percent
Salesmen's Commission	50
Sales Manager's Override	5
Salesmen's Bonuses	5.0
Advertising	
Classified	6.5
Display	2.5
Signs & Other	1.5
Rent	2.5
Insurance	1.3
Secretarial	4.2
Taxes—Payroll & Other	1
Car Expenses	3.3
Telephone	1.5
Dues, Subscriptions &	
Licenses	1
Travel & Entertainment	1.5
Professional Fees	.5
Office Expenses—	
Supplies, etc.	1.7
All Other Expenses	1.5
	90.5
Net Profit	9.5
	100.0%

INTER-OFFICE COOPERATION

It is usually sound real estate practice to cooperate with other real estate offices whenever feasible. If you are a Realtor, Article 22[6] of the Code of Ethics specifically calls for cooperation on properties the broker

[6]See page 292, Realtor's Code of Ethics.

has listed exclusively. On open listings, it is generally a matter of individual office policy. Most offices do cooperate, for in the long pull it means added sales and greater profits. The Realtor holding the exclusive listing should be first consulted and negotiations carried on through him, unless he gives permission to deal directly with the owner.

No experienced broker would proceed with another office's listing of any kind without first contacting the listing office. It must be determined: (1.) Will they cooperate? (2.) If so, what is the latest updated information regarding the property? (3.) When can the property be shown? (4.) What is the commission? (5.) How is it to be split? Once the ground rules are set, you can proceed in an orderly cooperative manner.

The basic commission split is generally, but not necessarily, 50/50.

INTRA-OFFICE COOPERATION

Instill a team approach among your staff by encouraging and properly compensating salesmen when they work as a team.

The basic office division for salesmen is usually 50/50, but when a salesman lists a property that is sold by another in the office, he should receive a listing fee of at least 10%. If this is the case, the salesman negotiating the transaction would receive 40%. The office share of the commission remains the same (50%).[7] Real estate market conditions dictate the percentage of division of inter-office commissions. If it is a seller's market and listings are hard to come by, the compensation for listing properties should be increased accordingly. Because it is a viable situation, a good broker will be attuned to the real estate market at all times, and structure his intra-office commission splits accordingly. Once you have worked out an equitable financial arrangement, encourage cooperation among salesmen. It will mean less internal friction and more sales for all.

PROFIT SHARING PLAN

A good profit sharing plan will serve as an incentive for everyone in an office to work as a team. It will mean annual bonus money and a

---

[7]In this situation some offices give the selling salesman 45% and retain 45% for the house.

retirement fund for salesmen and office workers alike, and will act as a cohesive force in assuring that personnel will remain in your employ. When properly structured, it will cost the firm little if anything more than the tax that would otherwise have to be paid to I.R.S.

Money for the profit sharing plan comes from a percentage of the net earnings a company makes. This amount may vary between 20 and 30 percent. It is wise to have your accountant and a good tax-oriented lawyer combine their talents in tailoring a plan for your specific needs. If they know their business, they will make certain that the plan is consistent with the requirements of the Internal Revenue Code relative to qualified profit sharing trusts, as well as seeing that it is in accordance with state laws. In basic terms, using 30 percent of net earnings as an example, here is how one such typical plan works.

Fifteen percent of the net profits are distributed annually as a cash bonus to employees in ratio to their earnings for the year.

The remaining 15 percent is put into a fund for investment purposes such as in real estate, mortgages, notes, stocks, bonds, or simply to be kept in an interest bearing account, as may be deemed advisable by the trustees of the profit sharing plan.

All employees become eligible after completion of six months of employment.

A percentage of the investment portion is returned to employees as a severance benefit. The percentage is based on the number of years the employee participated under the plan. Generally, 20 percent is returned to him for each year he was active with the firm. After five years, he would receive 100 percent of his share of the invested portion of the funds.

The above plan or one structured along similar lines serves the dual purpose of providing a yearly bonus for your employees and gives them a retirement fund to look forward to. The latter can mean much to your commission sales personnel particularly, who are only too aware that they are in a "feast and famine" business. Retirement plans are usually found only in large companies or when working for the government. When the relatively small, independent real estate office can set up such a fund, the financial security it engenders will have a stabilizing effect for the entire staff.

COMMISSION SCHEDULES

Though commission rates may vary slightly in different parts of the country, they follow a remarkably uniform pattern even in as geographically separated areas as New York, Illinois, California and Florida.

No state or federal law exists establishing rates of commission. It is a matter of negotiation between the real estate broker and his client. In the absence of a commission agreement, courts usually follow local customs, often relying on the advice of the area's real estate board in fixing an amount when a dispute arises.

The following rate schedule was compiled after researching real estate rates from several sections of the country.

Improved Property:

For selling or exchanging property up to $100,000—Between 6 to 7½% of sales price.

On the excess over $100,000 up to and including $1,000,000—6% of sales price.

On the excess over $1,000,000 up to and including $3,000,000—5% of sales price.

On the excess over $3,000,000—3% of the sales price.

Unimproved Land:

Including vacant lots, acreage, unplatted land, groves and farmland—10%.

Leaseholds:

For selling the interest in realty a tenant holds—6% of the consideration paid by the buyer.

Sale of Business:

10% of the sales price

Leasing:

For leases of from one to five years, 6% of the total rental. For leases of longer duration, 4% of the total rental for the next five years or part thereof; 2½% for the remaining term of the lease.

Leases for 30 years or longer are considered as sales. If it is a "net lease" whereby the tenant pays all costs of maintaining the property including taxes, the sale of the property (for commission purposes) is calculated by multiplying the average annual rental amount by 17. The charge is 6 percent of such total.

Sub-leases and assignment of leases are treated as if they were new leases; 6 percent of the gross amount of the transaction.

For the leasing of agricultural properties; 10 percent of the total rent. If the lease is on a sharecrop basis; 10 percent of the estimated amount the landlord will receive. The broker and the landlord may mutually agree to delay a portion of the commission payment until the crop proceeds are actually received. At that time, an accurate computation can be reached.

Management:

For collecting rents, leasing, supervising the maintenance and repairs of the property, hiring personnel, paying expenses, keeping accounts and rendering monthly statements; 5-6 percent of the gross receipts of the property.

TERMINATION AGREEMENT WHEN SALESMAN LEAVES AN OFFICE

It is wise to have a written agreement between a salesman and his broker when employment is terminated. It need not be a complex legal document, but rather a clearly stated letter of agreement that is signed by both parties. The simpler the better, but in preparing such an instrument, be certain to cover the following points:

1. *Disassociation Date.* Because valuable information is mutually known, with new clients and confidential information coming in daily, it is wise to end the association formally as soon as possible once a "parting of the ways" is agreed upon. Immediate disassociation is usually the wisest course. This entails promptly informing the state licensing agency. It is unwise to ask for or give a 30-day notice period. Cut the ties in as friendly a fashion as possible, but cut them you must, and without delay.

2. *Pending Closings.* Any deal of the departing salesman *that is under contract* but not closed, should be honored by the broker. The property in progress should continue to be jointly worked, and when it does close, the share of the commission due to the salesman should be paid him. The same holds true of any deferred commissions, notes, or mortgages mutually held.

3. *Written Matter Returned to Office.* Most states recognize that written matter of every description—customer cards, listings, office forms, legal forms, correspondence, manuals, photos, or whatever—are the property of the office, and must be returned upon termination. The law recognizes that what is in a person's mind can not be erased, but it also holds that he may not leave with written information other than personal matter. All such business matter, including listings and prospects are the property of the office.

4. *Relinquish Interest in Profit Sharing Plan.* Upon terminating employment prior to a specified retirement date, all accruing benefits are automatically relinquished by the salesman.

5. *Relinquish Interest in Deals Underway but Not in Contract.* The departing sales associate has no claim whatsoever to transactions he may have been working on that have not reached the contract stage. His listings and buyers may be assigned to others in the office and he should agree in writing that he cannot interfere in the progress of such deals after he leaves.

SALES CONTRACTS

The sales contract is the most important legal instrument you will be called upon to prepare. It can take many variations and forms with clauses being added and deleted to fit specific requirements. As a broker, your ethical concern should be with its fairness, while your business and legal obligation must focus on the contract being a legally binding document. To meet this later criteria five essential points must be present.

1. The parties to the agreement must be competent in the eyes of the law. They should be mentally capable of knowing and understanding what they are doing.

2. The contract should contain a statement of the consideration——something of value offered by the purchaser. Consideration usually takes the form of money, but personal services, merchandise, other real estate or any other benefit may be equally acceptable. Love and affection are also recognized as good consideration, as it may occur when one member of a family transfers title to property to another.

3. A valid contract must contain an offer and an acceptance. When the price, terms and conditions are acceptable to all parties, a "meeting of the minds" is said to exist. Both sides are agreeable to carrying out all of the provisions of the agreement.

4. The purpose for, and the subject matter of, the contract must be lawful ones. Courts refer to this as "legality of object."

5. Under the Statute of Frauds, almost all jurisdictions recognize that a contract has to be in writing and signed by all principals in order to become enforceable.

The contract form shown below was selected for its wide application in various types of real estate transactions as well as for its clarity of content. Its language protects the broker in the event of default by either party.

SALES CONTRACT

_____(City) , (State) ,_____ 19__

Receipt is hereby acknowledged of the sum of
(check/cash) Dollars ($_____) from_____proceeds to be held in
escrow by   subject to the terms hereof, as a deposit on account
of the purchase price of the following described property:

(Here include legal description)

Purchase price:

_____ Dollars ($ _____)

Terms and conditions of sale:

(Here include all of the special provisions
of the transaction)

Seller agrees to surrender possession of herein described premises to purchaser on _____ . Seller agrees to assume risk of any and all damage to above described premises prior to closing of this transaction, ordinary wear and tear excepted.

Taxes based on 19___assessments, insurance, .interest, rents and other expenses or revenue of said property shall be _____

Certified liens, if any, shall be paid in full by the seller. Pending liens, if any, shall be assumed by the purchaser. It is understood and agreed that this property is being sold and purchased subject to the zoning restrictions, reservations and limitations of record, if any. Seller agrees to convey title free and clear of all encumbrances, except as herein set forth, by a good and sufficient _____ deed.

Seller agrees to deliver to purchaser within_____days from the date hereof a complete abstract to said property, brought to date showing his title to be good, marketable and/or insurable, and in the event such abstract is not delivered within said time, seller hereby authorizes the undersigned broker to have an abstract made at seller's expense and delivered to purchaser, but, in the event title shall not be found good, marketable and/or insurable, seller agrees to use reasonable diligence to make the said title good, marketable and/or insurable and shall have _____ days so to do, but if after reasonable diligence on his part, said title shall not be made good, marketable and/or insurable within _____days, the money this day paid and all monies that may have been paid under this contract shall be returned to purchaser and the purchaser and seller shall be released from all obligations hereunder to each other. Or, upon request of the purchaser, the seller shall deliver the title in its existing condition.

It is mutually agreed that this transaction shall be closed and the purchaser shall pay the balance of the cash to close and execute all papers necessary to be executed by him for the completion of this purchase within _____days from the delivery of the aforementioned abstract.

Checks issued for the deposit on this contract will be deposited promptly for clearance and the holder of the deposit will not be responsible for non-payment of checks received. Deposit checks will be deposited and the funds held in an escrow account until the sale is closed. If the seller does not execute the contract, the deposit will be returned to the purchaser upon notification by the bank to the holder of the deposit that checks received have cleared.

When this contract is executed by the purchaser and the seller and the sale is not closed due to any default or failure on the part of the purchaser, the seller, at his option, may seek to enforce this contract; in which event, the purchaser shall be obligated to pay reasonable attorney's fees and court costs to the seller, or else the seller may direct the holder of the deposit to pay the broker his brokerage fee not to exceed one-half of the deposit and to pay the balance of the deposit to the seller as consideration for execution of this agreement, and the holder of the deposit shall be held harmless by all parties for disbursement in accordance with this agreement.

When the contract is executed by the purchaser and the seller and the sale is not closed due to default or failure on the part of the seller, the purchaser, at his option, may take action to enforce this contract; in which event, the seller shall be obligated to pay reasonable attorney's fees and court costs to the purchaser, and the seller shall be obligated to pay the full real estate brokerage fee to the broker. In the event it shall be necessary for the broker or brokers to enforce collection of the payment of the real estate brokerage fee, the seller shall be obligated to pay reasonable attorney's fees and court costs to the broker or brokers.

Time shall be of the essence and this contract shall be binding on both parties, their heirs, personal representatives, and/or assigns when this contract shall have been signed by both parties or their agents.

Singular pronouns of the first person shall be read as plural when the agreement is signed by two or more persons.

By _____

I, or we, agree to purchase the above described property on the terms and conditions stated in the foregoing contract, and do hereby approve, ratify, and confirm said contract in all respects.

Witness:

_____   _____ (Seal)
                                              Purchaser

_____   _____ (Seal)
                                              Purchaser

I, or we, agree to sell the above described property on the terms and conditions stated in the foregoing contract, and do hereby approve, ratify and confirm said contract in all respects. The undersigned acknowledges the employment of the broker named herein and agrees to pay said broker _____% of the purchase price of the said property as a brokerage fee for finding the above signed purchaser. Said brokerage fee shall be paid at time of closing of this transaction, except as otherwise provided herein.

Witness:

_____   _____ (Seal)
                                                Seller

_____   _____ (Seal)
                                                Seller

(Reproduced with permission of the Miami Board of Realtors, Miami, Fla.)

CLOSING COSTS DISCLOSURE

Some states require each broker to furnish the purchaser written notification that he will be charged certain closing costs before obtaining title to the property. A simple disclosure form, rather than a formal, explanatory letter is the clearest and most direct way to satisfy this requirement. Such a form is illustrated below.

CLOSING COSTS DISCLOSURE FORM

To: Prospective Purchaser

As a prospective purchaser of real estate you should be aware that additional acquisition costs may be demanded of you upon the closing of the sale. Some of the known closing costs are set forth below:

1. Survey
2. Title Insurance
3. Recording Fees
4. Roof Inspection
5. Termite Inspection
6. Insurance Polity
7. Attorney's Fees
8. Service Fee On Mortgage
9. Origination Fee On Mortgage
10. Intangible Tax
11. Documentary Stamps
12. Credit Report
13. Appraisal Fee
14. Mortgage Company's Attorney's Fees
15. Abstract Fee
16. Charge For Establishing Escrow Account
17. Other: _____

The broker(s) in this transaction (is)(are) _____, who (is)(are) the agent(s) for the seller and will be compensated by him upon completion of this transaction.

The purchaser acknowledges this instrument has been read and signed prior to the signing of the contract of sale.

Witness:

_____

_____   _____
                                                Purchaser

                                                _____
                                                Purchaser

                                                _____
                                                Broker

THE POLICY BOOK

The daily function of a busy real estate office puts in motion a myriad of procedural problems that can become quite chaotic if ground rules are not formulated beforehand.

A policy book is a compilation of the rules and regulations by which a real estate office functions. Adopting good, workable policies creates harmony and effective relations between management and personnel. It is simply good business to run an office from a set of thought-out solutions to predictable situations. In addition, a policy book should be inspirational in tone.

The policy book presented here is the result of tested procedures that can readily be adopted for use by every real estate office.

INTRODUCTION

Welcome to the_____Company, Inc. Realtors. You are joining a hard-hitting sales team of carefully selected professionals. Our success over the years did not happen by accident. It's the result of diligent, properly-directed work, that stems from a set of carefully thought-out, time-tested policies. Keep in mind that the company, by law, is responsible for your ethical and business activities. Do not do anything by word or actions that could put your license in jeopardy, or that of the company. Your success is our success. Be proud to be a member of this elite team. We'll benefit when your actions are a credit to us all.

OUR AIM

It is the company's intention to be Number 1 in sales in the county by working aggressively, knowledgeably and ethically, while functioning together as a team.

ETHICS AND INTEGRITY

As members of the National Association of Realtors we have pledged to abide by the Association's Code of Ethics,[8] which can be summed up in the golden rule, "Do unto others as you would have them do unto you."

Absolute integrity in all your dealings will result in added sales. Buyers and sellers place confidence in those they trust, and once you have a person's trust the job of selling becomes relatively easy.

KNOW THE FACTS

Know what you are talking about. Get exact information about any property you are presenting. If you don't know the answer to a question, don't guess. You will inspire confidence by admitting not knowing, and finding the answer later. If a buyer has confidence in you and feels he can rely on your representations, you are at a great advantage.

COMPANY REPUTATION

We feel our reputation is our most important asset. Each of us contributes to it by his daily actions. We are known in the community for our high standards, which makes it easier to get listings, prospects and repeat

---

[8]See page 291, Realtor's Code of Ethics.

sales. The company firmly believes that it is better to lose a sale than to make one by misrepresentation.

COMMISSION DIVISION

The commission division between office and salesman follows:

Basic Split	50/50
When Salesman sells own listing	60/40
When Salesman Sells outside Broker's listing (on what we receive)	50/50
When Salesman sells inside Listing (after listing fee)	50/50
Listing fee if Property is sold inside office	10%
Listing fee if Property is sold outside office (with office)	50/50
When Salesman sells office listing	50/50

BONUS PLAN

"Nothing succeeds like success," may be an old saw, but nevertheless, one we heartily believe in, and subscribe to. As an added incentive for salesmen to reach ever-higher plateaus, your commission will be increased from 50 percent to 60 percent for the balance of the year after you have earned $10,000. Calculations begin January 1st of each year.

HOW TO DRAW THE DEPOSIT RECEIPT

Taking a deposit is the single most important procedure you will do in real estate, so take great care in seeing that it is done properly. Proceed as follows:

1. Fill in the standard Deposit Receipt form completely and accurately. Double check the spelling of the principal names, and the legal description. Be certain the wording of all terms and conditions is not ambiguous. Be certain all necessary signatures are obtained, including the required <u>two</u> witnesses.

2. It is company policy to take 10 percent of the sales price as a deposit. Adhere to this amount in all instances. Any deviation from the rule must first be cleared with the office.

3. Have checks made out to the company's Escrow account.

4. Turn the check into the office for deposit the day you receive it. Any delay not only may jeopardize your sale, but it is also against state real estate law.

5. Make an original and four copies. After the purchaser has signed and given you the deposit, and you have also signed for the company, give him a copy. It serves as his receipt for the deposit money. When the seller has signed, leave him a copy. You now have one copy remaining for each of their attorneys. The original is retained by the company.

COMMISSION SCHEDULE[9]

We strictly adhere to our commission schedule. No salesman is authorized to deviate from it, or in any way negotiate our compensation with a client. If a question or dispute about commission arises, immediately take yourself off the griddle by stating the facts of the situation—<u>that you have no authority to change the standard commission</u>, and that matters of this nature have to be discussed with management.

If you deviate from this rule causing a cut commission, the entire amount lost will be deducted from your share of the deal.

RELATIONSHIP WITH ASSOCIATES

It's been our purpose to instill a cooperative, team effort among salesmen in this office. Be ready to work jointly with your fellow associates and share a commission when the occasion requires. Also, stand ready to be of

---

[9]See pages 51-53.

assistance on a courtesy basis when no monetary gain is immediately apparent. Courtesy begets courtesy. The shoe may be on the other foot next time.

RELATIONSHIP WITH CLIENTS

A good client-salesman relationship occurs when you are working with him on an equal footing. Do not talk down, or (at the other extreme) appear subservient to him. Look upon him as a business friend. You each have a common purpose, and it can best be achieved when you're working from the same level. Make your meetings together pleasurable. Don't tell him about your ailments, family misfortunes or other personal problems. No one wants to hear that! A good salesman is optimistic by nature. Make him want to see you again and do business with you in the future. Indeed, contact him periodically after a sale is made. If you have done your job well, he will always be a valuable source of repeat and referral business.

PERSONAL HABITS

Look prosperous. Dress well. Participate in community affairs. Be civic-minded. Join a service organization. Become active in your church. If politically motivated, you may want to take a fling at running for public office. Be socially active. Make "waves," for the more well-known you become, the more chance you will have of generating new business.

Drinking alcoholic beverages during business hours is strictly forbidden. Having alcohol on your breath is a sure way to lose a deal. Your respect and credibility are compromised in the eyes of your client. What you do after hours is your concern, but during the working day you must abstain from consuming alcohol. Violations of this rule will mean dismissal.

Be punctual. Do not develop a reputation for being late. Be reliable, reputable, and an all-around good person to do business with.

FLOOR TIME

We have initiated a rotation system to provide equal floor time for each salesman. During floor time, when the salesman is "up" he receives all prospect inquiries and property listings, whether by telephone or walk-in. The only exceptions are when he is already occupied or when a client or prospect specifically asks for <u>another</u> salesman. When he is occupied, the second schedule's "up" salesman takes his turn.

A good floor man will have done his homework. He will have prepared himself by knowing all current office listings, what is being advertised and what properties have "for sale" signs on them. He must be in a position to handle the floor with confidence and knowledge.

Your floor time lasts for one full day or until you show property to a walk-in prospect. After you complete your turn on the floor, your name is placed on the bottom of the list until your turn comes around again. From a standpoint of fairness and sales results, this system has proven one of the most significant innovations we have ever initiated.

OFFICE HOURS

We open at 8:30 A.M. and close at 6:00 P.M., seven days a week. You will be assigned floor time. A schedule is posted weekly setting forth when it is mandatory for you to be on duty or standing by, and when you will have a day off. If for any reason you cannot cover your floor assignment, be certain the sales manager is informed as far in advance as possible so that he can arrange for a substitute. You are expected to put in a minimum of a 40-hour workweek.

VACATIONS

A summer vacation schedule is prepared by management during the first week in May. Each of us will have two weeks off. In order to avoid a conflict of dates, list your first and second choice of vacation time with the office no later than April 30th.

GROUP INSURANCE

A low-cost major-medical group, hospitalization plan is available to all employees. It also offers an optional life insurance plan as a part of the package. It is available through our affiliation with the Board of Realtors. This is not a mandatory plan, but the wisdom in having such insurance should be apparent. Details will be furnished you upon request.

EXPENSES

The office is not liable for any unauthorized expenses incurred by the salesman.

If legal or other expenses are required to make the sale or protect the commission, the expenditures will be made by the office and deducted from the gross commission received before the usual division is made.

Office expenses such as secretarial, telegrams, advertising, printing, signs, photos, telephone, etc. will be paid for by management. Out-of-town calls and ads, however, must first be approved by the sales manager.

YOUR AUTOMOBILE

Each salesman must furnish his own automobile and is responsible for its maintenance, upkeep and insurance. The insurance shall cover bodily injury and property damage in the amount of $_____ and $_____ respectively, naming the company as additionally insured. A copy of the policy must be filed with the office.

OFFICE FACILITIES

The most modern electronic calculators, dictating equipment, typewriters, photo-copying machines, cameras, up to date plat books, aerial maps and tax rolls are available for you to use in the performance of your duties. In addition, you have access to our extensive library of real estate books, as well as all files and records. The secretarial staff is at your service, as, of course, is management. We will spare no reasonable expense or effort in helping you with the mechanics of performing your job.

YOU AS A PHOTOGRAPHER

A choice of several very good cameras and ample color film are always available to you. Learn how to use them with skill. There is nothing to equal a good visual presentation whether you're selling a country barn or a $10 million high-rise. A good photo or two speak the proverbial 1,000 words toward making your next sale.

ATTENDING CLOSINGS

It is mandatory that all salesmen attend the closing of sales they have negotiated. Last-minute problems can arise at a closing session that may only be worked out by the salesman who has been with the principals since the beginning. No one else knows their motivations and impulses better. More than one deal has been saved at the closing table by well-timed tactful words of wisdom by the salesman.

ADVERTISING PROCEDURE

It is our policy to advertise only Exclusive Listings. Display and classified ads will be written by the salesman and submitted to the sales manager for approval and final drafting. It is the salesman's responsibility to insert the ad, and then, after it appears, cut it out and place it in the "Advertising and Publicity Book" with the following information.

Date of Insertion —
Newspaper it Appeared in —
What Page and Section —
Results —

SHOWING AND SELLING THE PROPERTY

1. Never show more than three or four properties to a purchaser in a given day.

2. Plan your appointments by calling the sellers beforehand.

3. Show the properties in their best light by taking the most desirable routes to get there.

4. Don't just talk for the sake of making conversation. Make your words count, and remember, successful selling is also knowing when to be silent.

5. After showing the properties, offer the prospect a choice by asking "which one" he wants to buy. The "either or" method rapidly brings him around to the point of it all—deciding.

6. Don't be timid about asking for a depsoit. Be forceful, be bold, and with it all, be polite, but ask for the money.

7. Take an offer even if you feel it will not be accepted. Your job is narrowing the gap to where it will be acceptable even if it means going back and forth again and again.

REGISTERING PROSPECTS

You must register the name of your prospect with the office along with the properties you have actually shown him. Telling the buyer about it and giving him the address is not sufficient to qualify him as your prospect. You have actually to take him to the property.

The same prospect may, at another time, call regarding other properties. When this occurs, unless he specifically asks for you and you are available at the time, he will be assigned to the floor man. With our ads continually running, and "for sale" signs on many properties, this is the only equitable course we can follow.

In the event that a prospect calls for a second inspection of the property, and the salesman who had shown it to him is not available, then another salesman will be assigned to him. If a contract results, then the second salesman will receive 10 percent of the first salesman's commission.

REGISTERING LISTINGS

Any new listings you obtain, whether on an open basis or exclusive, must be immediately registered with the office. Be certain the listing form is completely filled out. An incomplete listing is a sign of inefficiency and it only means double work. Remember the old axiom, "A well-listed property is half sold." The salesman who lists the property first is the one who will receive the standard listing fee when it is sold.

THE "POCKET LISTING"

A "pocket listing" is one that a salesman either does not register with the office or delays registering. Hiding properties in this manner is completely unethical, and contrary to our team approach of operating. The practice will not be tolerated. A listing must be in the office the same day it is obtained. The seriousness of this violation cannot be minimized. A salesman caught "pocketing" a listing may be subject to dismissal.

DEAL WITH THE RIGHT PRINCIPAL

When dealing with an individual, corporation, or group, be certain the person you are negotiating with has the authority to act. You will be saving a lot of wheel-spinning if you first determine that the representative can indeed be a party to a contract, and that he is not just "bird dogging" for someone else, or a board of directors. A person's company designation is sometimes deceptive. Many a vice-president's title is just for promotional purposes.

SALESMAN BUYING OR SELLING FOR OWN ACCOUNT

The office has no objection to a salesman buying or selling real estate for his own account, providing the office's portion of the commission is received the same as if any other sale took place. Salesmen should be cautioned, however, that they must reveal their position as a principal to the other party when negotiating as such.

GENERAL POLICIES

To insure that a principal's rights are fully protected, it is incumbent upon you to recommend that he hire an attorney. Under no circumstances are you to dispense legal advice or suggest that a buyer or seller not retain a lawyer. This rule also holds true for giving tax, accounting, or any other professional advice, except real estate.

High-pressure selling is contrary to our ethics. Salesmen are cautioned against trying to force a sale in this manner. You will do far better to go the other route. Speak softly, but carry a velvet hammer.

Do not criticize our competitors even if you think it is warranted. The motives for making such criticism appear so obvious that whatever you say, would probably be discounted. It can only prove detrimental to you in the long run.

Be courteous and cheerful (a good salesman is an eternal otpimist), and always retain a professional bearing. Your continuing real estate education is important for enhancing your abilities. Therefore, it is a company requirement that you enroll in at least one college level, real-estate related course each year, or attend the weekly training programs conducted by this office.

POLICY CHANGES

Because real estate is such an active, viable business, in the interest of fairness and efficiency, the office reserves the right to make policy changes that it deems necessary.

FINAL WORD

You are a part of a leading, highly successful real estate organization. If you adhere to our policies, put in a good day's work, and apply yourself properly, success is sure to be yours. Good luck.

3

CONDOMINIUMS AND

COOPERATIVES

Condominium Defined . . . Declaration of Condominium . . . Bylaws . . . Articles of Incorporation . . . Condominium Common Area Contract . . . Condominium Unit Contract . . . Condominium Mortgage . . . Warranty Deed for Condominium Unit . . . Maintenance Contracts, Recreation Leases and Ground Leases . . . Selling the Condominium . . . The Prospectus.

Cooperative Defined . . . Tax and Other Advantages . . . Certificate of Incorporation . . . Bylaws . . . Subscription Agreement . . . Occupany Agreement . . . Cooperative's Place in the Housing Field.

CONDOMINIUMS

The concept of condominium ownership had its origin in Europe during the late Middle Ages and has had many peaks of popularity throughout history. In recent times, South America, Puerto Rico and some portions of Europe have utilized this form of ownership to a great extent, as has the United States since 1961. In that year, the National

Housing Act was passed, under which the Federal Housing Administration was authorized (through Title II, Section 234) to insure mortgages for people owning individual units in apartment dwellings. State laws throughout most of the nation soon followed, which, in the main, treat condominium ownership on a similar basis as any other fee simple possession of real estate.

A condominium owner receives title to his unit in the form of a deed, as do all property owners. He may arrange mortgage financing and insure the premises. The real estate taxes on the unit are assessed and billed him separately. All the advantages of fee ownership are his, such as being able to deduct the property taxes and mortgage interest charges from his federal income tax. In states where homestead exemption exists, he may take advantage of this form of tax savings. The condominium owner may repair and maintain the unit, and lease it or sell it as he sees fit.

There are certain common areas of a condominium structure—such as the corridors, stairs, elevators, swimming pool, heating plant, lobby and the ground itself—that are held jointly by all the owners of the condominium. Their rights to its use and the sharing of maintenance and other costs are usually clearly defined in the bylaws and other documents of the condominium.

To insure the legal rights of condominium owners, lengthy, and sometimes complex instruments are required. Some of those in general use and their main purpose are explained below:

Declaration of Condominium—This instrument details the conditions, covenants, restrictions and intentions for which the structure is created. The provisions of the declaration must follow state condominium requirements in those states that have enacted laws regulating offerings made to condominium buyers. It must also comply with federal standards and regulations when under FHA auspices.

Bylaws—Bylaws are standing rules and regulations that govern the condominium project. Subjects such as voting rights, holding of meetings, the election of officers and the extent of their powers are determined, as are the authority for leveling assessments, the ordering of repairs and improvements, and the issuing of maintenance contracts.

Articles of Incorporation—Condominiums, like cooperatives, are corporate in structure, and are generally organized as non-profit entities. The articles of a condominium corporation state the statutory powers it holds, the qualifications and requirements for membership, method of choosing officers and directors, and their indemnification by the corporation for expenses and liabilities.

Condominium Common Area Contract—This is a specialized contract that sets forth the purchase price, describes the common areas covered under the agreement, establishes the operation and maintenance of the facilities, and provides for a good and marketable title to be conveyed.

Condominium Unit Contract—Aside from a detailed description of the unit, together with the legal description of the entire premises, the condominium unit contract for sale is similar to contracts for the transfer of any other form of real property. A typical description is shown below:

> Condominium apartment unit #_____, of_____ Condominium, Inc., all as set forth in the Declaration of Condominium and the exhibits annexed thereto and forming a part thereof, recorded in Offical Records Book #_____, at Page_____, of the Public Records of_____County, State of_____; together with all of the appurtenances thereto including an individual_____% interest in and to the common elements of said condominium.
> All of the foregoing condominium apartment unit is situated on a portion of Lot_____, Block_____, in_____ Subdivision, according to the Public Records of County, State of_____. A more detailed metes and bounds description that the said condominium apartment unit is situated on is set forth in the said Declaration of Condominium.

Condominium Mortgage—As in the contract (with the notable exception of the legal description), the form used for condominium mortgaging is essentially similar to those in use for other forms of real estate ownership. The only area where they differ is in a reference clause linking it to the Declaration of Condominium document. A typical reference clause reads,

> "This mortgage is on an apartment in a condominium together with appurtenances thereto. The failure of the mortgagor to pay any assessments required to be paid pursuant to the Declaration of Condominium or to otherwise comply with any of the terms, covenants or conditions of said Declaration

shall constitute a default under this mortgage; and the mortgagee may at its option, immediately or thereafter, declare the indebtedness secured herewith due and payable.''

Warranty Deed for Condominium Unit—In addition to a full description of the unit as well as the overall property as shown in the Condominium Unit Contract, the deed should contain the following language:

This conveyance is subject to:

1. Taxes and assessments for the year 19___, and subsequent years thereto.

2. Conditions, restrictions, limitations, convenants running with the land, and easements appearing of record.

3. Zoning ordinances of_____County, State of
_____.

4. The Declaration of Condominium and exhibits attached thereto and the Articles of Incorporation and Bylaws of _____ Condominium Apartments, Inc.

The unit warranty deed is signed by the president of the condominium corporation, attested to by the secretary and generally witnessed by at least two people.

Maintenance Contracts, Recreation Leases and Ground Leases

Some condominium projects bind their members to maintenance contracts, recreation leases (whereby the recreational facilities are separately leased to them), and ground leases. The latter situation occurs when the land under the structure does not belong to the condominium corporation, but rather is leased for a long term (frequently 99 years). Contracts and leases of this nature, though sometimes necessary, are considered negative features. However, with state and federal regulations to contend with, most condominium builders offer overall real estate value, particularly in markets where condominium projects are highly competitive.

Throughout the country, real estate other than apartment buildings is moving into the condominium scene. Office buildings and warehouses, particularly, are being built or converted for condominium use. They, at once, offer the user tax advantages and most frequently prove to be sound investments.

Selling the Condominium

The first requisite for selling condominium units is an adequately budgeted, effective advertising campaign. The promotion must be planned to reach the type of buyer being sought. At one extreme, is the luxury-oriented campaign for the wealthy. Invariably stressed here is snob appeal, exclusivity and expensiveness. At the other, is the "bread and butter" condo sales program seeking to reach average-income families who want good living accommodations priced within their means. Somewhere in between, are the vast majority of projects up and down the economic scale, including those directed to special interest groups such as retirees, golf or tennis enthusiasts, families, religious groups, trade union members, etc.

Some advertisements go into meticulous details of the facilities, amenities or financing available. The story must be told with such enthusiasm, clarity and directness that the prospective purchaser will be sufficiently motivated to inspect the premises and later purchase a unit. The complete advertising campaign is often accomplished with elaborate fold-out color brochures (generally displaying site and floor plans), full-page newspaper advertisements, strategically placed billboards, as well as TV and radio commercials. Most developers seek out ad agencies that have had prior experience in this type of promotion; for the blending of copy and artwork and the use of the proper medium is a job for competent professionals.

The Prospectus

Falling within the area of promotion, yet a legally required presentation in some states, is the Prospectus, a preliminary printed statement concerning the offering. A typical Prospectus might read as follows:

PROSPECTUS

The following is a summary of the pertinent facts relating to (Name of Condominium), a residential condominium:

1. (Name of Condominium) consists of (# of Units) apartments located at_____(Address)_____.

2. There is no recreation or ground lease associated with this condominium project.

3. It is the developer's intention to sell all of the condominium apartments. In the event all are not sold, the developer reserves the right to lease any unsold apartments.

4. All of the apartment residences and facilities are owned in common by the unit owners, and in addition thereto, a parking area containing _____ parking spaces, lobbies and public areas, swimming pool and recreation deck area, card room and billiards area, men's and women's saunas, exercise room, tennis courts and dressing rooms. Adjacent areas will be landscaped.

5. ___(Name of Condominium)___ offers a choice of five different apartment floor plans:

Type "A" units, each with 1 bedroom and 1½ baths.
Type "B" units, each with 2 bedrooms and 2 baths.
Type "C" units, each with 2 bedrooms and 2 baths convertible.
Type "D" units, each with 2 bedrooms and 2 baths, plus a den.
Type "E" units, each with 3 bedrooms and 3 baths.

6. A copy of the site and plot plan designating the portions of the apartment building that are owned by the unit owners or the Association is attached to the Declaration of Condominium.

7. The estimated date for completion of _(Name of Condominium)_ is____(Date)____or earlier.

8. ___(Name of Condominium)___ provides the following wholly owned recreational facilities:

  (a)   A landscaped recreation and pool deck area of approximately _____square feet.

  (b)   A heated swimming pool approximately _____square feet, having a depth of _____feet at the shallow end and _____feet at the deepest point, and which facility has a capacity of approximately_____persons.

  (c)   A men's and women's sauna, each of which has approximately _____square feet of area and a capacity of_____persons each.

(d) A separate men's and women's dressing area, shower and bathroom facilities, each of which is approximately _____ square feet, and has a capacity of _____ persons each.

(e) An exercise room of approximately _____ square feet, which has a capacity of approximately _____ persons.

(f) A recreation room of approximately _____ square feet, which has a capacity of _____ persons.

(g) A crafts room of approximately _____ square feet, which has a capacity of approximately _____ persons.

(h) A kitchen of approximately _____ square feet, which has a capacity of approximately _____ persons.

(i) An office and reception area for the manager of approximately _____ square feet, which has a capacity of approximately _____ persons.

(j) _____ tennis courts of approximately _____ square feet, which have a capacity of approximately _____ persons.

(k) _____ laundry rooms of approximately _____ square feet each, which have the capacity of approximately _____ persons.

(l) Tenant's storage areas of approximately _____ square feet each, which have a capacity of approximately _____ persons, and which are located on each floor of the building.

9. It is represented that the minimum amount that will be expended for the personal property to be installed in and furnished to the common elements shall be the sum of $_____.

10. It is estimated that the recreational facilities referred to above will be available for use by owners on or before _____.

11. All of the recreational facilities referred to above shall be owned by the Association.

12. The cost for the operation and maintenance of the recreational facilities is included within the maintenance sum charged the apartment owners by the Association.

13. The following is a brief summary of the restrictions concerning the use of the condominium apartments which have been incorporated herein for the mutual benefit of all apartment owners:

(a) All apartments shall be used for residential purposes.

(b) No unlawful use shall be made of the condominium property or any part thereof.

(c) No sale or rent sign shall be permitted on any part of the property.

(d) Children shall not play in walks, corridors, elevators or stairways of the property.

(e) The common elements shall not be abused, defaced, littered or obstructed in any way.

(f) No structural changes or alterations to any unit (except as provided in the Declaration of Condominium) can be made.

(g) Pets shall be permitted provided that the maintenance of such pets shall not constitute a nuisance. The Board of Directors shall determine whether there has been any violation of this rule.

(h) No radio or television antenna, or any wiring for any purpose may be installed on the exterior of the building.

(i) Televisions, radios and musical instruments must be used at such times as will provide a minimum of disturbance to other unit owners.

(j) No unit owner or resident shall direct, supervise or in any manner attempt to assert any control over any of the employees of the Association.

(k) The Managing Agent of the Association shall retain a pass key to each condominium unit for emergency purposes.

(l) Nothing shall be hung or displayed on the exterior walls, balconies, terraces or staircases of the building.

(m) The halls and staircases shall remain free and clear of all garbage cans, supplies, milk bottles and other articles.

14. _____ Waterworks will supply water, storm drainage, and sewage disposal. Waste disposal will be provided by_____ Sanitation Co. Electricity will be supplied by_____. Telephone service will be supplied by_____.

15. There is a management agreement which the Association executed with_____ Realty Co. Said management agreement is for a period_____years. The services to be performed by the management company are as follows:

(a) To render to the Board of Directors of the Association, monthly statements of receipts, expenses and charges, and to remit receipts less disbursements.

(b) To employ and supervise a day manager and other employees, to supervise necessary decorating, repairs and replacements in the common elements, to insure the operation of the premises as a first-class apartment complex, with cleaning service as reasonably required, and all periodic cleaning and maintenance work reasonably necessary for operations.

(c) To provide experienced assistance and recommendations to the Board of Directors in connection with annual budgets and the analysis of operating results.

(d) To attend meetings and to keep the minutes thereof, of the annual meeting of the owners and each regular monthly meeting of the Board.

(e) To collect assessments due or to become due from the owners and to give receipts therefor.

(f) To keep detailed and accurate records in chronological order of the receipts and expenditures affecting the common elements, and to prepare a yearly budget for maintenance and operation of the building and to notify each owner on or before_____ of each year as to such estimate, wtih a reasonable itemization thereof. Further, to supply all owners on or before the annual meeting, an itemized accounting of the maintenance expenses for the preceding year and of all sums collected.

(g) To assist in the preparation and implementation of appropriate rules for the operation of the premises, including preparation and serving of appropriate notices to the owners with respect to breaches of such rules and reports to the Board concerning continuing infractions. Further, to handle paperwork and correspondence for officers and members of the Board, and to mail all notices of meetings, prepare a certified list of members qualifying to vote, and provide the owners with a summary of meetings and special reports.

(h) To maintain appropriate records of all insurance coverage required by the Declaration or reasonably required by prudent management, and to assist in the preparation of all claims and in the settlement thereof by cooperating with any insurance agent having the responsibility for the placement of insurance.

(i) To render on behalf of the Board any and all services and perform any and all duties and take whatever action is reasonably necessary, whether or not specifically designated or authorized in the management agreement, that may be deemed necessary to the efficient and proper management of the property.

(j) To hire, supervise, discharge and pay all day managers, and other employees and pay necessary taxes and file payroll tax returns for said employees. To arrange contracts covering laundry and other leased concessions as directed by the Board. To place purchase orders for such equipment, tools, appliances, materials and supplies as are necessary to maintain the property.

The compensation to be paid the management company is the sum of $_____ per month until one-third of the premises is occupied;

$_____per month until two-thirds of the premises is occupied; and
$_____per month after all the units are occupied.

16. Purchasers of condominium apartments in ___(Name of Condominium)___ shall receive a Fee Simple interest therein, plus an undivided interest in the common elements appurtenant thereto.

17. The developer has the right to retain control of the Association until a majority of the units have been sold.

18. The manner in which the apportionment of common expenses has been determined is by utilizing a fraction—the numerator of which is the square footage contained in a particular unit, and the denominator of which is the total square footage of all units.

19. The estimated monthly and annual expenses for the Association, and a schedule of the apartment owner's expenses is as set forth on the "Projected Budget" delivered with the Condominium Documents. There are no items of expense contemplated to be required to be payable by the apartment owners to persons or entities other than the Association. The total estimated monthly and annual expense is as stated in the budget. There is no rent payable to the Association or to other parties for recreation or other commonly used facilities. The estimated operating budget is for the first annual accounting period of the Association.

20. At the time of the closing, the purchaser will be required to pay a sum equal to_____percent of the purchase price of the apartment unit (exclusive of the cost of extras), which will pay for the documentary stamps on the deed, issuance of an owner's title insurance policy in the amount of the purchase price, and the recordation of the deed of conveyance. The purchaser shall pay for the cost of a complete abstract of title and any and all mortgage closing costs. The purchaser shall further pay the amount of $_____ , which shall be payable to the Association as an initial deposit.

(Adapted with permission of Kendall Gate-Invesco, Inc.)

COOPERATIVES

The cooperative form of ownership is corporate in structure, with each owner-occupant purchasing shares of stock in the corporation. As stockholders and participants, members are jointly and severally held responsible for the obligations and actions of the corporation. Each member of the cooperative is the lessor of the unit he occupies. His rental payments cover the proporationate share of mortgage payments, taxes insurance, repairs and maintenance.

Unlike the condominium form of ownership where each participant has a separate mortgage and deed to his unit, the mortgage and deed cover the entire property and are held by the cooperative corporation. In the event of a default on the mortgage, all owner-occupants are affected.

The value of the stock one possesses is usually pro-rated in proportion to the size of, and investment in, the apartment unit. It is generally calculated on a square footage and location basis. If a tenant-owner of a one-bedroom unit has, say, 750 square feet in apartment area, his interest and obligations in the cooperative corporation would be half that of another owner occupying a similarly located, multi-bedroom unit consisting of 1,500 square feet of space. The expenses to maintain the common areas such as the heating plant, corridors, pool, grounds, and so on, are likewise pro-rated.

Advantages of this form of ownership include:

1. Deducting pro-rated interest and property tax payments, as well as depreciation elements when paying internal revenue tax.

2. Some degree of control over monthly rental payments, as opposed to being subject to periodic lease increases at the hands of the landlord.

3. With appreciating real estate, as traditionally occurs with the passing of time, the value of a cooperative owner's shares will also increase.

4. Many states extend homestead exemption property tax benefits to cooperative apartment owners.

Some highly specialized real estate forms are used in creating and maintaining a cooperative building. Forms such as:

Certificate of Incorporation—This document sets forth the purpose of the cooperative, the number of officers and directors, the method of issuing capital stock in the corporation, rights and obligations of members, rules of conduct of affairs, contractual powers, remedy in the event of a default, and length of the agreement.

Bylaws—The rules governing the cooperative are covered in the bylaws. Subjects such as membership requirements, meetings, method of selecting officers and directors, fiscal management, and use of common area facilities are detailed.

Subscription Agreement—This document states the amount of shares in the cooperative and their par value that an individual owner-tenant agrees to purchase. Other matters provided for in the subscription agreement are the priority of the mortgage lien, the amount of the monthly carrying charges, occupancy agreement of the purchaser, and cancellation rights of the corporation in the event of a default.

Occupancy Agreement—This agreement is also referred to as a Proprietary Lease. The right to occupy a specific unit or units of the building is covered, as are the monthly carrying charges, renewal options, management, taxes and insurance provisions, maintenance and additional clauses, default remedies, and subordination of the owner-tenant's rights to the lien of the mortgage.

Cooperative apartment ownership is primarily a product of large urban areas. For the confirmed apartment dweller (who may be weary of collecting valueless rent receipts), it is a means of owning a portion of the project in which he resides. As a stockholder, he has a voice in the affairs of the building. In recent years, cooperative housing has experienced an unspectacular, but steady growth nationwide. It has taken its place somewhere between individual ownership of an apartment unit (condominium), and renting as a tenant under lease.

4

EXCHANGING

Exchanges Discussed . . . Tax-free Status . . . Depreciation Benefit . . . Uninterrupted Income . . . Properties Must Qualify . . . Like-Kind Properties . . . Boot . . . Trade-ins As Means of Financing . . . Broker As Middleman . . . Exchange Contract Forms . . . Exchange Listing Forms . . . Reasons for Exchanging Real Estate.

Bartering is inherent in Man. It occurred before the advent of money, and examples of it can be found in civilization's earliest recorded history. It has prevailed as a mode of conducting business through the ages. Today, it is proving to be a sophisticated, increasingly popular method of transacting real estate, with investors taking advantage of its capital gains tax benefits, depreciation, and other money-saving features.

Particularly when a tight money market prevails, with limited cash available to invest, and mortgage money obtainable only at disadvantageous terms, exchanging or trading real estate offers a logical way of making deals. Wise investors and brokers are learning the techniques of exchanging and the tax and other advantages it has to offer.

TAX-FREE STATUS

The single most important reason for exchanging investment real estate today is its "tax-free" advantages. As provided under Section 1031 of the Internal Revenue Code, once property that meets certain qualifications is exchanged for "like kind" property, tax payments can be indefinitely deferred. The word "tax-free," however, is a misnomer. What actually occurs is that the tax on the gain, or the deduction on the loss, is only postponed until the property changes ownership in a conventional (and taxable) sales manner. Deferring tax payments can continue over many property exchanges and for many years. Indeed, it could conceivably continue until the owner dies. Then his heirs would be forced to pay the tax on the property at the current, and invariably higher, assessed base.

DEPRECIATION BENEFIT

Being able to begin a new depreciation basis is another valid reason for exchanging productive or investment real estate. No matter how much depreciation an exchangor may have used up on the property he is disposing of, he invariably can start the process all over again with the property he receives.

UNINTERRUPTED INCOME

Yet another advantage of exchanging income properties is the assurance of continuity of income. With an outright sale, many months or a year or more can elapse before the seller finds a suitable, comparable property. The interim loss of income can never be regained.

PROPERTIES MUST QUALIFY

In order for an exchange to qualify as being tax-free, it must meet several requirements. The property traded must either be held for productive use, or for investment. This would exclude "dealer" or "speculator" properties, which are held for short periods of time and then sold to the dealer's customers for a profit. The government declares a person a dealer when a study of his real estate activity reveals frequent purchases and sales in a given year with the properties remaining in his possession for only a brief period. The property has to be held as an investment, or for productive use (as a ranch, farm, mine, etc.) to qualify. Also excluded is a person's residence, which cannot be construed as falling into either of the above categories.

LIKE-KIND PROPERTIES

Further, to satisfy IRS regulations when effecting exchange for tax benefits, that which is exchanged must be for "like-kind" property. The federal government regulations explain this as follows. "The words 'Like-kind' have reference to the nature of the property and not to its grade or quality. The fact that any real estate involved is improved or unimproved is not material, for such fact relates only to the grade or quality of the property and not to its kind or class."

The real estate exchanged may be vacant land for an apartment, city real estate for a ranch, a farm for an office structure, a hotel for a shopping center, a lease of 30 years or more for a fee interest, an apartment for an apartment, etc. To be eligible, that which is traded must not be for personal property of any kind. Merchandise, vehicles, boats and residential real estate do not qualify.

BOOT

In an exchange of properties, if one party receives something of value in addition to the property he takes in trade, it is referred to as "boot." Boot can be a mortgage, personal property, stocks, bonds, cash or a residence. It is that which is added to make the transaction an even or equitable one. However, the boot portion of the trade is invariably taxable.

TRADE-INS AS MEANS OF FINANCING

A popular means of financing real estate is the trade-in of an existing house for a new one, or a lower-valued property for a higher one. In practice it works not unlike the trade-in allowance used in the automobile industry. The equity value of the property used for the trade is applied to property being purchased. In the instance of a builder who takes a used house in trade for a new one, his profits are invariably tied up in the property he has accepted. Many such builders list their acquisitions with active, local real estate offices, knowing they have the clientele for such houses and can generally bring about a fast sale.

BROKER AS MIDDLEMAN

In creating an exchange of real estate, the broker is most often put in the position of being a middleman. When this occurs, he represents neither side, but rather has a fiduciary relation to both. This is an ethical and legal business arrangement as long as both sides are made aware of his role. For effecting a trade he is entitled to receive a commission from both parties.

CONTRACTS AND LISTING FORMS

An especially formulated contract is needed to bring about a meeting of minds in an exchange agreement. The legal description of the two properties must be given, as must the detailed terms and conditions of the exchange. Two forms have been selected as examples. One is recommended by the Florida Association of Realtors; the other by the California Real Estate Association. Both are in frequent use and acceptance in their respective states as well as in others. Also illustrated are Exchange Listing Forms.

EXCHANGE AGREEMENT

Florida Association Of Realtors Standard Form

Date _____, State _____

The undersigned, as First Part(1) _____

does agree to transfer and convey to, as Second Party (2) _____
_____

the following described property (show legal of (1)) _____

(Show mortgages and amounts, if any)

and (pay) (accept) $ _____
upon closing in consideration of the transfer and conveyance of the following described property to him or his assigns (show legal of (2))

(Show mortgages and amounts, if any)

TERMS AND CONDITIONS

The parties hereto shall execute and deliver within _____ days from the date of acceptance, all instruments, in writing necessary to transfer title to said properties and complete this exchange. Conveyance shall be by warranty deed. Abstracts shall be furnished by the owners showing their titles to be insurable in the usual form subject to easements and restrictions common to the subdivision. Liens of governmental agencies for work authorized or not completed at time of closing and the mortgages shown above which shall be _____, taxes, insurance, interest and rents shall be prorated to date of closing.

First Party agrees that the Real Estate Broker representing him in this exchange is:

_____ of _____   _____
      Broker   Address   Phone No.

First party agrees that Broker may cooperate with other Brokers and divide commissions in any manner satisfactory to them. The above Broker or (Brokers) is (are) authorized to act as Broker for all parties hereto and may accept commission therefrom. Should second party accept this offer, first party agrees to pay said Broker commission for services rendered as follows: _____
_____

This offer shall be deemed revoked unless accepted in writing within
_____ days after date hereof and such acceptance is communicated to first
party within said period. Broker is hereby given the exclusive and irrevocable right to obtain acceptance of second party within said period. Time is
of the essence of this contract, but Broker may, without notice, extend for a
period of not to exceed one month the time for the performance of any act
hereunder, except the time for the acceptance hereof by second party. __

_____

Signed, sealed and delivered in
presence of:

_____   _____ (Seal)

_____   _____ (Seal)

                                        First Party or Parties
Dated _____ , 19__.   Accepted:_____

                                        Broker: _____

                                        By_____

ACCEPTANCE

    Second party hereby accepts the foregoing offer upon the terms and
conditions stated and agrees to pay commission for services rendered to:

_____ of _____   _____
        Broker   Address   Phone No.

as follows: _____

Second party agrees that Broker may act as Broker for all parties hereto and
may accept commission therefrom, and may co-operate with other Brokers
and divide commission in any manner satisfactory to them.
Signed, sealed and delivered in presence of:

_____   _____ (Seal)

_____   _____ (Seal)

                                        Second Party or Parties
Dated _____ , 19__.   Accepted:_____

                                        Broker: _____

                                        By: _____

*(Copyright form of the Florida Association Of Realtors used with its permission in this
publication and not for reprinting)*

EXCHANGE AGREEMENT (Another Form)

California Real Estate Association Standard Form

_____

_____

hereinafter called first party, hereby offers to exchange the following described property, situated in _____ , County of
_____ , State _____ .

(Here include description)

For the following described property of _____
_____ hereinafter
called second party, situated in_____ ,
County of_____ State_____ .

(Here include description)

TERMS AND CONDITIONS OF EXCHANGE:

_____

_____

_____

_____

   The parties hereto shall execute and deliver, within_____days from
the date this offer is accepted, all instruments, in writing, necessary to
transfer title to said properties and complete and consummate this exchange. Each party shall supply Preliminary Title Reports for their respective properties. Evidences of title shall be Land Title Association standard
coverage form policies of title insurance showing titles to be merchantable
and free of all liens and encumbrances, except taxes and those liens and
encumbrances as otherwise set forth herein. Each party shall pay for the
policies of Title insurance for the property to be acquired_____conveyed
_____.

   If either party is unable to convey a marketable title, except as herein
provided, within three months after acceptance hereof by second party, or

if the improvements on any of the herein named properties be destroyed or materially damaged prior to transfer of title or delivery of agreement of sale, then this agreement shall be of no further effect, except as to payment of commissions and expenses incurred in connection with examination of title, unless the party acquiring the property so affected elects to accept the title the other party can convey or subject to the conditions of the improvements.

Taxes, insurance premiums (if policies be satisfactory to party acquiring the property affected thereby), rents, interest and other expenses of said properties shall be prorated as of the date of transfer of title or delivery of agreement of sale, unless otherwise provided herein.

_____ of _____   _____
Broker   Address   Phone Number

is hereby authorized to act as broker for all parties hereto and may accept commission therefrom. Should second party accept this offer, first party agrees to pay said broker commission for services rendered as follows:

_____

Should second party be unable to convey a marketable title to his property, then first party shall be released from payment of any commission, unless he elects to accept the property subject thereto. First party agrees that broker may cooperate with other brokers and divide commissions in any manner satisfactory to them.

This offer shall be deemed revoked unless accepted in writing within __ days after date hereof, and such acceptance is communicated to first party within said period. Broker is hereby given the exclusive and irrevocable right to obtain acceptance of second party within said period.

Time is of the essence of this contract, but Broker may, without notice, extend for a period of not to exceed one month the time for the performance of any act hereunder, except the time for the acceptance hereof by second party.

All words used herein in the singular shall include the plural and the present tense shall include the future and the masculine gender shall include the feminine and neuter.

_____

_____

                                          _____

                                          _____

                                          _____

Dated _____ 19____   _____

ACCEPTANCE

Second party hereby accepts the foregoing offer upon the terms and conditions stated and agrees to pay commission for services rendered, to:

_____ of _____   _____
        Broker   Address   Phone No.

as follows:_____

_____

Second party agrees that broker may act as broker for all parties hereto and may accept commission therefrom, and may cooperate with other brokers and divide commissions in any manner satisfactory to them.

Should first party be unable to convey a marketable title to his property then second party shall be released from payment of any commission, unless he elects to accept the property of first party subject thereto.

_____   ____   _____ _____

_____

_____

_____

Dated_____ 19___   _____

(Reproduced with permission of the California Real Estate Association)

REASONS FOR EXCHANGING REAL ESTATE

Because of the added difficulty of convincing two parties of the merits and value of property to be exchanged, many brokers shy away from exchange transactions. Yet, even for those not oriented to this type of sale, opportunities frequently are there to work a trade. He should be alert for the signs, for when a sale is not forthcoming in the conventional manner, an exchange may be the only logical conclusion. Many times during the course of a broker's career he will be confronted with the possibilities of effecting trades. To best serve his clients and to close more deals, he should know the various advantageous features of dual sales and the ways of making them.

Most major cities throughout the country have Exchange Clubs composed primarily of Realtors who are specialists in this type of transaction. These groups meet regularly to share their listings and discuss methods, new techniques and current governmental regulations affecting exchanges. The National Institute Of Real Estate Brokers, an affiliate of the National Association of Realtors published a pamphlet beamed to property owners, listing 11 reasons for exchanging real estate. Though no longer in print, this list nevertheless remains a valuable summation of the advantages of exchanging, and is reproduced below:[1]

1. Exchanging can be the more convenient way of selling your property. It is much simpler at times to exchange, rather than to sell for cash and then look around for a new property.

2. Properties difficult to sell are often easier to exchange.

3. Properties with large equities, or free and clear, adapt themselves to exchanging.

4. You, as owner, can pyramid your equity by using the exchange method.

5. Investment properties can be exchanged to defer capital gains tax, until the property taken in exchange is sold.

6. Many buyers have frozen equities in other properties, which you can take in exchange for cash out by your Realtor.

7. Offering your property for exchange can lead to a cash sale.

8. A property offered for either an exchange or a straight sale widens the field for the seller. This attracts many more potential buyers.

9. Exchanging develops more logical transactions for the seller because of current tax regulations on investment properties.

10. Exchanging helps secure for the buyer properties that might not be otherwise obtainable. Because of tax considerations, many owners will not sell for cash.

11. Exchanging may help you obtain a depreciation advantage. If you now own property which has been substantially depreciated, you may acquire a new depreciation level by exchanging.

---

[1]Reproduced with permission of the Realtors® National Marketing Institute of the National Association of Realtors.

EXCHANGE LISTING

Property_____Address_____City_____

Sellers_____Address_____City_____

Phone_____Legal Name in which Title is Held_____

Manager_____Began?_____Salary_____Phone_____

Price_____Location_____Listing No._____Customer No_____

Terms_____

Type Property_____Date_____Expiration_____

Assess. Val._____Ind. F.M.V._____Seasonal ( ) Year-round ( ) Key_____

Will Trade_____Cash Avail._____Boot Avail._____Take Back Mtg._____

Basis_____Attorney_____Accountant_____

Tax-Bracket_____Previous Owner_____Address_____

Allocation of Value: Land_____% Improvements_____% Personal Property_____%

Depreciation Schedule_____% Deprec. taken_____Remaining economic life_____

Type Ownership: FEE_____COMMON_____JOINT_____PARTNERSHIP_____CORPORATION_____LEASEHOLD_____

Can Sublet?_____Sellers Age_____Purchase Date_____How Acquired_____

Title Held by: ABSTRACT ONLY_____Where Avail?_____TITLE INS._____

Inventory $_____Equipment $_____Furniture-Fixtures $_____Display Signs_____

Insurance Agent_____Building Rating_____

ENCUMBRANCES	Original Amt.	Payment	Term	Interest Rate	Date	Balance Due	Prepayment Penalty	Mortgagee
Prime								
Secondary								
Secondary								
Chattel								

Equity_____FHA Commitment_____Conv. Commitment_____

Annual Gross Income (end |)	($_____)	TYPE	Assess. Due	As Of	Paid By

ANNUAL EXPENSES: Water _____

Taxes, exc. Fed.-State $_____   Sewer _____

Insurance   _____   Street _____

Interest   _____

Management   _____   Elec._____Gas_____St. Sewer_____

Utilities   _____   Lot Size_____Parking_____

Maintenance-Repair   _____   Zoning_____Acreage_____

Replacements   _____   Taxes yr._____Tax Arrears_____

Misc.   _____   _____   BLDG: Year Built_____Size_____

NET OPERATING INCOME $_____   Type Construction_____

Amortization   _____   Plot Plan Avail.?_____Sq. Ft._____

NET INCOME (before deprec.) $_____   Roof_____Floors_____

Depreciation   _____   Stories_____Air Cond._____

NET TAXABLE INCOME $_____   Insul._____Street_____

% Return on: Equity_____Investment   _____   Heating_____Bus Service_____

Tax Returns Avail?_____Fiscal Yr. _____   Schools_____Churches_____

Figure 4-1.

NUMBER AND TYPE UNITS_____

_____

_____

NEEDED REPAIRS_____

_____

LEGAL DESCRIPTION_____

_____

_____

WILL TRADE FOR (AID)_____

_____

REASON FOR SELLING - MOTIVATION_____

_____

DESCRIPTION OF CHATTEL:

REMARKS:

PHOTO OR PLAT:

☐ OPEN   ☐ EXCL.   ☐ EXCL. RIGHT   ☐ MLS   ☐ CO-BROKE

Approved: SALESMAN_____

_____   COMPANY_____
          Seller or Authorized Agent

(Reproduced with permission of the Florida Association Of Realtors)

Figure 4-1 (continued).

Name Of Owner _____

Address _____ Phone _____

Legal Description Of Property To Be Exchanged _____

_____

Price $_____ Terms _____

_____

_____

No. of Lots _____Zoned _____Taxes, City_____

Size of Lots _____Taxes, County_____

Paved Street_____Sidewalks_____Sewers_____

Equity_____Will Add Cash_____Needs Cash_____

1st Mortgage $_____Payments $_____Interest_____%

2nd Mortgage $_____Payments $_____Interest_____%

Other Encumberance $_____Payments $_____Interest__%

Property Desired _____

_____

Reason For Trading _____

_____

Remarks _____

_____

_____

_____

Figure 4-2. Exchange Listing (Another Form)

5

INVESTING IN REAL ESTATE

*Investment Real Estate Discussed . . . The Ten Invest-
ment Questions . . . Leverage–Money at Work . . .
Forms of Investment: Motels and Hotels . . . Office
Buildings . . . Apartment Houses . . . Apartment In-
vestment Rules-of-Thumb . . . Shopping Centers . . .
Mobile Home Parks . . . Industrial Properties.*

Brokers handling investment or income real estate should have a
working knowledge of the various types of properties thus classified, and
know what makes them attractive to a purchaser. Each has its own characteristics and with it, certain advantages and disadvantages. Some investments must be handled as full-time, operating businesses, With others,
virtually all the purchaser has to do is invest his money. Most, however,
are somewhere in between. Naturally, the investments requiring the most
time and risk are the ones that will throw off the highest yield.

THE TEN INVESTMENT QUESTIONS

The investor should be concerned with ten basic questions no matter
what type of property he is seeking to acquire. They are presented here,
not necessarily in order of importance, but for the conclusion that the
aggregate answers will reveal.

1. How much gross income will be generated?
2. What are the actual expenses?
3. How much cash is required to obtain the asset?
4. What is the anticipated net cash flow?
5. What is the annual amount of equity build-up?
6. Is the property structurally sound and in good repair?
7. Is the price realistic? Does it represent a good real estate value?
8. Are there hidden plus factors that do not show up on the balance sheet? (Factors such as additional income possibilities not explored, extra land for future expansion, increased leverage by refinancing, etc.).
9. What is the long-range prognosis for the property? For the area?
10. Will the asset best serve the purchaser's investment needs, both from a tax and income standpoint?

LEVERAGE—MONEY AT WORK

Leverage purchasing in real estate means effective use of money. It is usually accomplished by investing the least amount of capital to acquire property in order for it to bring the maximum percentage of return. By mortgaging to the highest amount practical, but not going beyond a point where the mortgage payments would throw the asset into an operating deficit, the greatest percentage yield can generally be obtained on the cash invested. One of the prime objects of the leverage purchaser is to control a large investment with the smallest capital outlay possible. Using leverage in this manner, however, can be a two-edged sword. It has its drawbacks. For example, to compensate for the lack of cash, the selling price of the asset is often increased, as is the interest rate when the maximum amount of money is borrowed. In prosperous times, with a rising real estate market, this works out well. The property appreciates and the increase is soon absorbed. The new owner can raise his rents as leases expire, pay his expenses and debt service (mortgage payments), and still realize a tidy profit. But when the situation becomes reversed and vacancies occur, or, in the case of condominiums, when sales begin to decline or cease altogether, the high-mortgage, leverage operator finds himself in difficulty.

To some degree, leverage plays a role in almost all real estate transactions today. It is rare to find a sizeable commercial venture totally free and clear of all financing. Indeed, only a small percentage of investors have sufficient funds of their own to acquire property 100-percent free of financing, and those having the funds prudently choose not to put it in one venture. If a mortgage can be obtained at a lower interest rate than from the rate earned on the investment, and this is generally the case, the investor can thus increase his overall yield by borrowing.

First-mortgage financing through established lending institutions (banks, savings and loan associations, life insurance companies, and mutual savings banks) accepts lower interest rates than those providing secondary financing. As a rule, they make a loan between 50 percent and 80 percent of the appraised value of the asset. Being a first mortgage holder, the risk of loss, should the owner default, is slight. Barring a serious and prolonged recession or depression, the property will almost always be worth more than the amount of the mortgage should it become necessary to put it on the market. With secondary financing, where the risk of loss is greater, it is understandable that the interest rates will be higher.

"Mortgaging out" is a term familiar to all involved in real estate. It means obtaining 100-percent debt financing. Although it does not occur frequently, mortgaging out is found in both new construction and resale projects. With new construction, the builder is able to complete the structure for the amount of mortgage he has obtained. In resale properties, it can be accomplished through second- or third-mortgage financing, wrap-around mortgages, short-term, balloon mortgages, or re-financing the existing mortgage completely. However achieved, it can be risky business. Usually, if subsequent vacancies occur in such a project, or if reduced income is necessitated by having to lower rents, the owner could find himself sustaining a loss, or negative cash flow instead of a positive one. Once the gross and net income are reduced, the market value of the property is automatically decreased. With no actual money invested in a mortgaged-out property, aside from his credit standing, an owner has little else to lose by abandoning it.

Leverage has its strengths and limitations. A knowledgeable leverage investor always studies the overall stability of a real estate transaction. He must determine if it is a well-located, sound project both structurally and economically. A responsible investor, exercising good judgment, can use to his advantage leverage that will both reward him financially and fill a community need.

An example of effective leveraging can be seen in the following actual case history of a 305-unit high-rise apartment building located in one of our large east coast cities.

ORIGINAL TRANSACTION

Purchase Price		$7,100,000
First Mortgage	$5,200,000	
Second Mortgage	960,000	
Cash To Close	940,000	$7,100,000
Income (from rents, parking, misc.)	$ 985,000	
Expenses (fixed & operating)	$364,050	
1st Mortgage Payment (at 6%)	415,200	
2nd Mortgage Payment		
(at 6½%)	100,000	−879,250
Cash Flow		$ 105,750

11¼% return on $940,000 invested.

Soon after acquiring the building, the owner was successful in obtaining a long-term, third mortgage on the property in the amount of $500,000 at 9 percent interest and payable $50,352 per annum.

The owner now had only $440,000 of his own funds left in the building. The original $105,750 cash flow was reduced by the new $50,352 debt service, leaving $55,398 remaining. The percentage of return on the reduced cash investment was increased by 1¼ percent, or

12½% + return on $440,000 invested.

In addition, the owner had the $500,000 in hand to invest in another, similarly structured property.

FORMS OF INVESTMENT

Presented in this section are some pertinent facts on the following forms of real estate investment: Apartment Houses, Shopping Centers,

Office Buildings, Motels and Hotels, Industrial Properties, and Mobile Home Parks.

Motels and Hotels

If one is not experienced in the intricate business of being an inn-keeper, an investor would be wise first to find a trained, qualified operator as a working partner. Motels and hotels are a 24-hour, 7-day a week operation. The percentage of return for the dollar invested is generally much higher than in an apartment house, shopping center or industrial property, but so is the risk. Knowledgeable resident management is one of the keys to success here.

One must also be aware of the trends when considering an investment that caters to the vicissitudes of the traveling public. Economy motels, for example, have come to the forefront in recent years. The $12- and $14-a-night inns with virtually all the trappings and amenities of Holiday Inns, Sheraton Hotels, Howard Johnsons and Ramada Inns have caused the established chains, as well as the local operators, to consider revamping their operation. The wise manager realizes that he must either compete in price, or offer more and better services if he is to remain in business.

Motel and hotel operators must be well-versed in several types of businesses to succeed. The restaurant and bar operation is a vital adjunct, as may be the running of a sundry-gift shop, convenience store, or even a gas station. These facilities may be leased out, of course, thus alleviating direct operation. The motel-hotel investor has one important fact to compensate him for the higher investment risk—he can expect to receive almost twice the cash flow of other forms of investment real estate if he is successful.

Office Buildings

A city should be thoroughly investigated for population and business growth before undertaking an office building investment. Geographically, some cities are natural administrative centers for large as well as small businesses. Certain cities are headquarters for specific industries and have developed as centers for offices that are far in excess of their per capita population. For example, the office space square footage in Hartford, Chicago, Atlanta, and San Francisco, in relation to population, is extremely high, while the opposite is true of Detroit, Los Angeles, and Philadelphia.

The surrounding locale of a building being considered for purchase should be carefully investigated. An investor should ascertain what the percentage of occupancy is in the vicinity as compared to the building under consideration. He should also determine the following: Is the square footage rate in line with the competition? Are growth trends favorable for the area, or is the neighborhood downgrading? Is the building accessible to major highways and public transportation? Are there adequate off-street parking facilities? Will new buildings coming in hasten obsolescence? Does the land the building is on allow for further development?

Office buildings offer a stable tenancy. A business firm's headquarters have a certain degree of permanency. Leases are generally made for long periods of time. This stability factor is a great advantage when projecting how an investment will fare in the years ahead.

From the standpoint of management, office buildings offer a minimum of problems. The running of an office building can be a smooth and relatively easy process, when in the hands of a competent property manager. His most important function, however, is the obtaining of new and renewal leases in order to keep the occupancy and income at the highest possible level. Most office buildings supply utilities and regular janitorial, vacuuming and clean-up services. (If you do not want to use your own employees to do this work, a maintenance company should be hired only after several reliable firms have competitively bid for it.) Parking facilities are frequently provided. Also, an office building practically shuts down after 6:00 p.m., making for less wear and tear of the premises.

With all the safety advantages, it is apparent why office building investors will be content to receive a modest cash return on their investment (often as low as current bank interest rates). Advantages, of course, manifest themselves in such ways as tax savings via depreciation, building up equity by reducing the mortgage, and in the normal appreciation of the property.

Apartment Houses

The vast apartment house market offers the investor favorable tax treatment in allowing him to take a faster method of depreciation[1] than in most other forms of real estate ownership, plus special tax benefits if he builds or operates low- and moderate-income housing. Also, as land cannot be depreciated for tax purposes, owners of apartment buildings are often able to assign the highest possible valuation to the improvements, leaving but a small percentage for the land.

The steady population growth has manifested itself in high occupancy rates, resulting in apartment houses appreciating more rapidly than some other forms of investment real estate. Surveys show that values are going up 10 percent—20 percent per year in many sections of our country, with the heaviest emphasis in the suburbs.

As in all forms of real estate, location is the single most important factor. Some of the things an apartment house investor should be aware of include: nearness to shopping, schools and churches, types of tenants, closeness to public transportation, desirability of the neighborhood, recreational and other amenities offered by the building, structural soundness, and a variety of size and apartment design. The knowledgeable apartment house investor also takes into consideration the adaptability of the property to conversion to condominium or cooperative ownership.

Competent resident management is important to the investor if he is going to be an absentee owner. For smaller buildings (up to 50 units) many experienced husband and wife teams pool their abilities to effectively run such buildings. Part of their remuneration comes in the form of a rent-free apartment and utilities.

There are several unknown quantities in calculating the income against the expense to operate an apartment house. First and foremost is the vacancy factor. Any investor would do well to make a survey of nearby competing units to determine their occupancy rate, and what they are offering in vying for the tenant's dollar. The leases of the building being considered should be studied. Their expiration dates, the number of

---

[1]See pages 182-185, Tax Advantages, Depreciation.

furnished against unfurnished apartments, and the amount of security deposit will help the purchaser discern a pattern. An apartment with many furnished apartments indicates a less stable tenancy.

Certain fixed expenses such as taxes, insurance, mortgage payments, ground rent, licenses, etc. can be readily checked from public records and legal instruments, but a building's operating expenses including repairs, maintenance, utilities, advertising, legal and accounting services, supplies, furniture replacement, garbage disposal, and a multitude of other items must be carefully checked and evaluated for accuracy. In addition, there are long-range, "nonrecurring" expenses such as roof replacement, exterior painting, replacement of air conditioning or heating plants, furniture, carpeting, etc. that have to be considered.

The percentage of return on an apartment investment varies with the size, age and type of building, as well as from one section of the country to another. In a rapid growth area where the general occupancy picture is usually high and the outlook is for continued growth, investors are content with between 7 percent and 10 percent cash flow. They are invariably counting on rapid appreciation, equity build-up through reduced mortgages, as well as the normal tax depreciation benefits.

Apartment Investment Rules-of-Thumb

The following are rules-of-thumb to help determine the reasonableness of apartment house properties listed for sale. The figures suggested are neither for slum nor luxury apartment buildings, but are compiled to cover middle to above average garden and high-rise housing facilities.

It should be emphasized that the "rules" given here are, at best, only rough guidelines and nothing more. They should not be looked upon as the final, authoritative factors in determining a building's true worth.

Equity per unit—$2,500 to $4,500

Cash flow—$350 to $450 per unit per year

Mortgage loan per unit—$12,000

Rent per square foot—25¢ to 30¢ per month

Total price per unit—$15,000 to $20,000

Mortgage loan constant—10% to 11% of loan amount

Utilities, if supplied by owner—$250 to $350 per unit per year

Cash flow—10% to 20% of gross income per year

Gross income—$2,500 per unit per year

Normal breakdown— 40%— 40% Operating and fixed expenses
40%— 50% Debt service
20%— 10% Cash flow
100% 100%

When estimating expenses to operate apartment units, the following general rules may be applied:

Operating and Fixed Expenses	% of Gross Income
Vacancy allowance	8
Supervisory management	3
Utilities (public area)	3
Insurance	2
Real estate taxes and licenses	8
Decorating and repair	5
Supplies	3
Reserves for replacements	4
Miscellaneous	2
Advertising	1
Exterminator	½
Accounting and legal	½
	40%

Shopping Centers

Shopping centers as an investment are always in demand. They range from the small neighborhood group of stores with perhaps one supermarket as the anchor tenant, to the mammoth regional shopping center of 50 or more acres, with air-conditioned, enclosed malls, theatres, a choice of several large department, discount and variety stores, and 100 or more retailers handling goods, food and services of every description. No matter the size, under normal circumstances, shopping centers present a highly desirable investment package.

From the standpoint of stability, shopping centers rate higher than most other forms of income real estate. They generally have a good proportion of AAA or AA rated, national tenants, who often are on overage or percentage[2] leases. Having rated tenants is desirable for a variety of reasons, but notably, with high advertising budgets, they attract a great many shoppers, thereby assuring the success of the rest of the center.

Managerial problems always exist, of course, but when one compares the complexities of managing an apartment house or a motel, running a shopping center is by far the least demanding. With the exception of single-tenant, net-lease investments,[3] few others forms of real estate lend themselves as readily to absentee management as do shopping centers.

Retail management analysts have determined that 23 stores are necessary to furnish the purchasing requirements of 1,000 families. With the steady increase in population and affluence, and the continued trend of suburban living, well-located shopping centers add up to prudent, safe investments. Because of this, the wise investor must (and be content to) accept a lower cash flow than found in other forms of income property investments. It is not unusual for a purchaser to realize a cash flow of as little as 6 percent to 8 percent or 9 percent on his invested dollar. As in other investments, however, he has the three usual additional compensating factors of increased equity by mortgage reduction, tax shelter, and appreciating real estate.

Mobile Home Parks

The surge of mobile home park construction has been dramatic in recent years. *Woodall's Mobile Home and Park Directory*, the "Bible" of the mobile home industry, estimates that in 1975 there were more than 24,000 parks throughout the United States and the number has been growing rapidly since. Housing shortages and the rising cost of living are the chief factors. To be profitable, a mobile home park should offer most, or all of the following features:

1. Adequate, nearby employment opportunities.

---

[2]See page 126 and 127, Leasing.

[3]Gas stations, Post Office buildings, Warehouses, Theaters, etc.

2. Shopping, schools and churches within a radius of a few miles.

3. Easy highway accessibility.

4. Low density, landscaped lots.

5. Underground utilities.

6. Social and recreational facilities.

Most parks are especially oriented to certain groups of people. As for example, the *military park* which is situated near the base of one of the armed forces. An investor would be wise to communicate first with the proper governmental authorities to determine if cutbacks of personnel, or a closing down of the facility are contemplated. He should also be aware of the on-base living facilities—the amount and adequacy of them—for this is what the military park will be competing with.

The *retirement park* is very popular in Florida, California, Arizona and Texas, as well as in other sunny, mild-weather sections of the nation. Here the emphasis is on adult community recreational facilities.

College-oriented parks are particularly popular as the number of married students increases. Extra amenities, such as a swimming pool and a recreational building, are not always necessary as colleges and universities have such facilities available. This, of course, will cut down on the cost and maintenance.

Industrial mobile parks are found near government projects or large corporation manufacturing plants. Here men with certain technical and artistic skills are needed sometimes just for limited periods of time. There is less permanent occupancy and the risks in building and operating such a park must be carefully evaluated.

Recreational vehicle parks are rapidly increasing nationally. Recreational parks cater to overnight or weekly hook-ups. Almost always found off the beaten trail, they nevertheless offer full conveniences such as water, garbage, electricity, and recreational facilities. Many have a convenience food and sundry store on the premises, as well as a gas station. Because of the outlying locations, land acquisition costs are considerably lower, as are taxes, than in other mobile park areas. The facilities, too, are less elaborate. As a consequence, an investor or builder can start a recreational vehicle park for a comparatively modest investment.

Many mobile home parks are a *combination* of the specialized parks discussed above. Such parks offer stability. A varied tenant-mix serves to lessen the investment risk, as a loss of one type of occupant will not necessarily cause an irreparable financial burden.

Because most mobile parks are not on or near main arteries but in outlying areas, the farsighted investor will seek to acquire additional adjoining land. He will then have room for expansion should business warrant it, and appreciating real estate as population and development come his way.

Industrial Properties

Acquiring industrial property for an investment can vary in character from the single, owner-user manufacturing plant or warehouse, to the modern, 500-acre, multi-tenanted industrial parks that dot the perimeter of our cities. Real estate men involved with industrial properties are aware of certain advantages and pitfalls that characterize this very specialized field. For example:

1. Reşale value may be restricted as most industrial buildings are custom-made for the first user. The floor plan and the structure itself are frequently designed for a specific need or process.
2. Factory buildings may rapidly become functionally obsolete as manufacturing techniques, machinery and equipment change.
3. Industrial land is generally in outlying, less desirable areas. On the other hand, land is less costly to acquire and real estate taxes are low.
4. A shift in a region's economy or fluctuation within an industry can, overnight, shut down an entire industrial area.
5. Because of the specialized nature of industrial buildings, tax benefits by way of rapid depreciation deductions can be taken. Due to lower land costs (which cannot be depreciated for tax purposes), the improvements upon it represent the vastly greater percentage of value.
6. The average factory or warehouse tenant is a permanent one. He often has a large investment in the premises he occupies, as the fixtures, equipment and machinery used are usually built-in, and it would be prohibitively costly to move. The span of his lease is traditionally for a longer term.

The modern *industrial parks* offer many advantages to industry and the community in which they are located. Today's industrial park occupies 50 to 500 acres, offers attractively landscaped sites of from 2 to 5 acres or more, has well-lighted, wide paved streets (to accommodate trucks of all sizes), and has railroad spurs at or near each site. They serve the community by alleviating traffic and parking congestion, and by attracting industry and jobs to the area.

What are some of the desirable features to look for when considering the purchase of industrial property? Here is a checklist of plus factors:

1. Truck-level bays for easy loading and unloading.
2. Adequate ceiling height.
3. Sufficient elevator capacity.
4. Fire sprinkling system.
5. Heavy floor-weight capacity.
6. Open span area for flexibility in space arrangement.
7. Finished office facilities.
8. Ample parking.
9. Attractively landscaped structure in an uncrowded area.
10. City sewer and water.
11. Paved, well-lighted streets.
12. Convenient, easy-to-reach location.
13. Nearby, or on-site railroad siding.
14. Low property taxes.
15. Low insurance rates.
16. No prohibitive deed restrictions or zoning regulations.
17. Readily available labor supply.

An alternative to owning investment property in one of the forms discussed here is to become a part of a group of investors. The various advantages and limitations of two forms of group ownership, syndications and real estate investment trusts, are explored in the next chapter.

6

INVESTMENT ALTERNATIVES—

SYNDICATES AND REITS

Real Estate Syndicate Defined . . . Improved Property Syndication . . . Vacant Land Syndication . . . SEC Function . . . Partnership-Joint Venture . . . Limited and General Partners . . . Syndicate Agreement . . . Broker-Syndicator Benefits . . . Syndicator's Code of Ethics.

Real Estate Investment Trusts Discussed . . . Special Tax Treatment . . . IRS Requirements . . . Equity Trusts . . . Mortgage Trusts . . . Advantages of Investing in REITS.

REAL ESTATE SYNDICATE DEFINED

A real estate syndicate is an association of investors who join together for the purpose of transacting business over a limited period of time. It is comprised of people who combine their knowledge, skills and finances for the common good of the enterprise. While there are any number of different types of organizations that a syndicate may use as a business vehicle (for example; partnership-joint venture, real estate investment trust, corporation, and tenancy in common), the partnership-joint venture structure is generally recognized by attorneys as the most satisfactory. It is used extensively in both large and small real estate syndications.

A syndicate is a special kind of business framework usually created for one purpose, such as for buying, improving and then selling a single entity for a profit. When that purpose is accomplished or fails to be achieved, the syndicate liquidates and is dissolved.

Aside from the business framework, two specific types of syndications exist—those that deal with improved, income-producing properties, and syndications concerned with vacant land. Each has its own characteristics and distinct investment advantages and disadvantages.

Improved Property Syndication

Most every form of income producing property lends itself to syndication, including retail stores and shopping centers, industrial park developments, office buildings, nursing homes, hotels and motels, mobile-home parks, service stations, apartment houses, factories, warehouses——even one-family residential properties. The list is limitless as long as the elements of a sound investment are present.

The main advantages of syndicating improved property are:

1. The tax savings it affords members by way of depreciating the improvement.
2. The net profit or cash flow generated while the property is being held.
3. Appreciation. The normal increase in value that good, improved real estate enjoys with the passage of time.
4. The tax shelter allowed participants on a portion of the money they receive from syndicate disbursements.
5. Equity build-up. The reduction of mortgages during the period the property is held.

The disadvantages are:

1. The need for skilled management to maintain the property, and the income it generates, at the highest possible level.
2. The necessity of accounting and legal services.
3. The wear and tear of the structure during the holding period frequently requires assessing members for repair and maintenance costs.

Vacant Land Syndication

Syndicators seek to acquire land that is in the path of progress, as well as acreage that will be able to sustain itself during a possible lengthy holding period. If it is agricultural land, for example, the ideal syndicate situation would be to lease it for farming while it is being held. In the instance of timber or mineral land, the granting of such rights would mean income to defray such expenses as taxes, insurance, and special assessments.

The prime advantages of syndicating vacant land and acreage are:

1. Little or no management problems.
2. The benefit of normal appreciation of well-located land with the passage of time.
3. The possibility of public improvements being made to the land, such as the addition of roads, sidewalks, electricity, telephone lines, bridges, canals, dams, etc., thereby enhancing its market value.
4. Tax deductions allowed the owners for real estate taxes, mortgage interest payments, insurance, and other expenses of maintaining unproductive property.

The disadvantages include:

1. Lack of tax shelter. (Land cannot be depreciated for tax purposes.)
2. Limited or no income received from the land.
3. As a rule, a much longer holding period is required of vacant land than for improved property.
4. Expenses such as taxes, insurance and mortgage payments have to be paid, necessitating periodic assessing of syndicate members.
5. The difficulty of financing unimproved real estate. Few lending institutions will grant mortgages on vacant land. Generally, the only way to finance such property is by the seller agreeing to take back a purchase money mortgage in lieu of receiving all his cash at closing.

The Security and Exchange Commission's Function

The SEC acts as a regulatory body for interstate syndicates. Its function is to protect the interest of the public and investors in the securities and financial markets. As a special form of financial venture, most of the larger real estate syndicates fall under its control. The SEC requires the filing of all real estate syndications *except* the following:

1. Syndicates that operate solely within their state.
2. Offerings made to not more than 25 people. When in excess of this number, it is viewed as a public offering and the necessary filing and complying with SEC regulations are required.
3. Syndicates that involve less than $300,000.

In addition, most states have their own filing requirements for syndicates and special laws that are sometimes intricate. Before attempting to form a syndicate, experienced legal counsel should be obtained to assure both compliance with such state regulations and that correct organizational procedures are being followed.

Partnership-Joint Venture Syndication

When properly structured, a (limited) partnership-joint venture form of syndication will avoid duplicate taxation, and it will allow for passing through the maximum depreciation benefits to the individual. However, for practicality and facility of operation, it is important that the characteristics of a corporation be retained. Care must be taken to insure that not more than half of such corporate characteristics are written into the agreement and observed. Otherwise it may be considered as a corporation, even though not actually one, and taxed accordingly. The government looks for the following elements usually found in a corporation:

The absence of personal liability.

Transferability of an individual's equity position to another.

Continuation of the organization in the event of the death, expulsion, bankruptcy, or resignation of one or more of its members.

The exercising of independent decisions in running the enterprise by properly authorized persons.

The regulations found in the Uniform Limited Partnership Act,[1] a part of the laws of most states, is a good guideline to follow when determining what constitutes a partnership for purposes of syndication. For example, such basic provisions as the liability of the general partner(s), and dissolution of the organization at the conclusion of a specific transaction are sufficient evidence that partnership treatment for tax purposes would be given the syndicate.

Limited and General Partner Distinction

The roles played by limited and general partners in a partnership-joint venture syndication form the basis for this type of business organization. As implied, a limited partner is limited in his liability to the amount he has invested. It likewise places a limitation on the profit he can take. Also, he is not given a voice in the management of the venture. Aside from investing his money, his role is primarily passive, resembling that of a silent partner.

The general partner is vested with the power of conducting the business. He is authorized to buy, sell, or exchange the property, execute leases, hire and release employees, erect buildings, obtain mortgages, etc., yet no action taken by him can increase the liability of the limited partners.

Syndicate Agreements

Syndicate agreements differ greatly as to content and form. Each takes on its own general characteristics. Though the contents of the document vary, all should cover the following basic grounds:

1. The specific purpose of the syndicate is defined. For example, it may be to acquire a building, complete a project, or buy a tract of land; then to hold and improve it, and sell at a profit. Whatever the plan or operational strategy, it should be stated in the agreement.

---

[1] A limited partnership is a partnership formed by two or more persons having as members one or more general partners and one or more limited partners. The limited partners are not bound by the obligations of the partnership.

2. The roles of the general and limited partners must be detailed. The general partner, being the working member, bears the responsibility of the debts, obligations, and the overall running of the operation. The limited partners are liable only to the extent of their capital contributions.

3. The percentage of interest each participant has in the enterprise is stated. Such a list might read as follows:

Name	Cash Contribution	Percentage Interest
James Smith	$100,000	25%
Able Pension Fund	100,000	25%
Dr. John Doe	50,000	12½%
Mary Roe	50,000	12½%
Col. Peter Hoe	50,000	12½%
Robert Jones	25,000	6¼%
Estate of A. Bland	12,500	3⅛%
Martin Meeker	12,500	3⅛%

4. A provision for the distribution of periodic profits, if any, as well as the assessing of partners in the event of loss, is shown. Also, the manner of distribution of monies from the ultimate sale of the asset.

5. The rights of the remaining partners in the event of death, retirement, incapacity or bankruptcy of a general partner.

6. Means by which limited partners can assign or dispose of their interest. (They generally are permitted to transfer it by sale or assignment to an heir.)

7. The method by which the agreement is terminated.

The above represents the salient points of a typical syndication agreement. Other matters that are sometimes covered in depth include the manner of keeping the records and bank accounts, mortgage refinancing and methods of assessing members.

Broker-Syndicator Benefits

If a broker acts as the syndicator, his form of compensation and position in the syndicate must be clearly revealed. All forms of his compensation—acquisition, management and selling fees—should be openly disclosed. It is further incumbent upon him to perform in a manner that will serve to protect those he is dealing with, as well as the general public.

Syndicator's Code of Ethics

The Association of Real Estate Syndicators, Inc. has adopted the following code of conduct:

1. The principal consideration of every syndicator shall be to protect the interest of the investing public.
2. Full and truthful disclosure of all material facts shall be made to all investors. A written prospectus or brochure, in clear, factual language, shall be made available to every prospective investor and shall fairly and honestly set forth the material facts respecting the investment, including without limitation:
   a) A full and accurate description of the property.
   b) A statement of estimated income and expenses.
   c) Complete information of mortgages and other liens against the property stating by whom held, terms of payment, maturity, etc.
   d) A statement of any interest, direct or indirect, owned by the syndicator in the property being offered.
   e) The syndicate managers and any other persons who will direct the affairs of the syndicate shall be identified and brief resumes of their experience in the real estate field shall be set forth.
   f) Projections, if any, into the future shall be clearly identified as estimates by the syndicators and stated as such.
   g) A statement of all compensation and profit, direct or indirect, of any nature, paid or to be paid to any of the syndicate managers or to any other person who will direct the affairs of the syndicate.
   h) A statement of the amount of compensation, if any, paid or to be paid for the management of the property or for the management of the syndicate.
   i) If the property is under contract, the salient terms and conditions of the contract of purchase.
3. Participants shall be given all necessary protection for funds deposited with the investment managers. Such funds shall be deposited in a special account and shall not be commingled with the syndicator's personal funds.

4. False, misleading or exaggerated claims or statements in advertisements or other publicity are expressly condemned.

5. The purchase contract and all other documents in connection therewith, pertinent to the transaction, and which are in the possession of the syndicate manager shall be made available for inspection by prospective participants.

6. In all their dealings with each other and with the public in general, syndicators shall maintain the highest standards of honesty, frankness, fair dealing and dignity.

7. The foregoing basic code of ethics may be clarified, supplemented or amended from time to time as provided in the Bylaws of the Association.

REAL ESTATE INVESTMENT TRUSTS

An investor's choice over real estate syndication may be the real estate investment trust. This investment form has made such a broad impact on the realty field that today it represents a twelve-billion-dollar industry. More than 175 of the larger ones are traded on leading stock exchanges throughout the country. And the number of REITS is continually growing. As originally intended, trusts afford the small investor an opportunity to become a part of multi-million-dollar transactions that are put together by skilled professionals, and give him a chance to participate in the profits they generate.

Special Tax Treatment

Present day trusts stem from 1960 when Congress enacted legislation[2] that made several important changes in a portion of the Internal Revenue Code. By this newly created statute, REITS that distribute 90 percent or more of their ordinary income to shareholders are taxed at corporate rates and only on their retained earnings. They pay no federal tax on the income distributed. Shareholders, nevertheless, must (a) pay taxes on the monies they receive from the trust at capital gains rates on the capital gains distributed; (b) pay the normal tax rate on the portion of a

---

[2]Public Law 86-779 adding Sections 856, 857 and 858 to the Internal Revenue Code of 1954.

REIT distribution that comprises ordinary income; and (c) pay no tax on any distribution that is not considered capital gains or taxable income.

IRS Requirements

However, to obtain this special tax treatment, the trusts are obliged to conform to certain requirements as outlined by the IRS.

1. To be eligible under the statute, a real estate company must:
   a. Be organized under state law as an unincorporated trust or association managed by one or more trustees;
   b. Have transferable shares or certificates of beneficial interest;
   c. Be a type of organization which would be taxed as an ordinary domestic corporation in the absence of the provision of these Sections of the Internal Revenue Code.
2. The beneficial ownership of qualifying real estate investment trusts must be held by 100 or more persons with not less than six individuals directly or indirectly owning more than 50 percent of the trust.
3. The real estate investment trust must elect to be treated as such and may not hold any property primarily for sale to customers in the ordinary course of trade or business. This provision, together with certain other provisions restricting trusts from providing services to tenants except through an independent contractor, is designed to make sure that the trust operates as a conduit strictly for investment income.
4. Income requirements are divided into the three following categories, all three of which must be met by a trust in order to qualify:
   a. Ninety percent or more of a trust's gross income must be obtained from dividends, interest, the rents from real property, gains from the sales of securities and real property, and abatements and refunds of taxes on real property.
   b. Seventy-five percent of the trust income must be derived from real property. Another 15 percent must be derived from either real property or from sources from which a regulated investment company may derive 90 percent of its income. The remaining 10 percent is not limited as to source. The difference in the 90 percent and 75 percent tests is that for the 90 percent test, the additional items which may qualify as investment income are dividends, interest on any obligations, and gain from the sale or other disposition of stock or securities.
   c. Not more than 30 percent of the trust's gross income may be obtained from sales of securities held for less than 6 months or from sales of

real property held for less than 4 years apart from involuntary conversions. This test relates to the requirement that the trust not hold property for sale to customers in the ordinary course of business.

d. At the close of each quarter at least 75 percent of the trust's assets must be in real estate assets, cash and cash items, and government securities. The remaining 25 percent may be in other investments, but the trust may not invest more than 5 percent of total assets in the securities of any one issuer. When it has bought the wrong kind of property or securities, the trust has 30 days after the close of the quarter to meet the tests.

There are two distinct types of REITS. They are *Equity Trusts* and *Mortgage Trusts*.

Equity Trusts are engaged in the business of either owning outright or having partial ownership of income-producing real estate. Everything from apartment houses, shopping centers, hotels or motels, office buildings, hospitals and warehouses to productive acreage, leaseholds and sale-leasebacks are the stock in trade of equity trusts. This form of REIT operates beneficially in the following ways:

1. The cash flow realized from the operation of the property.

2. Tax depreciation benefits while the property is held. Depreciation may be passed through to the shareholders and serve as a tax shelter on the dividends they receive.

3. Appreciation. The increase in market value through normal inflationary trends when the property is sold.

Mortgage Trusts strive to invest in secure real estate mortgages. They are active in both commercial and residential mortgaging. Some specialize in short-term construction loans. This mortgage form generally is for the length of time it takes to complete the structure. Other trusts adopt a policy of loaning money on completed buildings and on a long-term basis. Still other mortgage-oriented REITS diversify their portfolios between the two.

Advantages of Investing in REITS

REITs have brought a new dimension to real estate. The combination of tax advantages, diversification, skilled management and liquidity that REITs offer investors has resulted in what amounts to a newly-created industry within the real estate field.

Taxwise, REITs offer all the advantages and protection of the corporate framework, and at the same time shareholders and their beneficiaries are taxed on an individual basis.

Heretofore, an investor was limited because of his resources as to the size and number of diversified investments he could make. Even when he invested in a syndication or a partnership he would generally find his investment limited to one specific property. If that one did not turn out profitable he would have little or no chance to recover. All his eggs were in the proverbial one basket. On the other hand, REITs offer a high degree of *diversification*, and with it a corresponding high percentage of safety. When a great number of investors pool their funds, many mortgage and equity investments can be made. If one proves a bad investment, the others are there to absorb the loss. Through diversification, an investor's loss ratio is at a minimum.

Many REITs have talented professionals at the helm. Their combined experience and brainpower offer *skilled business management* and incisive decision-making. Also, the quality, size, and choice of investments made available to trusts having the necessary capital further reduce the margin for error that is always present.

In the past, real estate ownership was looked upon as lacking liquidity. The REITs have changed this concept. With most of the large and middle-size trusts traded on leading stock exchanges throughout the country, they are as liquid as any stock, bond or mutual fund issue.

Real estate investment trusts experience alternate growth and contraction pains as our economy fluctuates. As in all forms of endeavor, the weak cannot keep up, and falter by the way. The strong survive. But in the long run, most real estate experts are in agreement that the concept of the modern-day real estate trusts is not only here to stay, but will continue to make an ever-increasing impact on the financial community.

7

LEASING

Essentials of a Lease Agreement . . . Short-Term Leases . . . Long-Term Leases . . . Ground Leases . . . Percentage Leases . . . Net Leases . . . Leasehold Valuation . . . Light and Air, Mineral, Grazing Leases . . . Types of Tenancy Defined . . . Sample Lease Forms: Business Property Lease . . . Residential Lease . . . Sub-Lease

Leases are made for the use of land, the improvements upon it, or for both. Leases also are devised for utilization of the area below the surface and for the light and air above it. They take many forms and may cover periods of time from one day to (conceivably) 999 years. To be enforceable in most states, leases for one year or over must be in writing. As evidence of constructive notice and for legal protection, business leases are frequently recorded.

ESSENTIALS OF A LEASE AGREEMENT

While a lease agreement need not follow a specific form, it should contain certain basic essentials and characteristics, as follows:

1. Date of the agreement.
2. Names of the parties to it.

3. Full description of the property and how title is held.

4. Length of the lease (*Habendum Clause*).

5. Amount of rental and manner of payment (*Reddendum Clause*).

6. Purpose for which the property is to be used.

7. Lessor's maintenance responsibilities.

8. Lessee's maintenance responsibilities.

9. Insurance requirements.

10. Default remedies in the event either party fails to comply with the terms of the lease.

11. Lessee's right to quiet enjoyment of the premises.

12. Lessee's right or prohibition to assign the lease to another.

13. Termination provision. The lessee's agreement to vacate premises, leaving it in good condition.

14. Options, if any, for the renewal of the lease or purchase of the property.

15. Signatures and witnesses to the lease.

SHORT-TERM LEASES

The great preponderance of leases are for short terms. While the definition of what determines a short- or long-term lease is an arbitrary one that varies with the type of lease being made, for this study we will consider a lease of less than 10 years as constituting a short term.

Most residential leases (of homes or apartments) are of short duration, as are office, store and warehouse leases. On the other hand, ground leases, mineral and air rights leases, pipe line leases, the lease of an entire structure, etc. are generally for a longer term.

The charge is sometimes made that short-term leases are written strictly in favor of the lessor. This is entirely understandable when one considers that the tenant usually has no financial stake in the property beyond his security deposit. Primarily, all he wants is the use and quiet enjoyment of the property, while the owner has a costly, highly valuable, vulnerable asset to maintain, protect and pay taxes on. He is within his rights to expect the premises to be returned to him in the same general condition he gave it, ordinary wear and tear excepted.

As a rule, in short-term residential (home) leases, the tenant is expected to maintain the property both inside and out, with the possible exception of major structural or mechanical repairs or failures. When dealing with a store, loft building, manufacturing plant or warehouse lease, the landlord usually assumes responsibility for the exterior maintenance of the property, and the tenant the interior. Any improvements made by the tenant invariably remain with the property at the expiration of the lease. The leasing of office space generally provides for the landlord to supply electricity, heat, air conditioning, janitorial services and public area maintenance. The rate of commercial leases is usually computed on a square foot basis, and varies with the quality and location of the space. Office accomodations can be as low as $2 or $3 per square foot for older buildings bordering on obsolescence, and as high as $12 to $14 per square foot for new, modern, 100 percent-located edifices.

Under most short-term leases, the owner is responsible for the tax and insurance payments. As a protection to the owner, certain escalation clauses covering the cost of living index, and operating expense increases are frequently written into leases of more than two or three years.

In short-term leases, the tenant may be prohibited from assigning or subletting the leased premises. If he is permitted to do so at all, he usually must first obtain the consent of the owner.

LONG-TERM LEASES

As indicated earlier, short- and long-term leases are relative terms. Some areas of our country consider leases of more than 18 or 20 years as being long-term. In any case, the longer the lease, the more detailed and explicit should be the terms. The tenant's obligations on long leases more closely approach the responsibilities of ownership. Also, cost-of-living clauses and the various other escalation provisions (taxes, insurance, maintenance, etc.) have to be carefully written into the agreement. Many leases made a decade ago are so out of step with economic advances as to cut the property's market value drastically, or render it unsalable for all practical purposes. Inflation has wiped out the true values of an inordinate amount of properties saddled with short-sighted, ill-conceived, long-term leases.

GROUND LEASES

Leases for use and improvement of the ground are frequently made for 50 or 99 years, or longer. Because they closely approach fee-simple ownership, the terms and conditions are necessarily both detailed and lengthy. They are sometimes quite complex in their thoroughness. Some states actually treat 99-year leases as if they were conveying real estate ownership. The lease is recorded and has the effect of a deed. Ground leases are nearly always "net" leases, with all the costs of maintenance, taxes, insurance paid by the lessees.

Most ground leases are made on vacant land or land with existing improvements that are to be demolished. The purpose of such a lease, of course, is to allow for the erection of a new structure. In addition, some ground leases are created on improved property where the lessee intends to continue occupancy over a long period of time. With the security of a 50- or 99-year lease, for example, a lessee would feel free to make major improvements to the premises to suit his long-range needs.

Ground leases often provide for periodic advances in the lease payments. The privilege of buying the land outright, sometime in the future and at a fixed amount, also is frequently written into ground leases. It is referred to as a *recapture clause*.

Because of their length and stability, ground leases sometimes serve as an important method of financing. A 99-year ground lease offers the lender practically the same advantages of collateral as when a mortgage is given on the basis of fee simple ownership. Rather than a lessee purchasing the land outright, his money is available for construction purposes. Tax-wise he benefits also, as he may depreciate, for tax purposes, all of the costs of the improvements he makes.

PERCENTAGE LEASES

Most percentage leases provide for a fixed minimum (base) rental to be paid before the percentage of gross business is added on. Others provide for a straight percentage of the gross income. Still others have a maximum ceiling that a tenant need pay. Certain safeguards are also written into percentage leases. For example, if a minimum volume of business is not reached, the landlord or the tenant may cancel the remainder of the lease.

The percentage of the volume of business varies with the type of retail establishment. Where a lease of a gas station or a supermarket might provide for a fraction of 1 percent of gross business after a certain business volume is reached, a specialty or drug store lease might be structured to call for between 3 percent and 10 percent of the volume. In the instance of hotels and motels, a lessee may pay as high as 25 percent or 30 percent. In every instance, the mark-up of products sold, type of establishment and the volume reasonably expected to be reached enter into negotiating the percentage lease. Percentage leases particularly must be fair for both tenant and landlord if they are to survive.

A lessor is entitled to receive monthly or quarterly reports from his percentage-lease tenants. He also should have the right to inspect the books and records at reasonable intervals.

NET LEASES

A net lease is one that requires the lessee to pay all, or substantially all, of the cost to operate and maintain the leased property. When items such as taxes, insurance, interior and exterior repairs, structural additions, utilities, and even special assessments are paid for by the lessee, it is defined as a "net-net" or "100 percent net" lease. If exceptions, such as taxes and/or insurance, are paid for by the lessor, it may still be referred to as a net lease, with the exceptions noted in the lease agreement. The only items traditionally not included in a net lease are the mortgage principal and interest payments. Most net leases are found in long-term agreements.

The opposite of a net lease is called a *gross lease*. Here all the expenses of operating maintenance, taxes, insurance, etc. are paid by the landlord.

LEASEHOLD VALUATION

A lease may be enhanced in value with each passing year. It can occur by an increase in comparable rentals in an area caused by an economic upsurge, or by improvements made to the property by the lessee. Thus, unless the lessor is prohibited from assigning or subleasing, a valuable and marketable commodity has been created for the lessee. The lessee may also obtain financing by putting up his leasehold interest as security.

On the other hand, whether he is aware of it or not, the lessor has effectively established the market value of his property by the quality of the tenant he has obtained and the terms and conditions of the lease. With the income of the property established, a knowledgeable broker or investor can deduct the taxes, insurance, mortgage payments and all operating expenses, to arrive accurately at the net profit of the property. Once the net profit is known, the true market value of the property can be readily established.

LIGHT AND AIR, MINERAL, GRAZING LEASES

Some leases provide for the preservation of light and air, as when a property owner enters into a lease with his neighbor who agrees not to erect a building over a certain height, or not to build at all for a specified number of years. The first property owner will thus be assured that light and air will not be blocked from his property.

Air leases also occur when one party leases the rights to build or otherwise use the space over railroad tracks, highways or existing structures.

One may lease the ground below the surface of the land for purposes of exploration or for extracting oil, coal, gold, silver or other valuable minerals from the land. Likewise, leases to farm or graze cattle upon the surface of land are familiar to us all.

TYPES OF TENANCY DEFINED

There are leases for many purposes created to meet every conceivable tenancy situation. Some frequently used leases and definitions of leasing terms include: *Month to month tenancy*—A lease for a month that is cancellable by either party on short notice—usually two weeks. This occurs when a tenant signs a lease for one month at a time. Also, when a tenant remains in possession after his lease has expired. He is referred to as a *holdover tenant* or *tenant at will*. Though he may legally occupy the premises, he has no fixed term or lease. Also called a *periodic tenancy*, his occupancy is based on the express or implied permission of the owner. When, however, a tenant remains in possession after his lease expires without the approval of the landlord, he is legally known as a *tenant at sufferance*, and has no rights whatsoever in the premises.

When a tenant leases his interest to a third party, he creates a *sublease*. It is also referred to as an *assignment of lease*. When the holder of a sublease in turn sublets to another, he creates a *sandwich lease*. His position is that of being sandwiched between the original lessee and the second sublessee. When property is subleased, the original lessee is called the *prime tenant*.

An *oral* or *parole lease* is one not in writing. Under the statute of frauds, most states require leases for more than one year to be written (to be enforceable).

SAMPLE LEASE FORMS

Two sample leases and a sub-lease, which have wide application and are easily adaptable to a variety of situations, are illustrated below.

BUSINESS PROPERTY LEASE

General Form Suitable For, Stores, Offices,
Lofts, Warehouses, Etc.

THIS AGREEMENT, made this_____day of_____19__, by and between_____

_____,
as Landlord, and _____ a corporation
of the state of_____, with its principal
office and place of business in _____
as Tenant: _____

WITNESSETH: That the said Landlord does hereby demise and lease to Tenant and Tenant does hereby hire from Landlord the following described premises:

together with all appurtenances thereto and with easements of ingress and egress necessary and adequate for the conduct of Tenant's business as hereinafter described, for the term of _____ years, running from and including the _____ day of _____ , 19___ up to and including the _____ day of _____ , 19___, for use in Tenant's regular business of or in any other legitimate business, subject to the terms and conditions of this lease.

AMOUNT OF RENTAL

Tenant covenants to pay to Landlord at Landlord's office at _____
_____
or such other place in _____
as Landlord shall designate in writing as rent for said premises, the sum of $ _____ per month, payable in advance commencing
_____ .

In addition to the above, Landlord and Tenant mutually convenant and agree as follows:

TENANT'S MAINTENANCE AND REPAIR OF PREMISES

1. Except as hereinafter provided, Tenant shall maintain and keep the interior of the premises in good repair, free of refuse and rubbish and shall return the same at the expiration or termination of this lease in as good condition as received by Tenant, ordinary wear and tear, damage or destruction by fire, flood, storm, civil commotion or other unavoidable cause excepted; provided, however, that if alterations, additions and/or installations shall have been made by Tenant as provided for in this lease, Tenant shall not be required to restore the premises to the condition in which they were prior to such alterations, additions and/or installations except as hereinafter provided.

TENANT'S ALTERATIONS, ADDITIONS, INSTALLATIONS, AND REMOVAL THEREOF

2. Tenant may, at its own expense, either at the commencement of or during the term of this lease, make such alterations in and/or additions to

the leased premises including, without prejudice to the generality of the foregoing, alterations in the water, gas, and the electric wiring system, as may be necessary to fit the same for its business, upon first obtaining the written approval of Landlord as to the materials to be used and the manner of making such alterations and/or additions. Landlord covenants not to unreasonably withhold approval of alterations and/or additions proposed to be made by Tenant. Tenant may also, at its own expense, install such counters, racks, shelving, fixtures, fittings, machinery and equipment upon or within the leased premises as Tenant may consider necessary to the conduct of its business. At any time prior to the expiration or earlier termination of the lease, Tenant may remove any or all such alterations, additions or installations in such a manner as will not substantially injure the leased premises. In the event Tenant shall elect to make any such removal, Tenant shall restore the premises, or the portion or portions affected by such removal, to the same condition as existed prior to the making of such alteration, addition or installation, ordinary wear and tear, damage or destruction by fire, flood, storm, civil commotion or other unavoidable cause expected.

All alterations, additions or installations not so removed by Tenant shall become the property of Landlord without liability on Landlord's part to pay for the same.

LANDLORD'S MAINTENANCE AND REPAIR OF PREMISES

3. Landlord shall, without expenses to Tenant, maintain and make all necessary repairs to the foundations, load-bearing walls, roof, gutters, downspouts, heating system, air conditioning, elevators, water mains, gas and sewer lines, sidewalks, private roadways, parking areas, railroad spurs or sidings, and loading docks, if any, on or appurtenant to the leased premises.

UTILITIES

4. Tenant shall pay all charges for water, gas and electricity consumed by Tenant upon the leased premises.

OBSERVANCE OF LAWS

5. Tenant shall duly obey and comply with all public laws, ordinances, rules or regulations relating to the use of the leased premises; provided, however, that any installation of fire prevention apparatus, electric rewiring, plumbing changes or structural changes in the building on the

leased premises, required by any such law, ordinance, rule, or regulation shall be made by Landlord without expense to Tenant.

DAMAGE BY FIRE, ETC.

Damage Repairable Within One Hundred Twenty (120) Days

6. In the event the said premises shall be damaged by fire, flood, storm, civil commotion, or other unavoidable cause, to an extent repairable within one hundred twenty (120) days from the date of such damage, Landlord shall forthwith proceed to repair such damage. If such repair shall not have been completed within one hundred twenty (120) days from the date of such damage, delays occasioned by causes beyond the control of Landlord excepted, this lease may, at the option of Tenant, be terminated. During the period of repair, Tenant's rent shall abate in whole or in part depending upon the extent to which such damage and/or such repair shall deprive Tenant of the use of said premises for the normal purposes of Tenant's business. In the event that Landlord shall fail promptly to commence repair of such damage, or, having commenced the same shall fail to prosecute such repair to completion with due diligence, Tenant may at Tenant's option upon five (5) days written notice to Landlord, make or complete such repair and deduct the cost thereof from the next ensuing installment or installments of rent payable under this lease.

Damage Not Repairable Within One Hundred Twenty (120) Days.

7. In the event the said premises shall be damaged by fire, flood, storm, civil commotion, or other unavoidable cause, to an extent not repairable within one hundred twenty (120) days from the date of such damage, this lease shall terminate as of the date of such damage.

SIDEWALK ENCUMBRANCES

8. Tenant shall neither encumber nor obstruct the sidewalk in front of, or any entrance to, the building on the leased premises.

SIGNS

9. Tenant shall have the right to erect, affix or display on the roof, exterior or interior walls, doors and windows of the building on the leased

premises, such sign or signs advertising its business as Tenant may consider necessary or desirable, subject to all applicable municipal ordinances and regulations with respect thereto.

TERMINATION BY REASON OF DEFAULT

10. In the event that either of the parties hereto shall fail to perform any covenant required to be performed by such party under the terms and provisions of this lease, including Tenant's covenant to pay rent, and such failure shall continue unremedied or uncorrected for a period of fifteen (15) days after the service of written notice upon such party by the other party hereto, specifying such failure, this lease may be terminated, at the option of the party serving such notice, at the expiration of such period of fifteen (15) days; provided, however, that such termination shall not relieve the party so failing from liability to the other party for such damages as may be suffered by reason of such failure.

CONDEMNATION

11. In the event that the leased premises shall be taken for public use by the city, state, federal government, public authority or other corporation having the power of eminent domain, then this lease shall terminate as of the date on which possession thereof shall be taken for such public use, or, at the option of Tenant, as of the date on which the premises shall become unsuitable for Tenant's regular business by reason of such taking; provided, however, that if only a part of the leased premises shall be so taken, such termination shall be at the option of Tenant only. If such a taking of only a part of the leased premises occurs, and Tenant elects not to terminate the lease, there shall be a proportionate reduction of the rent to be paid under this lease from and after the date such possession is taken for public use. Tenant shall have the right to participate, directly or indirectly, in any award for such public taking to the extent that it may have suffered compensable damage as a Tenant on account of such public taking.

ASSIGNMENT

12. Tenant may assign this lease or sub-let the premises or any part thereof for any legitimate use, either with or without the consent of Landlord. If any assignment or sub-lease is made by Tenant without Landlord's

consent, Tenant shall remain liable as surety under the terms hereof notwithstanding such assignment or sub-lease.

TAXES

13. Landlord shall pay all taxes, assessments, and charges which shall be assessed and levied upon the leased premises or any part thereof during the said term as they shall become due.

TENANT'S LIABILITY INSURANCE

14. During the term of this lease, Tenant at its own expense shall carry public liability insurance in not less than the following limits:

Bodily Injury—$100,000/$300,000
Property Damage—$50,000

LANDLORD'S RIGHT TO ENTER PREMISES

15. Tenant shall permit Landlord and Landlord's agents to enter at all reasonable times to view the state and condition of the premises or to make such alterations or repairs therein as may be necessary for the safety and preservation thereof, or for any other reasonable purposes. Tenant shall also permit Landlord or Landlord's agents, on or after sixty (60) days next preceding the expiration of the term of this lease, to show the premises to prospective tenants at reasonable times, and to place notices on the front of said premises, or on any part thereof, offering the premises for lease or for sale.

RENEWAL OF LEASE

16. Tenant shall have the option to take a renewal lease of the demised premises for the further term of_____( ) years from and after the expiration of the term here granted at a monthly rent of _____ dollars ($_____) and under and subject to the same covenants, provisos and agreements as are herein contained. In the event Tenant desires to exercise the option herein provided, Tenant shall notify Landlord of such desire in writing not less than sixty (60) days prior to the expiration of the term hereby granted.

AND IT IS MUTUALLY UNDERSTOOD AND AGREED that the covenants and agreements herein contained shall inure to the benefit of and be equally binding upon the respective executors, administrators, heirs, successors and assigns of the parties hereto.

IN WITNESS WHEREOF, the parties hereto have executed this lease the day and year first above written.

_____ (L.S.)

_____ (L.S.)

Signed, Sealed and   _____ (L.S.)
Delivered in the
presence of   _____ (L.S.)

_____   Landlord(s)
_____

Attest:
_____   _____
      Assistant Secretary   Vice-President
                                (Tenant)
(Reproduced with permission of PPG Industries, Inc., Pittsburgh, Pa.)

RESIDENTIAL LEASE

This agreement, entered into this_____ day of_____, A.D. 19___between_____hereinafter called the Lessor, and_____ _____ hereinafter called the Lessee, and _____hereinafter called the Rental Agent.

Witnesseth, that in consideration of the covenants herein contained, on the part of the said Lessee to be kept and performed, the said Lessor does hereby demise and lease to the said Lessee that certain

(Here describe property)

To hold the said premises hereby demised unto the said Lessee from the_____day of_____ , A.D. 19__, to the_____day of_____, A.D. 19__, the said Lessee paying therefor the rent of_____Dollars as follows:

(Here include how rents are to be paid, security deposits
held and any other special terms and conditions.)

The Lessor covenants with the Lessee that the Lessee paying the rent
when due as aforesaid, shall peaceably and quietly use, occupy and possess
the said premises for the full term of this lease without let, hindrance,
eviction, molestation or interruption whatever, except as provided below,
and the said Lessee covenants with the Lessor:

1. To pay said rent herein before reserved at the times at which the
same is made payable.

2. To pay all water, electric, gas, and telephone charges which may
be assessed upon the demised premises during the term hereof.

3. Not to suffer or commit any waste of the premises, nor make any
unlawful, improper or offensive use of same.

4. Not to assign this lease or underlet the said premises or any part
thereof without the previous consent of the said Lessor being first obtained
in writing.

5. That this lease shall terminate when the Lessee vacates the said
premises, providing all payments have been made hereunder or a sub-lease
agreement has been executed.

6. At the termination of said tenancy quietly to yield up the said
buildings and grounds in as good and tenantable condition in all respects
(reasonable wear and use and damage by fire and other unavoidable causes
excepted) as the same now are:

It is hereby agreed that all expenses in connection with upkeep of the
grounds including all water used for irrigation purposes will be paid for by

_____.

Provided always that if the rent hereby reserved, or any part thereof,
shall be in arrears, or in event of any breach of any of the covenants and
agreements on the part of the Lessee herein contained, the Lessor may at
his option declare the entire rent for the term for which said premises are
leased, due and payable, and/or may declare this lease terminated and
re-enter upon the said demised premises.

Provided always that if the premises or any part thereof shall at any
time during the said term be destroyed or rendered uninhabitable by fire or
storm, then the payment of the rent hereby reserved, or a proportionate part
thereof, according to the extent of the damage incurred, shall be suspended
until the premises shall have been reinstated and rendered fit for habitation.

I. COMMISSION AGREEMENT:

Lessor acknowledges that Lessee was procured by_____ and
agrees to recognize said Rental Agent on extensions or renewal when

made. On month-to-month extensions, commission shall be paid monthly or quarterly.

If the property on which the premises are a part is sold by Lessor to Lessee during the term of this lease, or during the term of any further extension or renewal agreement (any continued occupancy of the premises by the Lessee after the expiration of this lease shall be considered a further extension or renewal agreement), the Lessor will pay said Rental Agent a commission on the selling price, said commission to be based upon the rates recognized as standard in the area, deducting from such sales commission any unearned leasing commission previously paid by Lessor from date of expiration of lease.

Witness our hands and seals, in triplicate, on the day and year first above written. Signed, Sealed and Delivered in the presence of

_____   _____(Seal)

_____   _____(Seal)

    (Witnesses to Lessor)

_____   _____(Seal)

_____   _____(Seal)

    (Witnesses to Lessee)

_____ By: _____(Seal)

_____

    (Witness to Rental Agent)

T 193—Sub-Lease.

This Sub-Lease *made the*   *day of*   19   *, between*

hereinafter referred to as Lessor, and

hereinafter referred to as Lessee

WITNESSETH, *that the Lessor hereby leases to the Lessee, and the Lessee hereby hires and takes from the Lessor, the following premises, to wit;*

in the building known as

to be used and occupied by the Lessee for

and for no other purpose, for a term to commence on the   *day of*   19   *, and to end on the*   *day of*   19   *, unless sooner terminated as hereinafter provided, at the ANNUAL RENT as hereinafter provided, payable in equal monthly instalments in advance on the*   *day of each and every calendar month during said term, except the first instalment, which shall be paid upon the execution hereof.*

The said premises are the same premises, or a part of the premises, referred to in a lease between

as the landlord and the Lessor herein as the tenant therein, dated the   *day of*   19

The Lessee represents that the Lessee has read the said lease (an exact copy thereof is attached hereto).

The terms, covenants, provisions and conditions of said lease are hereby incorporated herein and shall be binding upon both parties hereto, those applying to the landlord therein shall apply to the Lessor herein and those applying to the tenant therein shall apply to the Lessee herein with the following exceptions:

    a.   *The annual rent payable hereunder shall be $*

    b.   *The security, if any, to be deposited hereunder shall be $*

    c.   *The following numbered paragraphs of said lease shall not apply to this sub-lease:*

The following numbered paragraphs of said lease are amended to read as follows:

IN WITNESS WHEREOF, *the parties have executed this sub-lease in duplicate the day and year first above written.*

Signed, sealed and delivered in the presence of

         ....

         ....

         ....

Strike out words within parenthesis if they do not apply.

(Form Courtesy Julius Blumberg, Inc., 80 Exchange Pl., New York, N.Y. 10004)

Figure 7-1. Sub-Lease

8

LISTING PROPERTIES

It is an old axiom in real estate that a well-listed property is half sold. It follows then, that at least half of a salesman's time should be occupied in its pursuit. Listing real estate is the lifeline of every brokerage office. Knowing the types of listing agreements and their legal ramifications is important, along with knowing the various methods of obtaining them.

Listings may take one of four distinct forms: Exclusive Right of Sale, Exclusive Agency, Multiple, or Open.

An *exclusive right of sale* is a written agreement employing a brokerage office for a specified period of time to the exclusion of all other offices. In this form of exclusive, not only is the broker protected in the event of a sale by another office, but he is also entitled to a commission even if the owner sells the property himself.

The *exclusive agency* listing is a written agreement which an owner gives exclusively to one brokerage office to sell or lease his property for a specified period of time. Should another agency be the procuring cause of the sale, the one possessing the exclusive agency is also entitled to collect a commission. The only time the broker is not entitled to compensation upon a sale being made is if the owner sells the property himself.

A *multiple* listing is a form of an exclusive right of sale agreement. It is given to one brokerage office for the express purpose of his distributing it to other agencies. Many local real estate boards have a central clearing house where such multiple listings are submitted by member brokers. Photos and brochures are printed and sent to participating offices. In this way, the client is assured that his property will be getting wide distribution. At once, hundreds of offices receive his listing with all the necessary information to consummate a sale at hand. The commission is shared by the listing and selling broker, with a small percentage going to the multiple listing board or organization for their "clearing house" services.

The *open* listing is the most common form of handling an owner's property. It may be implied simply by oral consent, or it can be in writing. The first broker to bring about a sale under the terms and conditions of the open listing is the procuring cause of the transaction, and is the only one entitled to receive a commission. When the sale of an open listing is consummated, it is not necessary for the owner to notify the other listing offices. The listing agreement is automatically terminated by the sale, Sample forms of a multiple-exclusive, an open listing and two exclusive right-of-sale agreements are shown at the conclusion of this chapter.

FOURTEEN WAYS OF OBTAINING LISTINGS

It cannot be emphasized too strongly that obtaining new listings should be a never ending campaign. Successful real estate practitioners have long realized that this function, by necessity, occupies more time and energy than any other single activity, including that of selling. Without sufficient properties of comparable nature, the selling process becomes, at best, a hit or miss proposition. Good listings are a broker's inventory . . . his stock in trade, and he must make a daily, organized effort to secure them. And, just having them on an open listing basis is not the final aim by any means. All good listers try for the exclusive right of sale. Getting exclusives can mean that extra something that leaves the competition behind. It gives the offices that have them virtual control over the destiny of the property for the term of the agreement.

Sources of getting listings are endless, if you know where to look and how to go after them. The more listings of similar properties one has, the more chance there is of bringing home a contract. This is one of the secrets of successful real estate selling. Having comparable offerings. Give the buyer a choice to pick from—the "either/or" method. In any event, you make a sale.

Because of the importance of having a healthy inventory of good listings, salesmen should be given a financial incentive to go after them. A fee of 10 percent- 15 percent as extra commission is fair compensation, whether the listing salesman brings about the sale himself or someone else does. If his normal commission split with the office is, say, 50 percent, he should receive the extra percentage over and above that if he sells his own listing.

Here are 14 proven ways of obtaining salable listings:

1. *Telephoning Owners*. Following up owner ads that appear in the classified columns and "For Sale by Owner" property signs. Also, following through by phone when a friend tips you off that an owner would like to sell. Whatever the origin, listing property by phone requires a smooth, friendly technique. Put a "smile" in your voice, yet try not to appear overly-solicitous. After all, the call can be as important to him as it is to you. Be pleasant and sincere. The owner must be quickly convinced that you are reliable and he can realize as much *or more* money by listing with you; that your office can get the job done fast and efficiently; that you have the professional know-how to set the technical and legal details in motion; that you have qualified buyers; that your experience in financing will help bring about a sale; and that you carefully qualify prospects before bringing them out.

A little tact and understanding of the seller's problems and desires can go a long way toward converting a five- or six-minute phone call into a valuable listing. After establishing favorable contact, immediately set up an appointment to view the premises.

2. *Mailings*.[1] One of the surest ways of obtaining a steady flow of

---

[1]See Letters Seeking Listings, pages 208 and 209.

listings is by direct mail. Its purpose is to get the seller to respond in a positive manner by filling in and mailing the return portion of a post card or letter, or by phoning. Real estate offices usually work from cross-reference lists presented alphabetically by streets. Most cities have publishing companies offering such books for sale at a nominal price. Brokers in smaller towns can go directly to the phone book for names. By using the former type list, an office can blanket a specific area in which it may have interested buyers. To be successful, direct mail should be a steady campaign. By utilizing one or more office workers on a part-time basis you can usually accomplish this end.

A 4-percent response on bulk mailings of this nature is considered good. (4 replies per 100 sent) Even if just one of these ultimately results. in a salable listing, you will be on your way to building a valuable inventory.

3. *Cold Canvassing.* Knock on enough doors on any given work day and you are bound to come up with properties to sell. Be sure to go about it in an orderly manner, though. Concentrate in a section of town for which you have buyers. If, for example, you are working with a family that wants a 3-bedroom, 2-bath ranch house in a specified school district, price range, say, $40,000 to $45,000, you can hone in and concentrate on this specific area and type of property.

An owner, who does not want to sell, can still be of help. If tactfully questioned, he may tip you off as to who in the area is thinking of selling. The corner storekeeper, gas station operator or even neighborhood children can also prove a valuable source. By simply stating that you, "are looking for the house that is for sale on the block" you will often elicit an answer that will direct you to the right property. People, young and old, usually like to show that they are knowledgeable and friendly. If none is known to be for sale, you are free to proceed to the next block.

To insure the most complete coverage when canvassing, many brokers leave specially-worded printed forms when the owner is not at home. A practical idea is to design the shape of the form so that it may fit over the door knob.

SORRY

I missed you. We are currently working with buyers interested
in obtaining houses in this area. If you are contemplating sell-

ing at this time or in the foreseeable future, please call me at 844-3035. We look forward to being of service.

John Jones
Leader Realty

Remember, there is nothing like face-to-face contact for results. The percentage of listings gotten through canvassing will be much higher than by telephone, advertising or direct-mail solicitation.

4. *Sold Signs*. Nothing succeeds like success. One of the first things a broker should do upon making a sale is to tell it to the world by placing a large, bright "sold" sticker over the "For Sale" portion of his sign. Some offices use a phrase such as "Sold, but we have others," or have special signs made up entirely devoted to announcing the sale. The more eye-catching the better. Shout it to the rooftops. Other sellers will peg your office as an active one, and will want you to work on their property.

5. *Newspaper Publicity*.[2] Most newspapers gladly publish news items of real estate sales. It is human interest and the public wants to be informed. A sale is positive proof of real estate value, and almost everyone either owns, wants to own or wants to sell real estate. Many editors will publish a photo of the property if one is furnished. A clear 5″ × 7″ glossy print will do, with a one- or two-paragraph story attached giving details such as names of the principals, addresses of the property, mortgage information, price, the salesman who made the sale and the office he is affiliated with. Make it easy for the busy editor to use your items by presenting them in as direct and professional a manner as possible. It has been said that free newspaper publicity is worth ten advertisements of comparable size.

6. *Local News Items*. Another source of leads is in training your eye to spot certain newspaper items. A person taking a new business position in another town often has his residence as well as other real estate to sell. Following up legal notices such as tax sales, foreclosures, probate of wills, as well as divorce items and death notices can prove a good source of getting properties listed.

7. *Personal Contacts*. The more active and prominent in the com-

---

[2]See Letters To Real Estate Editor, pages 218-220.

munity a broker is, the more listings will come his way. Personal contacts can prove an endless source of drawing both sellers and buyers to your office. Begin by becoming active in your church, take part in youth organizations, charity drives, join at least one business club or participate in local politics. Develop a reputation of service to your community. You will be widening your personal contacts and at the same time creating an atmosphere of trust and confidence that only can result in obtaining more listings and closing more sales.

8. *Representing Builders*. There is no better source of assuring a steady flow of salable listings than by representing one or more builders. Builders may range in size from the large developer who needs full time coverage, to the customer or "spot" builder who buys up vacant lots and puts in one to half a dozen houses on speculation, and will need only part time sales help.

The advantages of having new, modern houses in your inventory are at once apparent. They are relatively easier to sell and the chances are obviously much better for the broker to step up his volume of sales. The disadvantages lie in the amount of commission a builder is generally able to pay. The builder's profit usually precludes giving a 6 percent-7 percent fee. A flat amount is often agreed to beforehand. Here, even more than with resales, a broker should try to represent a builder on an exclusive basis. Multiple sales is the name of the game. A workable arrangement with a good builder can often guarantee a successful year for the broker.

A builder is generally engulfed in the details of construction. It's to his advantage to have a full-time team of professional salesmen representing him. But you must seek him out and sell him on your services. Point out that you have a ready-made organization that will work evenings and week-ends (when most sales are made) when necessary. Emphasize that you will give him full sales coverage of his model houses. Also, that many prospective buyers already have a home and you are in the best position to sell it rapidly for him (or work out a trade-in plan). In short, you will be freeing the builder to pursue his main function—that of building more and better homes.

9. *Broker Cooperation and Multiple Listing Services*. Half a loaf is better than none. Cooperating with other brokers can mean sales that otherwise would have been lost. It makes good sense to seek out a broker who is active in a certain area or specializes in a specific type of real estate rather than to lose your customer for lack of something to sell.

Many real estate boards have highly organized multiple listing services. Brokers who are members of a MLS send their listings to a central clearing office where they are printed and sent out to other subscribing members. When a broker thinks he has a buyer for a multiple listing, he generally contacts the listing broker who makes the necessary appointment with the owner to show the premises. Upon consummating a sale, the commission is divided between the two with a small percentage taken "off the top" for the central clearing office to cover operating expenses. Sellers usually like this service because with many offices working on the property, the added exposure usually brings faster results.

10. *Former Customers*. Make it a point to keep in contact with former buyers. A phone call every six months, or a personal letter or a card at Christmas will maintain the relationship. All factors being equal, when he is ready to sell, you will get the nod again to handle the property.

11. *Advertising*. Newspaper display or classified ads will keep your name before the public, as will billboards, radio and the yellow pages. A modest, continual advertising campaign will bring better results than infrequent large blasts. A true case in point is a short classified ad used daily for over 10 years by a highly successful New York real estate firm. It simply stated, "List with us if you *really* want to sell. Cash buyers waiting." The broker attributed numerous sales every year to this little ad that far outweighed its moderate cost.

12. *Envelope Stuffers*. Every piece of mail that leaves your office should contain a circular giving background information of your organization. Theme: Why and how it pays rather than costs to deal through you. It can be a cleverly worded short message or a more detailed one, perhaps containing a biographical sketch and photo of each sales associate. The long-range effect of this simple, inexpensive advertising method will prove just another plus factor in building up your inventory.

13. *Window Displays*. The majority of real estate offices are on the ground floor in high traffic-count areas. Utilize this valuable window space to best advantage. Because the passer-by will be gone in a matter of 3 or 4 seconds, your message must be kept simple, to the point and tell but a single message.

14. *Old Listings*. Many listings are not worked on after being taken; the most obvious reason is that they were overpriced. Perhaps at the time you didn't have anyone for this type of property, or the owner may have

been uncooperative. Whatever the reason, it pays to periodically check and up-date old listings. You may find the seller with a remarkably changed attitude, and with it a realistic price. Keep periodic tabs on old listings. You have already done the bulk of the work. A brief phone call is all it takes to revive it.

SIGNING UP THE LISTING

Ten points to drive home when signing up an owner:

1. The all-out effort in time and money that you will devote to advertising, photographing and brochuring the property.
2. Your experienced, highly qualified staff, invaluable mortgage contacts and all around real estate expertise will assure a sale at the highest possible price in the shortest possible time.
3. That you have cash buyers waiting who will be immediately offered the property.
4. Your willingness to work cooperatively does not close the door to other offices making the sale.
5. The property will take precedent over oral listings which are, at best, a nebulous arrangement.
6. A property offered around by too many offices is known among brokers as a "football." Buyers soon recognize these offerings and automatically conclude that something is wrong and avoid the property.
7. Brokers are understandably reluctant to advertise open or verbal listings for fear of the competition picking up the property and selling it out from under them.
8. Your entire office will make an earnest and continual effort to sell the property until the listing agreement is terminated.
9. The owner will not be bothered by unqualified prospects, or the annoyance of having to deal with many brokers. Buyers will be carefully screened before being shown the property.
10. For the least trouble and fuss from contract to closing of title, one hard-hitting real estate office is all that's needed.

It's so easy to follow the path of least resistance by not trying for the Exclusive Right of Sale. This is a mistake that can prove costly. A concerted effort should be made first to list the property exclusively for as long a period as possible. Begin by using an already filled in form calling for at least a 180-day exclusive. If the owner balks at this, reluctantly agree to revise the figure to 90 or 60 days (which is all you really should expect in the first place). If tactfully done, this sort of "compromise" will tend to satisfy the owner and remove his resistance to signing.

A seller may already be working closely with other brokers or for other reasons will not, under any circumstances, give out an exclusive listing. If all efforts have failed, have him sign a non-exclusive (open) listing. It obligates the owner to sell at the specified price and terms. You know he means business and cannot change his mind if you produce a ready, willing and able buyer. The written agreement also serves as legal proof that the broker is entitled to his commission when he performs. Without a listing contract, a broker is looked upon as merely volunteering his services. In most states he would have a difficult time collecting, should the owner change his mind or if a dispute arises as to the commission amount. All listing agreements should precisely spell out the compensation due the broker. Four typical listing agreements follow. Included are an open listing agreement, two exclusive right of sales, and a multiple-exclusive.

OPEN LISTING AGREEMENT

In consideration of the services of _____ _____, hereinafter called broker, I hereby list with said broker for a period of _____ days from date hereof, the following described property and at the following description price and terms:

ADDRESS: _____

LEGAL DESCRIPTION: _____

SELLING PRICE: $_____ FURNISHED _____ UNFURN. _____

EXISTING MORTGAGE(S) _____

MORTGAGE COMMITMENTS: _____

MINIMUM CASH REQUIRED: _____

I agree to pay to the broker a commission of _____ per cent (_____%) of the selling price should the broker find a purchaser ready, willing and able to buy at the above price and terms, or if he sells the property at other price and terms agreeable to me.

It is understood that this listing agreement in no way prohibits me from selling the property direct. I retain the right to sell to any party not first contacted by the broker. I also retain the right to list my property for sale with any other broker or brokers. I also have the right to withdraw the property from the market upon notice to the broker.

Should a sale be made within six months after this authorization terminates to parties with whom the broker may negotiate during the term hereof, and whose name has been disclosed to me, then I agree to pay said commission to said broker.

Should the property be sold, I agree to furnish the purchaser a good and sufficient Warranty Deed, and a complete abstract of title.

Should deposit money paid on account of purchase be forfeited by the purchaser, one half shall be retained by the broker, providing said amount does not exceed the commission.

I hereby acknowledge receipt of a copy of this authorization to sell.

Signed on the _____ day of _____ , 19__. _____

_____   _____ (Seal)
Witness   Owner

_____   _____ (Seal)
Witness   Owner

In consideration of the foregoing listing and authorization, the undersigned broker agrees to use diligence in procuring a purchaser.

_____
                                                    Broker

Exclusive Right of Sale

In consideration of the services of _____
hereinafter called broker, I hereby list with said broker, exclusively and irrevocably, for a period of_____days
from date hereof, the following described property and at the following described price and terms:

ADDRESS: _____

LEGAL DESCRIPTION: _____

SELLING PRICE: $_____ FURNISHED _____ UNFURN. _____

EXISTING MORTGAGE(S): _____
_____

MORTGAGE COMMITMENTS: _____

MINIMUM CASH REQUIRED: _____

I hereby agree to pay said broker as commission _____ (_____%) per cent
of the selling price should, during the time set forth herein, said property be sold by said broker, or by me, or by
another broker, or through some other source, or whether said property be withdrawn from sale, transfered, conveyed, or leased without approval of said broker, either at the above price and terms, or at any other price and terms
agreeable to me.

Should a sale be made within six months after this authorization terminates to parties with whom
said broker, or a co-operating broker, may negotiate during the term hereof, and whose name has been disclosed
to me, then I agree to pay said commission to said broker.

In case the above described property is sold or disposed of within the time specified, I agree to make
the purchaser a good and sufficient warranty deed to the same and to furnish a complete abstract of title brought
down to date at my expense. Interests, taxes, insurance, rents, if any, shall be prorated as of date of closing.

I agree to refer to said broker all prospective purchasers or brokers who may contact me directly,
and to furnish said broker with their names and addresses.

The said broker is given the exclusive right to place his sign upon the premises and to remove any
other sign found thereon, and to advertise said property at the price and terms above set forth.

Should a deposit or amounts paid on account of purchase be forfeited, one half thereof may be retained by said broker, providing however, that the brokers share of any forfeited deposit or amounts paid on account of purchase, shall not exceed the commission.

I hereby acknowledge receipt of a copy of this authorization to sell.

Signed on the _____day of _____, 19_____

_____   _____ (Seal)
Witness   Owner

_____   _____ (Seal)
Witness   Owner

In consideration of the foregoing listing and authorization the undersigned broker agrees to use
diligence in procuring a purchaser.

_____
Broker

By _____

Figure 8-1.

THIS IS A STANDARD FORM OF THE MIAMI BOARD OF REALTORS
A Realtor Designates Only Professional Members   of the National Association of Real Estate Boards
Realtors are required to meet rigid standards   *Realtors adhere to a code of professional ethics*

LISTING AGREEMENT
EXCLUSIVE

Date ....

1. In consideration of your agreement to use your professional efforts to find a purchaser for that property situate in Dade County, Florida, described as follows:

   LEGAL DESCRIPTION: ....

   ....

   ....

   ....

   INCLUDED IN SALE: ....

   ....

   STREET ADDRESS: ....

   the undersigned owners hereby give you for a period of .... days from this date the sole right and authority to find a purchaser for said property at the following price and terms, or at any other price and terms acceptable to the undersigned owners, to-wit:

   SALE PRICE: ....

   TERMS: ....

   ....

   ....

   ....

2. Upon finding a purchaser for said property, the undersigned owners agree to enter into a written contract with purchaser on a form the same as or similar to the Miami Board of Realtors standard Purchase and Sale Contract.

3. For finding a purchaser ready, willing and able to purchase the above property, the undersigned owners jointly and severally agree to pay you a brokerage fee of ....% of the sales price of said property, said fee to be paid you whether the purchaser is found by you or by the undersigned owners or by any other person, at the price and upon the terms set forth above, or at any price or terms acceptable to the undersigned, or if the undersigned agree to sell or exchange said property within four months next after the termination of this agency to a purchaser to whom you or any cooperating broker submitted said property for sale during the continuance of said agency. In any exchange of this property, permission is given you, by the undersigned owners, to represent and receive brokerage fees from both parties.

4. If the property herein concerned is a single family residence, and said property is leased during the term of this agreement, it is understood and agreed by the undersigned owners that a brokerage fee of   for such leasing shall be paid to you, the listing broker.

5. In consideration of the above, the undersigned owners agree:

   (A) To immediately refer to you for attention all inquiries relative to said property.

   (B) To make said property available for showing at reasonable hours.

   (C) To close and/or give occupancy within..from date of execution of Purchase and Sales Contract.

   (D) To furnish a complete Abstract of Title to the property brought to date showing a marketable and insurable title thereto. Upon finding a purchaser for the property, the usual and customary practice for the examination, curing title and for closing the transaction shall apply. We agree to execute and deliver to the purchaser a good and sufficient warranty deed with dower rights, if any, released, free and clear of all liens and encumbrances except those which the purchaser shall assume as part of the purchase price and which are specifically detailed above.

   (E) We further grant the herein named broker the sole right, for the duration of this agreement, to install and display a real estate sign on our herein described property in keeping with all Metro and City Ordinances currently in effect.

6. As our broker, you are authorized to act as escrow agent at such time as a Purchase and Sale Contract is drawn.

7. It is hereby certified that we are the owners of the property described above.

WITNESSES:

....(SEAL)
                                         Sole Owner ( )   Joint Owner ( )

....(SEAL)
ACCEPTED BY:

By ....
      As Realtor   Salesman

Figure 8-2.

Miami Multiple Listing Service, Inc.

MULTIPLE LISTING AGREEMENT

Date _____

1. In consideration of your agreement to use your professional efforts to find a purchaser for that property situate in Dade County, Florida, described as follows:

LEGAL DESCRIPTION: _____

INCLUDED IN SALE: _____

STREET ADDRESS: _____
and to brochure such property to other Realtors through the services of the Miami Multiple Listing Service, Inc., in accordance

with its Rules, the undersigned owners hereby give you for a period of _____ days from this date the sole right and authority to find a purchaser for said property at the following price and terms or at any other price and terms acceptable to the undersigned owners, to wit:

SALES PRICE: _____

TERMS: _____

2. Upon finding a purchaser for said property, the undersigned owners agree to enter into a written contract with purchaser on a form the same as or similar to the Miami Board of Realtors standard Purchase and Sales Contract.

3. For finding a purchaser ready, willing and able to purchase the above property, the undersigned owners jointly and severally

agree to pay you a brokerage fee of _____ % of the sales price of said property, said fee to be paid you whether the purchaser is found by you or by the undersigned owners or by any other person, at the price and upon the terms set forth above, or at any price or terms acceptable to the undersigned, or if the undersigned agree to sell or exchange said property within four months next after the termination of this agency to a purchaser to whom you or any cooperating broker submitted said property for sale during the continuance of said agency. In any exchange of this property, permission is given you, by the undersigned owners, to represent and receive brokerage fees from both parties.

4. If the property involved is available for leasing, the undersigned owners agree that all negotiations for leasing will be made by and through the listing Realtor. The undersigned owners further agree in negotiating any lease to utilize the Realtors Standard Receipt for Deposit and Contract to Lease or a similar form which will be signed by the undersigned owners and the lessee. The undersigned owners further agree to pay a brokerage fee of _____ for the leasing transaction.

5. In consideration of this multiple listing, the undersigned Realtor agrees:

  (A) To carefully inspect said property and secure adequate information regarding it.

  (B) To advertise said property as he deems advisable.

  (C) On cooperative sales with participating members of the Service, the listing member shall retain _____ % of the brokerage fee; the balance shall be paid to the selling office.

  (D) To permit the undersigned owners to cancel this listing prior to the termination date as set forth above by payment to the undersigned Realtor of one-half of the agreed brokerage fee.

6. In consideration of the above, the undersigned owners agree:

  (A) To immediately refer to you for attention all inquiries relative to said property.

  (B) To make said property available for showing at reasonable hours.

  (C) To close and/or give occupancy within _____ from date of execution of Purchase and Sales Contract.

  (D) To furnish a complete Abstract of Title to the property brought to date showing a marketable and insurable title thereto. Upon finding a purchaser for the property, the usual and customary practice for the examination, curing title and for closing the transaction shall apply. We agree to execute and deliver to the purchaser a good and sufficient warranty deed with dower rights, if any, released, free and clear of all liens and encumbrances except those which the purchaser shall assume as part of the purchase price and which are specifically detailed above.

  (E) We further grant the herein named broker the sole right, for the duration of this agreement, to install and display a real estate sign on our herein described property in keeping with all Metro and City Ordinances currently in effect.

7. As our Realtor, you or any cooperating Realtor are authorized to act as escrow agent at such time as a Purchase and Sales Contract is drawn.

8. It is hereby certified that we are the owners of the property described above.

WITNESSES:

_____   _____ (SEAL)
                                      Sole Owner ( )   Joint Owner ( )

_____   _____ (SEAL)

ACCEPTED BY:

By _____   _____
          As Realtor   Salesman

Original copy to Realtor.
Duplicate copy must be mailed to the Miami Multiple Listing Service, Inc. within 24 hours.
Triplicate copy must be delivered to seller within 24 hours.
7/1/74

Figure 8-3.

9

THE MORTGAGE MARKET

Financing Discussed . . . Institutional lenders: Savings and Loan Associations . . . Mutual Savings Banks . . . Commercial Banks . . . Life Insurance Companies : . . Private Investors: Purchase Money Mortgages . . . Pension, Trust and Endowment Funds . . . FHA-Insured Mortgages . . . VA-Guaranteed Mortgages . . . Conventional Mortgages . . . Creative Financing: Variable-Rate Mortgages . . . Wraparound Mortgages . . . Participation (Kicker) Loans . . . Balloon Mortgages . . . Piggyback Financing . . . Sale-Leaseback . . . Sale-Buyback . . . Sale-Leaseback-Buyback . . . The Mortgage Instrument Analyzed . . . Additional Clauses in Mortgages . . . Truth in Lending Act.

At the base of most successful real estate transactions lies its financing. Sales usually hinge upon obtaining satisfactory mortgages, for it's a rare transaction these days that does not involve the placing of one or more mortgages, or the assumption of an existing one. This section will cover all the traditional methods of financing, along with the new innovative techniques—techniques that can often make the difference between completing a sale or losing it.

The mortgage market is closely allied to other money markets in that it reflects an area's economy. Money is not unlike any other commodity. When it is readily available, the price to obtain it (the interest rates) understandably goes down. Those of us in real estate must know when and where to go to find the most advantageous mortgages, and how to present the property we are attempting to mortgage in the most favorable light.

There are four principal sources of obtaining mortgage money. They are:

1. Institutional lenders
   a. Savings and loan associations
   b. Mutual savings banks
   c. Commercial banks

2. Life insurance companies

3. Private investors

4. Pension, trust and endowment funds

INSTITUTIONAL LENDERS

SAVINGS AND LOAN ASSOCIATIONS

One of the main purposes of the federal savings and loan associations is to finance homes by granting conventional as well as FHA- and VA-insured mortgages. To a lesser degree they also finance commercial properties. By so doing, they are fulfilling the prime purpose of their charter; that of safely investing the depositors money at a reasonable rate of return. Most conventional mortgages offered by savings and loan associations are for 75 percent to 85 percent of the purchase price, while FHA- and VA-insured loans can reach as high as 90 percent-100 percent. The length of the loan can be for as long as 30 years, though most are in the 20-25 year time period. Over 80 percent of the total assets of all federal savings and loan associations are committed to the financing of residential real estate.

MUTUAL SAVINGS BANKS

Mutual savings banks are active in 18 heavily populated northeastern and northcentral states and have over 500 separate banks. Like the savings and loan associations, they invest heavily in mortgages for dwellings, both for government-insured and conventional loans. For conventional mortgages they often make loans up to 90 percent of the sales price. Some of the urban savings banks are heavily insured in commercial real estate of all types. Unlike the savings and loan associations, mutual banks are involved in certain long-term investments other than real estate mortgages. Also, unlike savings and loan associations, their scope of activity frequently extends outside their immediate locality and into other states. It is estimated that approximately 65 percent of their investments are in mortgages.

COMMERCIAL BANKS

Commercial banks comprise the state- and federally-chartered banks that obtain almost all their funds from "demand deposits" or checking accounts as they are more familiarly called. They are known for giving short-term business loans, though their charters permit them to make amortized mortgages for terms up to 20 years and in amounts as high as 80 percent of the appraised value. Traditionally, however, loaning money for long-term mortgages is generally more of a sideline with commercial banks. They rarely have large mortgage departments with mortgage officers and staff appraisers. They are neither geared for nor do they seek this type investment, though some do give permanent mortgage financing on a limited basis or to certain preferred customers. Their importance to real estate financing lies in short-term loans. They give builders, developers and investors interim loans until other lending institutions consent to give permanent financing.

Commercial banks also administer to trust funds placed in their care. These monies are often invested in secured second mortgages.

LIFE INSURANCE COMPANIES

Working through local mortgage brokers, or directly with their own representatives, life insurance companies finance a multiple of high-rise and other larger projects. Ventures such as regional and suburban shopping centers, PUDS, urban office buildings, apartment housing and condominiums of all types comprise a large share of their real estate lending activity. The insurance companies have been innovators in creating "participation" mortgages, whereby they come in for "a piece of the action" as well as the usual interest rate of return. Participation can take two forms; either as a share in the annual profits, or as part of the actual ownership of the project. Participation, or a "kicker" as it is sometimes referred to, is objectionable as far as a developer or investor is concerned. It is only in a tight money market when no other means of obtaining financing is available that a mortgagor would be willing to submit to participation.

Residential and rural real estate mortgaging by life insurance companies plays a significant role through FHA and VA financing. Also, before granting conventional mortgages, some insurance companies require a "tie in" purchase of a life insurance policy. In certain regions, single and multiple family communities have been entirely financed by them. With their vast amount of investment capital available, insurance companies are well-known for buying up portfolios of other lending institutions. While the insurance companies may then own the mortgages, the original lenders or local mortgage brokers frequently continue to service the mortgages for an agreed upon fee.

The insurance industry estimates that approximately 35 percent of their resources are invested in real estate financing.

PRIVATE INVESTORS

Individual investors play a leading role in second or junior mortgaging. The private investor's bailiwick is where the institutional lenders fear to tread. Because of the added risk involved (of being behind a first mortgage), the private investor is entitled to, and invariably receives, a greater return for his investment. Many such mortgages are made at the highest legal interest rate allowable.

The one instance when this does not necessarily hold true is with *purchase money mortgages*, whereby the seller of real estate takes back a mortgage, usually to facilitate the sale. It can be a first or second mortgage that he "takes back." The interest rate is generally more in keeping with the current first-mortgage market rate, but it can be higher or lower. It is a point to be negotiated when making a sale.

At times, motives other than those for profit govern the terms of a private mortgage, as in the case of a father passing on property to his heirs. The terms of such a mortgage are understandably liberal.

The extent and variations found in private mortgages dictate that only the most general reference statements be made. No statistics exist as to the part private mortgages play in financing real property. But those active in real estate for any length of time soon realize the impact and importance such financing has.

PENSION, TRUST AND ENDOWMENT FUNDS

With the advent of government-insured (FHA) and guaranteed (VA) loans, union and industry pension funds, university endowments and private trusts have appreciably increased their investments in real estate. Heretofore, certain safe, readily convertible securities and government bonds comprised the great bulk of the investment portfolio of such funds. In recent years, they have substantially invested in first mortgages of large commercial properties, and as principals in real estate acquisitions. In this manner, many trusts have safely increased their investment yield and gained valuable tax savings while holding appreciating real estate.

The three familiar types of mortgages that everyone in real estate should be on intimate terms with are the following:

1. FHA-Insured Mortgage
2. VA- (or GI) Guaranteed Mortgage
3. Conventional Mortgage

FHA-INSURED MORTGAGES

An FHA loan is one that is insured by the Federal Housing Administration. The FHA does not loan the money, but rather insures the lending institution that does to the extent of 97 percent of the first $15,000 loaned, plus 90 percent of the next $5,000, plus 85 percent of the remainder up to $33,000, at the time of this writing. The loans are made for a maximum of 30 years. There are numerous FHA programs covering low-income housing, housing for the elderly, programs for nursing homes, condominiums, cooperative apartments, and for repair and improvements to housing. The one most widely used is the Section 203 loan, which deals with single-family, owner-occupied residences. It will be used as the basis for discussion here because of its extensive usage in real estate transactions across the country.

Primarily due to the low down payment, and the FHA inspections necessary assuring the purchaser true market values, the program is most desirable from the buyer's standpoint.

With practically no risk involved because of FHA insurance, lending institutions are constantly seeking to make FHA loans, even though their terms and conditions, as well as the interest rate are controlled by the FHA. Because interest rates vary as economic circumstances dictate, FHA rates have always remained competitive. In fact, statistically, they are fractionally below the prevailing conventional mortgage rates.

The government, too, protects itself by charging the borrower ½ of 1 percent of the loan for insurance. This amount is collected by the lender monthly and paid to the FHA. When the loan is eventually paid off, a portion of the ½ of 1 percent insurance may be returned to the borrower.

VA-GUARANTEED MORTGAGES

The Veterans Administration's function in real estate is to guarantee mortgage loans made by private lending institutions, such as banks and savings and loan associations, to honorably discharged veterans of W.W. II, the Korean War and the Vietnam conflict. Also eligible are unremarried widows of veterans who died as a result of service.

Interest rates on GI loans vary with the changing mortgage market, but like FHA loans, are usually slightly less than those in conventional financing. The loans can be used for buying, building, repairing and improving a home or farm, or to buy land or a building for business purposes. The veteran can also obtain the loan for supplies, equipment or working capital to go into a business or profession.

A real estate loan can be made for up to 35 years (although most are made for 30 years); for farms, up to 40 years, and for non-real estate, up to 10 years. The G.I. is protected by a VA appraisal before the loan is approved. The amount and approval of the loan are determined by the appraised value and the income ability of the veteran.

The VA also makes certain direct loans to veterans who are satisfactory risks in credit-shortage areas, such as certain small towns and rural locals that do not have nearby private lending institutions.

Like the FHA mortgage, the VA exercises certain controls over the terms and conditions of the loan in return for guaranteeing its repayment. Unlike an FHA loan, however, the borrower is not charged for insurance. Loans are permitted to be made for 100 percent of appraised value. Thus, the mortgage can be made with no money down.

CONVENTIONAL MORTGAGES

A conventional mortgage is one which is based on real estate as the security, and is neither FHA-insured nor VA-guaranteed. First mortgage money from any lending institution, such as savings and loan associations, banks, life insurance companies, etc. is classified as a conventional mortgage. Most such mortgages require more cash equity than in government-sponsored mortgages. Conventional mortgages have much more latitude as to terms and conditions, but are, nevertheless, regimented by state and federal regulations in their charters.

CREATIVE FINANCING

Imaginative, creative financing of real estate involves knowing the needs of both lender and borrower, and then applying that knowledge to produce an intelligent, acceptable mortgage arrangement. Some of the more accepted and modern methods and techniques will be described here in detail.

VARIABLE-RATE MORTGAGES

With the mortgage market in an unending state of flux, lenders are utilizing the technique of "tieing" the interest rate to a given percentage amount above the bank prime lending rate, or to an institution's weighted average cost of savings money. The object of course, is to keep the interest rate up with the times. If the banks' prime lending rate currently is, say 9 percent and the agreed upon variable rate is 3 percent over prime, the borrower will be paying 12 percent interest as long as the prime rate stays at 9. (The prime rate generally refers to the interest that one or more of the major New York banking houses charges its prime, blue-chip borrowers.)

WRAPAROUND MORTGAGES

The "wraparound" is created when a lender gives a mortgage in a higher amount than the existing first mortgage which remains on the property. The lender of the wraparound mortgage assumes the first mortgage, taking over its payments. The wraparound, second mortgage he gives is not only for a higher amount, but bears a higher interest rate. With the continued trend toward appreciating real property values and steadily rising interest rates, the wraparound mortgage technique has gained greatly in use and popularity.

PARTICIPATION (KICKER) LOANS

When mortgage financing becomes more difficult to obtain, lenders seek something more than just a fixed interest rate. They may want to participate in the income or profits of the property or take an equity position in it. They may also want high closing fees and discounts (points). Whatever the something extra they are seeking, in the jargon of real estate it is referred to as a participation or kicker loan.

BALLOON MORTGAGES

A balloon mortgage is one that provides for periodic payments which do not completely amortize the loan at the time of its termination. The resulting final, larger payment that becomes due is the balloon amount.

Balloon mortgages are generally used for financing income-producing properties. They are particularly useful when there is a limited cash flow and normal mortgage payments would be prohibitive. The periodic payment required to reduce the loan is less than the usual amount, allowing for a higher annual net income.

PIGGYBACK FINANCING

When two or more lenders pool their resources to make one loan it is referred to as piggyback financing. This may occur when a borrower is seeking a higher amount (for example a 90 percent loan) than an institution's loan-to-value ratio permits. The originating lender may agree to take, say 70 percent of the loan, but allow another lender (generally a private party) to take up the additional 20 percent needed. Though it has about the same effect as a second mortgage, it is in fact but a single first mortgage. To protect his interest, the private lender can take out mortgage insurance, for his position is subordinated to that of the prime lender.

SALE-LEASEBACK

This financing technique occurs when a seller simultaneously leases back the property he has just sold. The sale-leaseback transaction has decided advantages for both buyer and seller-lessor. The seller-lessor receives cash from the sale and remains in possession of the property. (The public is often unaware of the ownership change.) From the buyer's point of view, he is assured a tenant, and thus a fixed return on his investment, as well as all the tax shelter advantages that go with real estate ownership.

SALE-BUYBACK

In this form of transaction, the seller repurchases the asset by means of an installment sales contract. Even though actual title to the property is vested in the new owner, the one buying it back retains a certain equitable interest in the title. As a consequence, a portion of the tax depreciation benefits will fall to him. Another advantage is that the sale-buyback deal allows the seller to receive the full amount of the sales price in cash, whereas if the property was mortgaged in the conventional manner, only a percentage of the sales price would be realized.

SALE-LEASEBACK-BUYBACK

This three-phase transaction allows the seller-leaseholder to repurchase his former property by way of an option written into the leasehold agreement, after a specified period of time has elapsed. The length of time before the repurchase takes place is an important factor. It cannot occur too soon, as the government could interpret the entire transaction as an elaborately structured loan. Some tax experts believe that a minimum of five years should elapse before the final buyback can take place.

A word to the wise is in order concerning leaseback and buyback situations. Each transaction has distinct tax ramifications that may require federal interpretation. Check with an experienced CPA or tax-oriented attorney before committing yourself or your client to any form of re-purchase or leaseback transaction.

THE MORTGAGE INSTRUMENT ANALYZED

The purpose of the mortgage instrument is to pledge real property as security for the payment of a debt or the performance of an obligation. It can take many forms and may include special clauses to fit specific situations. A sample form and its basic divisions are shown below.

Date And Place Of Origin

THIS MORTGAGE made in ____ (City)____ of the County of_____ and State of_____ , entered into this_____ day of_____ , in the year of our Lord One Thousand Nine Hundred and_____ .

Parties

BY AND BETWEEN_____, hereinafter called the Mortgagor, which term as used in every instance shall include Mortgagor's heirs, executors, administrators, successors, legal representatives and assigns, and shall denote the singular and/or plural and the masculine and/or feminine and natural or artificial persons whenever and wherever the context so requires or admits, party of the first part, and _____, hereinafter called the Mortgagee, which term as used in every instance shall include Mortgagee's heirs, executors, administrators, successors, legal representatives and assigns and shall denote the singular and/or plural and the masculine and/or feminine and natural and/or artificial persons whenever and wherever the context so requires or admits, party of the second part;

Amount Of Indebtedness, Interest Rate, Manner Of Payment

WHEREAS the said Mortgagor is justly indebted to the said Mortgagee in the aggregate sum of_____Dollars ($_____), lawful money of the United States, for money actually loaned to the Mortgagor, with interest thereon to be computed from the_____ day of_____, 19__, at the rate of_____% per annum, and to be paid_____ according to a certain bond, note or obligation bearing even date herewith.

Description Of Property

THE MORTGAGOR hereby mortgages to the Mortgagee, ALL that certain

(Here include legal description)

Conveyance Of Property[1]

NOW, THEREFORE, for and in consideration of the sum of one dollar in hand paid by the Mortgagee, receipt whereof by the Mortgagor is hereby acknowledged, and also for the better securing of the payment of the said sum of money and interest thereon, and for the better securing of the performance of the covenants and agreements hereinafter contained, the said Mortgagor has granted, bargained, sold and conveyed, and by these presents does grant, bargain, sell and convey unto the said Mortgagee, that certain lot, piece or parcel of land above legally described.

Signed, Sealed, Witnessed

IN WITNESS WHEREOF, the Mortgagor on the day and year first written, has executed these presents under seal

---

[1]This clause can be omitted in lien theory states.

Signed, sealed and delivered
in the presence of

_____   _____ Seal

_____   _____ Seal

(Acknowledgement of Mortgage)
State of _____)
)ss
County of _____)

    I, an officer authorized to take acknowledgements according to the laws of the State of _____ duly qualified and acting, HEREBY CERTIFY that _____ to me personally known, this day personally appeared and acknowledged before me that _____ executed the foregoing Mortgage, and I further certify that I know the said person(s) making said acknowledgement to be the individual(s) described in and who executed the said Mortgage.

ADDITIONAL CLAUSES IN MORTGAGES

    Clauses in mortgages can take many forms to cover most every conceivable situation. A few examples of typical mortgage clauses are illustrated.

    Subordination Clause—This mortgage is subject and subordinate to a mortgage given to secure the payment of _____ thousand dollars ($ _____) and interest, recorded in the Clerk of the County Court, _____ County, _____ (state) _____ , O.R. Book _____ , Page _____ , on _____ , 19 ___ on which there remained due the sum of _____ thousand dollars ($ _____) and interest, which mortgage now is a prior lien on the premises; and this mortgage shall be and remain subject and subordinate, at all times, to that mortgage, and to any renewal or extension of it, or to any new mortgage given to replace it, to secure an amount not to exceed the sum of _____ thousand dollars ($ _____) and interest not to exceed _____ % per annum.

    Purchase Money Mortgage—Said property is the same premises conveyed to the Mortgagee by the Mortgagor by a deed bearing even date with these presents, which are given to secure the (payment) (part payment) of the purchase money of the said mortgage.

Balloon Mortgage—This mortgage provides for periodic payments that do not completely amortize the loan at the time of its termination. The final payment of the balance due upon maturity is $_____ together with accrued interest, if any, and all advancements made by the Mortgagee under the terms of this mortgage.

Acceleration Of Mortgage On Default—It is hereby expressly agreed that if default be made in the payment of any principal or interest on said note, or in the performance of the covenants or agreements herein contained, or any of them, then at the option of the legal holder of said note, the whole of the principal debt herein secured shall become due and payable, and be collected by suit or by proceedings hereunder.

Acceleration Of Mortgage For Not Maintaining Building—The whole of said principal sum shall become due at the option of the Mortgagee, if the building or said premises are not maintained in reasonably good repair, or upon the actual or threatened alteration, removal or demolition of any building on said premises, or any building to be erected upon said premises, or upon the failure of any owner of said premises to comply with the requirements of any governmental department claiming jurisdiction within _____ months after an order making such requirement has been issued by any such department.

Warranty Of Good Title To Premises And Personal Property—The Mortgagor represents and warrants the title to the premises and to the fixtures, chattels and personal property covered by this mortgage, that the mortgaged premises is free of all liens and encumbrances except those herein specifically stated. If the Mortgagor is a corporation, the Mortgagor warrants that the execution of this mortgage has been duly authorized by its board of directors and that no provision of its certificate of incorporation or by laws requires the consent of its stockholders to the execution and delivery of this mortgage.

Prepayment Privilege—The Mortgagor shall have the right and privilege to prepay the mortgage indebtedness in whole or part upon _____ days prior written notice to the Mortgagee, provided that interest at the rate of_____% per annum is paid to the date of prepayment on the amount of principal prepaid. This right to prepay shall apply only if the Mortgagor is not in default of the covenants, conditions or agreements contained in the aforesaid mortgage.

Mortgage Debt Payments—In the event of the passage after the date of this mortgage of any state law deducting from the value of the land for the purposes of taxation any lien thereon, or changing in any way the laws for the taxation of mortgages or debts secured by mortgage for state or local purposes, or the manner of the collection of any such taxes, so as to affect this mortgage, the holder of this mortgage and of the debt which it secures, shall have the right to give _____ days written notice to the owner of the mortgaged premises requiring the payment of the mortgage debt. If such notice be given the said debt shall become due, payable and collectible at the expiration of said _____ days.

Fire Insurance Coverage—The Mortgagor will keep the buildings on the premises insured against loss by fire for the benefit of the Mortgagee; he will assign and deliver the policies to the Mortgagee; and he will reimburse the Mortgagee for any premiums paid for insurance made by the Mortgagee on the Mortgagor's default in so insuring the buildings or in so assigning and delivering the policies. The fire insurance policies shall contain the usual extended coverage endorsement.

Late Charge Clause—In the event payments of any kind that are due on this mortgage, or on the real estate tax payable on the property encumbered by this mortgage, are not made on or prior to the due date, a late charge of_____% per annum on the sums overdue shall accrue from the due date, and shall become due and payable the first day of the month following. If the Mortgagor fails to pay late charges when due, the entire principal and interest amount shall become due at the option of the Mortgagee. In the event the Mortgagee fails to strictly enforce the late charge obligations by the Mortgagor it shall not constitute a waiver by the Mortgagee of its rights to enforce the provisions of this clause; nor shall the acceptance of the late charges be construed as an extension of time for future principal and interest payments.

TRUTH IN LENDING ACT

As a protective measure for the purchaser of real estate, particularly the residential buyer, the federal government has enacted the Truth In Lending Act and Federal Reserve Regulation Z. This act and regulation require professional lenders to give notice of interest rates and detailed finance charges to individuals for all loans under $25,000. As further protection, the individual has the right to rescind the entire sale within three business days after the required finance charges and interest rates have been clearly disclosed to him. If he elects to rescind the transaction, he is not liable for finance charges. All deposits given by him must be returned within ten days.

10

PROPERTY MANAGEMENT

Management Discussed . . . Selecting a Management Company . . . Specialized Management . . . Management Duties and Responsibilities . . . Sample Management Agreement Form.

The field of property management is the natural outgrowth of absentee ownership by lawyers, doctors, out-of-state investors, public companies, trusts and others who invest in income-producing real estate. Because these people or organizations do not have the time, inclination, or (in most cases) training to manage their properties effectively, they wisely look to professional property managers to do the job.

Selecting a management company or an individual manager may mean the difference between success or failure of a project. Good real estate management encompasses the following basic requisites:

1. Knowing the rental market in order not to over- or under-price the available space.
2. Then, properly presenting it to the public.
3. Drawing a lease with the necessary legal and financial clauses included to adequately protect the owner.
4. Maintaining the property in such a manner as to enhance its value, yet so doing at the most economical cost possible. This may involve preventive maintenance—the repair and maintaining of property before it shows signs of neglect or deterioration. Costly breakdowns and permanent damage to the property may thus be avoided. In addition, a better

outward appearance is maintained. Wise preventive maintenance invariably results in long-range savings.

5. Collecting rents, keeping proper accounts, making mortgage payments, and submitting periodic (usually monthly) reports to the owner.

6. Taking complete charge of the property. Such duties as hiring repair and maintenance personnel, ordering service contracts (elevator, oil burner, air conditioning, pest control, janitorial, lawn care, etc.), contracting for insurance policies, and dispossessing undesirable tenants, to name just some. In short, vigorously and effectively running the property in an economical manner to realize the most profit for the owner.

SPECIALIZED MANAGEMENT

Specialized management "know-how" is required for the running of certain types of property. Condominium and cooperative projects, mobile home parks, and motels are wide-ranging examples of specialized management. This form of management often has to deal with groups of people (tenant organizations) as well as individuals. Good management demands that no one person or segment of the whole receives preferential treatment.

Likewise, the management of hospitals, medical office buildings, shopping centers, warehouses and other specialized forms of real estate ownership demands particular, in-depth knowledge of the daily operating problems that will arise and must be dealt with. To be done properly and effectively, good management results from careful planning and design, as well as from constant attention.

THE MANAGEMENT AGREEMENT

The duties of a property manager should be spelled out in a detailed contractual agreement entered into by both owner and managing agent. The form can be in a lengthy Letter Of Agreement or as a formal contract. The duties and obligations of each to the other should be clearly stated, covering in detail the following areas:

1. *Length of Employment.* The manager should be employed for a

specified length of time. A period of at least one year is usual, at which time the agreement should continue automatically on a month-to-month basis. Either party may then have the right to terminate the contract by giving the other formal (written) notice at least one month in advance.

2. *Bonding.* The agent and all other employees he may hire for the administration of the property, should be adequately bonded by a properly licensed insurance or bonding agency.

3. *Income and Expense Statements.* The owner should expect to receive itemized monthly income and expense statements prepared by the manager from his books and records.

4. *Escrow Account.* The manager should maintain a separate escrow (trust) account in the name of the property or its owner. While the manager will be responsible for its proper administration, he should not be held liable in the event of failure to meet obligations or bankruptcy.

5. *Scope of Management Authority.* (a) The manager generally orders repairs and maintenance done if the expenditures do not exceed a specified amount. In the event of an emergency, however, he should have the right to exceed the stated amount. (b) The manager should have the authority to prepare copy and advertise available vacant space in the appropriate media. When vacancies exist, he should have a fixed, monthly advertising budget to work from. (c) The manager must be given the authority to prepare and sign leases up to a specified number of years, cancel leases, collect rents and give receipts for same, to evict undesirable tenants, or those delinquent in paying rent. He may also be given the authority to institute legal action against a tenant or make a settlement of money owed to the property. All of the aforementioned should be done in the owner's name and with his expressed approval. (d) The manager should be given the right to employ, supervise and discharge personnel at his discretion. (e) His duties should include entering into maintenance contracts such as for elevators, heating, trash removal, window cleaning, garden care, and for other needed operating services. All such contracts entered into are made on behalf of the owner who assumes responsibility for them. (f) The manager should pay all salaries, taxes, special assessments, insurance premiums and the general operating and fixed expenses of the property. He also may be expected to make the mortgage payments.

6. *Exclusive Right of Sale.* In the event the owner decides to sell the premises during the term of the management agreement, he may agree to

employ the managing agent (who must be a licensed real estate broker) as his exclusive sales agent for a specified period of time.

7. *Owner's Responsibilities*. The owner should be responsible for all legal actions taken against the property or the management. He should take out public liability insurance and workmen's compensation as a means of protecting himself and his agent from damage suits of any kind.

8. *Manager's Compensation*. Managing agents should have their fees clearly defined to avoid any misunderstanding. Payment for his managerial services is generally based on a percentage of the gross income. He also should be paid separately for obtaining new leases and renewing those that have expired. If he performs extra services such as supervising new construction, modernization of the premises or when extra work is performed for supervising flood or fire restoration, the amount and manner of payment should be mutually agreed upon beforehand.

A sample agreement form follows:

MANAGEMENT AGREEMENT FORM

Parties

    In consideration of the covenants herein contained_____ (hereinafter called "Owner"), and_____(hereinafter called "Agent"), agree as follows:

Exclusive Agency

1. The Owner hereby employs the Agent exclusively to rent, lease, operate and manage the property known as_____ upon the terms hereinafter set forth for the period of_____beginning on the_____day of _____ 19__, and ending on the_____day of _____19__, and thereafter for annual periods unless on or before sixty (60) days prior to the date last above mentioned, or on or before thirty (30) days prior to the expiration of any such renewal period, either party hereto shall notify the other in writing of an intention to terminate this agreement in which case this agreement may be terminated prior to the last mentioned date. Either party may terminate this agreement upon thirty (30) days written notice after the expiration of_____months of the original term.

Renting And Managing Premises

2. The Agent accepts the employment and agrees:

a) To use due diligence in the management of the premises for the period and upon the terms herein provided, and agrees to furnish the services of its organization for the renting, leasing, operating and managing of the herein described premises.

b) To render monthly statements of receipts, expenses and·charges and to remit to Owner receipts less disbursements. In the event the disbursements shall be in excess of the rents collected by the Agent, the Owner hereby agrees to pay such excess promptly upon request of the Agent.

c) To deposit all receipts collected for Owner in a Trust account separate from the Agent's personal account.

Agent's Authority

3. The Owner hereby gives to the Agent the following authority and powers and agrees to assume the expenses in connection herewith:

a) To advertise the availability for rental of the herein described premises, and to display "for rent" signs thereon; to sign, renew and/or cancel leases for the premises or any part thereof; to collect rent due or to become due and give receipts therefor; to terminate tenancies and to sign and serve in the name of the Owner such notices as are appropriate; to institute and prosecute actions; to evict tenants and to recover possession of said premises; to sue for in the name of the Owner and recover rents and other sums due, and when expedient, to settle, compromise, and release such actions or suits or reinstate such tenancies.

b) To make or cause to be made and supervise repairs and alterations, and to do decorating on said premises; to purchase supplies and pay all bills therefor. The Agent agrees to secure the prior approval of the Owner on all expenditures in excess of $_____for any one item, except monthly or recurring operating charges and/or emergency repairs in excess of the maximum, if in the opinion of the Agent such repairs are necessary to protect the property from damage or to maintain services to the tenants as called for in their leases.

c) To hire, discharge and supervise all labor and employees required for the operation and maintenance of the premises; it being agreed that all employees shall be deemed employees of the Owner and not the Agent; and that the agent may perform any of its duties through Owner's attorneys, agents or employees and shall not be responsible for their acts, defaults or negligence if reasonable care has been exercised in their appointment and retention.

d) To make contracts for electricity, gas, fuel, water, telephone, window cleaning, rubbish hauling and other services or such of them as the Agent shall deem advisable; the Owner to assume the obligation of any contract so entered into at the termination of this agreement.

Save Harmless

The Owner agrees to save the Agent harmless from all damage suits in connection with the management of the herein described premises.

Compensation

The Owner agrees to pay the Agent as follows:
a) For Management _____
b) For Leasing _____
c) For Sale _____
d) Other Items Of Mutual Agreement _____

_____
_____
_____
_____
_____
_____
_____
_____

This agreement shall be binding upon the successors and assigns of the Agent, and the heirs, administrators, executors, successors and assigns of the Owner.

IN WITNESS WHEREOF the parties hereto have affixed or caused to be affixed their respective signatures this _____ day of _____, 19 ___.

Witness

_____   Owner _____

_____

_____   Agent _____

_____

11

PROPERTY TAXATION AND

TAX ADVANTAGES

*Property Taxation Discussed . . . Determining Tax
Revenues . . . Assessed Valuation . . . Evaluating Land
. . . 4-3-2-1 Depth Rule . . . Other Methods of Assessing Land . . . Evaluating Improvements . . . Tax Appeals . . . Tax Exemptions*

*Tax Advantages Discussed . . . Capital Gains . . . In-
stallment Sales (Why 29 Percent Down?) . . . Deferred
Payments . . . Dealer vs. Investor . . . Section 1231
Assets . . . DEPRECIATION . . . Qualifying Property
. . . Non-Qualifying Property . . . Methods of Taking
Depreciation (Straight Line, Declining Balance, Sum
of Digits) . . . Component Depreciation . . . Advanta-
geous Closing Dates . . . Changing Regulations.*

PROPERTY TAXATION

The present and contemplated future property tax burden of real
estate is an important factor in its marketability. Taxes influence how,
where and when areas are developed. Sales are sometimes made or lost by
what the tax outlook indicates. The whole aspect of how and how much
properties are assessed is a prime element in real estate. To serve his

client more effectively, a broker should clearly understand the assessing process and in turn be able to converse with knowledge and authority on this basic yet sometimes technical subject.

DETERMINING TAX REVENUES

The assessing process is fundamentally the same throughout the country. Tax revenues for almost all communities are determined by the local government, the school board and the county government. To prevent duplication of effort, many areas have one county assessing office for the cities and townships within its borders.

Though the federal government is prohibited by the Constitution from levying local real estate taxes, it does receive revenue in the form of capital gains taxes when a property is sold. (See Capital Gains, page 180.)

Tax rates are arrived at after a community estimates its budget for the coming year. When the expenses and income are determined, the amount needed from assessing real property can be calculated. Expressed in formula, it would be shown as:

$$\text{Tax Rate} = \frac{\text{Estimated Expenses} - \text{Estimated Income}}{\text{Total Assessed Valuation}}$$

A local government's estimated expenditures would include, among other operating expenses, such matters as road and park maintenance, the school budget, police, fire and sanitation departments, as well as the salaries of government employees from the mayor and commissioners on down.

As the expenditures are estimated, so must be the income. Revenues from traffic fines, parking meters, recreation facility fees, licenses of various kinds, building and occupational permits, state rebates, etc. must be estimated. Once it is determined how much revenue is required for the government to function properly, the community's assessing process can begin.

Assessed Valuation

Although the overall assessing procedure is quite similar throughout the nation, the methods of arriving at the evaluation varies. Some municipalities assess at 60 percent of fair market value; others at 50 percent or 40 percent. Still others take the value to be that which the property would bring at a forced (distress) sale. Increasing in popularity, however, is full market value assessment. That is, what a property will bring on the open market in ordinary circumstances.

The assessment consists of two parts.

1. Valuation of land.
2. Valuation of the improvements.

Land assessments are set by a typical valuation placed on a lot in the immediate neighborhood. If the lot size used, for example, is 50′ × 100′, then the larger size parcels are valued proportionately. In mass appraising of land, assessors frequently use the *4-3-2-1 depth rule*. By this method, property is divided into four equal parts from front to rear. The first quarter, having street frontage, is evaluated at 40 percent of the total value; the next quarter 30 percent; the next 20 percent; and the rear portion 10 percent. Deeper lots are also assigned percentage values. For example, 125′ deep lots are evaluated at 109 percent; 150′ deep lots = 117 percent; 175′ lots = 124 percent; 200′ lots = 130 percent, and so on.

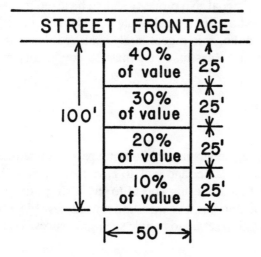

4-3-2-1 DEPTH RULE

Figure 11-1.

Oversized, corner, and odd-size lots are specially treated by assessors. Corner lots have several formulas for arriving at value. In the "Baltimore Method," for example, a corner lot is worth the total of the inside lots on each side.

Regarding commercial lots, the "Zangerle Curve," is a method that shows the percentage of side-street frontage value to be added to the main-street frontage value to arrive at an estimated worth of the corner lot.

Still another method of assessing corner lots is the "Bernard Rule." Here a lot is evaluated first as if it were a side street, inside lot, then as a main street, inside lot. The average of the two is the appraised value.

There are, in addition, other methods. Good assessors and appraisers merely use these as tools. Always to be taken into consideration are the future of the property, its salability, growth patterns and the general economic conditions of the area.

The evaluation of improvements upon the land takes a multitude of factors into account; factors such as replacement cost, a building's income, utilization for the area it occupies, remaining life, obsolescence, structural condition, depreciation, as well as others.

Evaluating Improvements[1]

Assessments should be uniform according to value (*ad Valorem*). This is the assessor's goal. No property should be taxed more or less than another of equal value. But as real estate is a viable commodity, and no two are precisely alike, it is a goal rarely achieved. Neighborhoods improve and deteriorate. Reassessments must be continually made.

Tax Appeals

It is, therefore, understandable that taxpayers sometimes feel their assessments are inequitable, and seek to have them reviewed. The property owner must first make his appeal to the taxing officials in proper form. Each jurisdiction has its own filing procedures. Most have special Boards of Equalization set up to handle such grievances. Using logic and

---

[1]For a further study of evaluation, see Chapter on Appraisal, page 17.

reasoning, the taxpayer should set out to prove that similar (preferably neighboring) properties have been given lower assessments, or that the assessments have been levied in an irregular, or even illegal manner. This could occur, for example, when "blanket" assessments are made for entire areas without the assessors having checked specific properties. The taxpayer has further recourse if he fails to win a reduction in his assessment. He may appeal the decision in a court of law.

Tax Exemptions

Certain classifications of real estate ownership are wholly or partially exempt from paying taxes. For example:

Property used for religious purposes.

Property used for hospitals, education or for other public benefit.

Many states have long standing *homestead laws* by which a portion of a homeowner's taxes is exempt.

Other instances of tax exemption may occur when a state or community deems it economically advisable to grant a tax exemption (usually for a limited number of years) to industry. It serves as an inducement to bring business into an area, thereby creating employment and the need for homes, goods and services that follows.

The main criterion for allowing tax exemptions is that it be socially and economically desirable to do so, thereby being in the best interest of the general public.

An entirely different form of property taxation is that which the federal government levies on profits made from real estate investments. There are many intricate and detailed tax saving advantages of investing in commercial real estate over non-realty business ventures. A discussion of these advantages follows.

TAX ADVANTAGES OF REAL ESTATE INVESTING

The real estate investor has to think in terms of what effect the Internal Revenue Code will have on his purchase or sale, because the tax saving effects can be substantial when dealing with income properties. Likewise, the negative effects can be costly if these benefits are not utilized to best advantage. Because of the wide scope of real estate taxation, it is wise for everyone to consult a qualified CPA or tax-oriented attorney, even if one has a basic knowledge of taxation. Tax laws and regulations are ever changing and new court decisions are handed down continually. Bear in mind that no two transactions or their tax consequences are exactly alike, nor will the position of the principals ever be duplicated. Therefore, each situation is unique in itself and must be treated accordingly. The purpose of the following is to acquaint (or in some instances reacquaint) you with certain basic tax advantages and pitfalls.

Capital Gains

Capital gains taxes are classified as either long- or short-term by the government. Short-term refers to property held for less than six months before being sold. The profits for short-term transactions are fully taxable at ordinary tax rates. Long-term capital gains are taxed at preferential rates which vary. Corporations, for example, are taxed at a flat 30 percent, while individual estates and trusts are taxed 25 percent of the first $50,000 of long-term capital gains, and at graduated rates (depending on the income bracket) for gains in excess of $50,000.

Installment Sales (Why 29 Percent Down?)

Many real estate transactions provide for terms of 29 percent down and the balance in mortgages or notes, in order for the seller to take advantage of a tax option which allows him to prorate the gross profit on the transaction over the period in which payments are received. Sales in which payments during the year of the transaction do not exceed 30 percent of the selling price qualify for the option, while sales in which the year of sale payments exceed 30 percent do not qualify, and the entire gain has to be reported in that year. Payments include cash or property, but do not include the purchaser's evidence of debt (mortgages).

Deferred Payments

With most real estate transactions involving mortgages and notes rather than all cash, the 29-percent down rule provides the best tax shelter and is most frequently applied. Promissory notes received in lieu of cash may even be assigned by the receiver to another without being considered as payment for purposes of taxes. However, stocks, bonds, debentures or other readily negotiable instruments are looked upon as payments when considering year-of-sale payments for the 30-percent rule.

Dealer vs. Investor

The thin line between being declared a dealer or an investor can result in far reaching tax consequences. Like all business enterprises, the dealer in real estate is taxed on his full profits. He may also deduct all of his losses. A combination of factors may enter into determining an individual's status. Obviously, one engaged full time in the business of buying, selling and leasing real estate is clearly a dealer. But what of the buyer of real estate who wants simply to hold until a satisfactory profit is realized? When does he become a dealer? How many transactions can he make? At what point does he lose his all important, tax savings "investor" status? These sometimes vexing questions have been confronting the IRS and the courts for years. Experts agree that it will continue to be a matter of individual interpretation. Such factors are taken into consideration as:

1. The number of transactions one makes during the tax year.
2. How and for what purpose was the property acquired?
3. Is real estate the full-time and only occupation the individual is engaged in?
4. Is he really a long-term investor or does he actively seek to sell after the six months "tax break" period has elapsed?

5. Does he advertise, engage a broker or in other ways systematically promote the sale of his real property?
6. Does he exhibit the physical trappings of a dealer in real estate, i.e. a sales force, broker's license, full-time office staff working primarily on real estate matters?

Actually the distinction can be so closely defined that an individual may be declared a dealer on one portion of land he is subdividing, and receive an investor status on the other that he is holding for future enhancement.

Section 1231 Assets

The Internal Revenue Code makes a tax distinction between property held for sale or trade in the ordinary course of doing business and property maintained as a taxpayer's business, plant site, or for rental income. When the latter situation occurs, it is looked upon as a "Section 1231 Asset." Once so classified, the most favorable tax treatment can be expected. Net gains (held for more than six months) are treated as capital gains, and enjoy maximum tax advantage, while if net losses result, ordinary loss benefits can be utilized.

DEPRECIATION

Tax shelter through depreciation plays a prime role in investment real estate. In many instances, it is an investor's prime or only purpose for obtaining the property. It often is more important to him than cash flow.

Tax depreciation methods usually are at variance with the actual economic depreciation (or loss in value) of a real estate asset. Depreciation methods utilized are usually designed to recover the greatest part of invested capital as rapidly as possible. They generally do not coincide with actual depreciation of a structure caused by physical exposure and wear, or functional obsolescence.

Qualifying Depreciable Property

1. The property must be used in the normal course of the owner's business (such as a factory, office or warehouse), or held for productive income (apartment house, mobile home park, office building, shopping center, etc.). Depreciation deductions may be claimed by any person, corporation or other taxable entity having a financial interest in the property. However, losses cannot be taken in excess of that which is invested.

2. There must be a capital investment to qualify for depreciation benefits. Merely holding title is not enough. A true monetary investment must have been made.

Non-Qualifying Property

1. Land. It is held by the IRS that land remains constant in value and is not subject to depreciation through use.

2. One's personal residence. A home lived in by the owner will not qualify. A single-family home that is not the owner's residence, but is being held for investment purposes is depreciable, as is half of a duplex, or ⅔ of a triplex in which the owner occupies one portion and leases out the remainder.

3. Homes or other buildings erected by a contractor for purposes of resale are considered a builder's stock in trade, and he would not be permitted to take depreciation advantages.

Methods of Taking Depreciation

The three most commonly used formulas for taking depreciation are straight line, declining balance, and sum of the digits.

1. *Straight Line*. This method simply takes the cost of the improvement,

less salvage value, if any, and divides by its estimated economic life. Payments are made in equal annual installments. For example:

Cost Of Structure	$550,000
Estimated Salvage Value	$-$ 50,000
	$500,000

Estimated Life = 25 years

$500,000 ÷ 25 = $20,000 or 4% per year.

2. *Declining Balance*. The principle behind this method is that depreciation in the early years of a structure's life is greater than in later years. Therefore, depreciation rightfully should be computed on the undepreciated balance. It is also referred to as "double declining balance" or "200-percent rate" when double the straight line is used. This method is available for new apartment house construction. Resale (used) apartment houses with a remaining life of 20 years or over frequently use the 125-percent declining balance method. Newly constructed buildings other than residential (apartment) units may qualify for the 150-percent rate.

The largest depreciation deductions are taken in the early years of the building. With each succeeding year the depreciation amount becomes less and less.

3. *Sum Of The Digits*. This formula, used on newly constructed buildings, takes into account the total years of useful life of the property, and divides it by the sum of these digits. For example, if the estimated life of an asset is 15 years, the first year's depreciation would be expressed in the formula of $\frac{15}{120}$. The denominator of the fraction is totaled:

$1+2+3+4+5+6+7+8+9+10+11+12+13+14+15=120$. The second year's depreciation would be $\frac{14}{120}$, the third $\frac{13}{120}$, then $\frac{12}{120}$, and so on. The denominator represents the cost of the asset, less any estimated salvage value.

There are other lesser-used methods of taking depreciation that are designed to best meet specific property situations. Tax depreciation experts at times combine methods, and also take *component depreciation* whenever possible. But whatever method or methods are utilized they must be followed consistently.

Component Depreciation. The IRS recognizes that certain parts of a structure have a shorter life span than others. For example, an elevator might be depreciated over 10 years, air condition compressor given 5 years, heating plants—15 years, etc. Other portions of a structure may be assigned a useful life as follows:

Component Part	Assigned Useful Life
Plumbing	15 years
Wiring	12 years
Roof	15 years
Paving	11 years
Floor	15 years
Ceiling	10 years
Heating Plant	10 years

By utilizing component depreciation an original owner, or one who holds the property during its early life, can at first step up the depreciation rate. In later years, however, it will catch up with him. Then the pendulum will begin to swing the other way. With the bulk of the depreciation gone, builders and investors often wisely choose to sell, then build or purchase another property where accelerated depreciation can begin anew. It should be noted that each owner commences a new depreciation base all over again. The fact that a prior owner took heavy depreciation benefits does not preclude the new owner from beginning a new cycle of depreciation computed on his acquisition costs, whether higher, lower or similar to that which the previous owner received.

Advantageous Closing Dates

A full year's depreciation may be taken if an asset is purchased anytime between January 1 and June 30. If it is acquired after June 30, and on or before December 31, then six months depreciation is allowed. For this reason, transaction closings are frequently timed for the end of June or December. In this manner, a full six months depreciation advantage can be taken though the property may have been actually owned for as short a period as a day.

Changing Regulations

Getting the full tax advantage of a real estate investment is not without its complexities. Real estate tax law is a study involving continual research. The laws that govern taxation are ever changing, and highly qualified experts are needed to tailor the proper depreciation method or methods for a specific asset. With IRS regulations continually being modified, and challenged in the courts, the services of a tax attorney or CPA should be utilized. A broker dealing in income properties would do his investors an invaluable service by recommending this course of action, should an unfamiliar, major tax problem arise.

12

REAL ESTATE LAW

Federal and State Laws Discussed . . . Statute of Frauds . . . What Is Real Property? . . . What Constitutes Personal Property? . . . Types of Estates: Freehold . . . Less Than Freehold . . . Fee Simple . . . Life Estates . . . Estates for Years . . . Periodic Estates . . . Estates at Will . . . Estates at Sufferance . . . Condemnation . . . Adverse Possession . . . Forms of Ownership: Sole Ownership . . . Co-tenancy . . . Tenancy in Common . . . Tenancy by the Entireties . . . Joint Tenancy . . . Partnerships . . . Corporations . . . Syndicates . . . Investment Trusts . . . Contracts . . . Deeds . . . Leases . . . Mortgages . . . Other Legal Instruments: Assignment . . . Bond . . . Easements . . . Extension Agreement . . . Lien . . . Option . . . Promissory Note . . . Power of Attorney . . . Release . . . Satisfactions . . . Legal Descriptions: Lot, Block and Subdivision . . . Metes and Bounds . . . Government Survey . . . Monuments . . . Forms of Verification: Acknowledgment . . . Affidavit . . . Affirmation . . . Certificate . . . Notarizing . . . Seal . . . Witness.

Federal laws pertaining to real estate are consistent throughout the country. They act uniformly and need no special state or local jurisdictional interpretation. State real estate laws, however, have certain variations that must be reckoned with. Variations notwithstanding, the basic principles of real estate law are remarkably similar in all 50 states. This similarity is understandable when one studies the history of our real property laws. In large part they are based on early English law when the feudal system[1] gave way to a free system of individual ownership (allodial).

Besides legal differences, American laws dealing with real property are continually changing. Judges daily make decisions that challenge or change existing state, county and municipal rulings. Some of the more significant elements of real estate law that apply in all states are outlined in this section. Where state and local jurisdictional laws differ, they are appropriately noted.

The limitation imposed by devoting just one chapter of this book to covering so vast and complex a subject as real estate law is apparent. A further, more detailed study, and the seeking of legal advice, is suggested when an unfamiliar or complicated matter of law arises.

STATUTE OF FRAUDS

Every state has adopted the statute of frauds principle that all real estate transactions, to be enforceable, must be in writing and duly signed. If there were no written instruments such as contracts, deeds, mortgages, leases, promissory notes, options, wills, etc., disputes as to true ownership would be endless. The chance of fraud would be obvious and claims and counter-claims would create chaos in our courts. Indeed, they would be impossible to settle. Thus, legal documents must be written to substantiate real estate transactions.

WHAT IS REAL PROPERTY?

Real property is land itself and everything permanently affixed to it. It includes not only the soil upon the surface, but also the minerals, oil

---

[1] The feudal system prevailed in England during the 11th, 12th and the early part of the 13th centuries. It maintained the ancient concept that all land belonged to the king or his designates. Servitude or money were rendered for its use and occupancy.

and gas below it, and the air space above. Legally, land ownership may be viewed as if the property were an inverted pyramid, with the tip commencing at the center of the earth and extending upward, past the surface of the earth to the outermost reaches of the heavens.

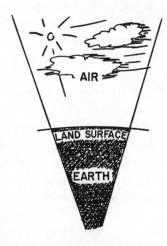

Figure 12-1.

WHAT CONSTITUTES PERSONAL PROPERTY (CHATTEL)?

That which is immovable and permanently attached to the land is considered realty. The rest are movables and constitute personal property. While trees, grass, and houses are real property, annual crops such as flowers, vegetables, as well as furnishings and automobiles are personal property. They are referred to as chattel, and ownership is transferred by means of a *bill of sale* if over a certain dollar value. Most states set the amount at $500. Below that, the transfer of personalty need not be in writing.

TYPES OF ESTATES

One's interest in real estate can be held in a variety of ways. Estates are broadly classified as either *Freehold* or *Less Than Freehold*.

Freehold interests include fee simple ownership and life estates, while less than freehold estates cover estates for years, periodic estates, estates at will and estates at sufferance.

The most familiar form of ownership is that of *fee simple*. It is the highest form of interest and conveys complete ownership. (It is also referred to as fee, or fee simple absolute.) It is the largest and best possible estate one can possess in real estate. The holder has every legal possession with virtually unconditional power and right to dispose of it in his lifetime or retain it for his heirs upon death.[2]

A *life estate* is limited to the lifetime of the holder, for it terminates upon his death. A life estate can also be for the length of another's life, or it may be contingent upon some future event, such as being terminated when the recipient is married. In return for use of the property, the person holding the life estate must maintain it and pay all taxes and liens. He cannot sell the property during his lifetime or after death. The disposition of the property after death is generally provided for by the donor when the estate for life is made.

An *estate for years* is one for a fixed term. The period of time may be for less than a year or for longer than the recipient's lifetime.

Periodic estates are tenancies that exist from one period of time to another, as in the instance of a month-to-month lease. This form of tenancy may exist with or without a written lease and extends only for the period of time that the rental payments cover.

An *estate at will* is one of indefinite duration that allows the lessee possession as long as both lessor and lessee mutually agree to it. If this reciprocal agreement is changed by either party, the estate at will may be terminated.

An *estate at sufferance* is created when one who originally was in rightful possession remains after his lawful title has terminated, and has been vested in another. When the term *tenancy at sufferance* or *holdover tenancy* is used, the reference is to a lessee and not one who held title.

The actual acquisition of real estate generally occurs by deed, will or descent. However, there are still other ways of obtaining title to property—such as by condemnation and adverse possession.

Condemnation is the taking of private property for public use. This is accomplished when the government exercises its power of *eminent*

---

[2]The only way property can be taken without consent from one having fee simple ownership is by eminent domain, the power of the government to expropriate property for public use by condemnation proceedings.

domain. To expropriate property in this manner two conditions must be met.

1. The property being acquired must be for public use and benefit.
2. Just compensation must be paid for it. That is, a fair market value has to be established.

Adverse possession occurs when an individual takes over land, and stays in possession for a specified statutory period of years. A court may then adjudge him the true owner even though he may have entered the land without any rights to it whatsoever. The government's reason for allowing the acquisition of title in this manner is twofold: 1. It promotes the use of otherwise vacant land. (If land is allowed to lie fallow over a period of many years, it serves no beneficial function to mankind.) 2. It legally settles uncertain ownership of land. To acquire property by adverse possession a person must be in "actual, open, notorious, exclusive and continuous" occupancy of the land for a prescribed statutory period. The length of time varies in different states. In some, the period is only 5 or 7 years; whereas in others, it can be for as long as 20 years.

FORMS OF OWNERSHIP

Sole or *several ownership* of realty is an estate held by one individual. When more than one person has an ownership interest, they are said to hold a *co-tenancy*. Co-tenancies can take the following forms: *tenancy in common, tenancy by the entireties* and *partnership interest*.

Real estate held by *corporations, syndicates* and *investment trusts* are other legal entities that constitute special forms of ownership. Each of the foregoing will be briefly defined and discussed.

Sole ownership has the distinct advantage of absolute control to dispose of or improve the property as one sees fit. Other forms of ownership present more complex legal rights. For example:

Tenancy in common occurs when two or more individuals, who are not husband and wife, own property. Each possesses a separate and individual interest. Upon the death of one, his interest will go to his heirs or to anyone he may name in his will. There is no right of survivorship as found in joint tenancies and *tenancies by the entireties*.[3]

A *joint tenancy* occurs when an estate is held by two or more people with equal and undivided interest and ownership. Property held by husband and wife is an example. Upon the death of one, that individual's interest automatically accrues to the remaining owner(s). Four unities are created in a joint tenancy: unity of interest, unity of title, unity of time, and unity of possession.

A *partnership interest* is the co-ownership of a business, property or other asset by two or more individuals for profit. Forty-seven states recognize the Uniform Partnership Act,[4] which provides that a partnership is a legal entity and real property may be acquired in the partnership name. Likewise, title to real estate belonging to the partnership can only be conveyed in the partnership name. The partners, however, may be held liable for the acts of their copartners.

A *corporation* is a separate legal entity comprising an association of individuals, formed within the framework of law, to act as a single person. A corporation is said to be an artificial body created by law. Its officers, directors and stockholders are not responsible for the debts of the corporation in case of default or bankruptcy. Corporations are registered with and chartered under state statutes and must conform to their numerous regulations. Officers and directors have to be registered with the state, and most require that an annual financial statement be filed. While most corporations are formed for commercial and industrial endeavors, many are founded for charitable, scientific, fraternal, educational or political purposes.

The *syndication* of real estate has certain unique advantages. A syndicate is created when a group of individuals or corporations combine their forces and resources to acquire, lease or sell realty for a limited period of time. It is a joint venture often used to acquire large real estate holdings that otherwise would be beyond the financial means of one individual or corporation. It also serves to limit liability and to capitalize on the expertise and the accumulated judgment of the others in the syndicate. Most syndicates are taxed by federal and state governments as if they were partnerships. Each member of the venture is taxed in proportion

---

[3]Some states recognize a form of joint tenancy called tenancy by the entireties. This tenancy is equally owned by husband and wife, with the surviving member receiving the entire estate.

[4]All states except Georgia, Louisiana and Mississippi.

to the interest he holds. See page 111 for further details of syndicates and how they function.

Real Estate Investment Trusts (REITS) are comprised of a group of investors, having one or more trustees, who hold title to the assets for the trust and control its acquisitions, management and sales. Though unincorporated, the trust must be owned in the form of shares by one hundred or more people (no five of whom are to possess over 50 percent interest). The major advantage of a business structure of this nature is the tax benefit, as no corporation tax need be paid. A disadvantage is the strict federal and state regulatory requirements as to the type of investments that can be made. When a real estate investment trust has shareholders in more than one state, it is also subject to Security and Exchange Commission regulations. See page 118 for further details of REITS and how they function.

CONTRACTS

Contracts for the sale of real estate can take many specialized forms. There are installment sales contracts, construction contracts, sale-leasebacks, option agreements, exchange contracts, binders, deposit receipts, letters of intention, parol contracts, as well as numerous others.

By definition, a contract is an agreement between competent parties, with sufficient consideration given, to do or refrain from doing something. It is an agreement that is enforceable by law. However, before a contract can be considered legally binding it should contain certain essentials, as follows:

1. The parties to the agreement must be competent in the eyes of the law. They should be mentally capable of knowing and understanding what they are doing.
2. The contract should contain a statement of the consideration —something of value offered by the purchaser. Consideration usually takes the form of money, but personal services, merchandise, other real estate or any other benefit may be equally acceptable. Love and affection are also recognized as good consideration, as it may occur when one member of a family transfers title to property to another.
3. A valid contract must contain an offer and an acceptance. When the price, terms and conditions are acceptable to all parties, a "meeting of

the minds'' is said to take place. Both sides are agreeable to carrying out all of the provisions of the agreement.

4. The purpose of the contract must be a lawful one. Courts refer to this as ''legality of object.''

5. Under the Statute of Frauds a contract has to be in writing and signed by all principals in order to become enforceable.

A valid, complete contract should contain the following basic information:

Date
Parties to the agreement
Offer and acceptance
Legal description
The consideration
Terms and conditions
Type of deed to be conveyed
Closing date and place
Properly witnessed signatures

DEEDS

A deed is the document by which a property owner transfers his title to another. The essential elements that must be present for a deed to be valid are:

Competent parties
A valuable consideration
An accurate description of that which is being conveyed
Words of conveyance
Properly signed and sealed
Delivered to the grantee

Other elements often present in a deed, though they need not be there for it to be valid, are warranties of title, a statement of encumbrances upon the land, witnesses to the deed, documentary stamps, and an acknowledgement. Deeds are almost always filed and duly recorded with the clerk of the county court or similar governmental agency.

There are many types of deeds used for various specific purposes, such as: Executor's Deed, County Deed, Referee's Deed in Partition, Referee's Deed in Foreclosure, Grant Deed, Administrator's Deed, Gift Deed, Deed of Release, Deed of Surrender, Guardian's Deed, Committee's Deed, Cession Deed, Deed in Lieu of Foreclosure, Deed in Trust, Mineral Deed, Deed of Confirmation, Support Deed, as well as numerous others. The ones primarily used to convey real property are the following:

General Warranty Deed—sometimes referred to as a Full Covenant and Warranty Deed, this deed conveys a convenant of warranty. By it the grantor will warrant and defend the title against all claims. From the grantee's standpoint, it is the best form of deed he can receive.

Special Warranty Deed—used when the grantor warrants only claims against him or his heirs, and not that of previous owners. It is frequently used to convey tax title. (In the state of Michigan, the term Warranty Deed is used in place of Special Warranty Deed).

Bargain and Sale Deed, with Covenants Against Grantor's Acts—contains covenants stating, "the party of the first part (grantor) has not done or suffered anything whereby the premises have been encumbered in any way whatsoever."

Bargain and Sale Deed, without Covenants Against Grantor's Acts—used to convey all the rights, title and interest of the grantor and nothing more. This is one of the simplest forms of a deed and carries with it no promises by the grantor.

Quit Claim Deed—in which the grantor states that he releases all rights, title and interest he may have in the property, but gives no warranties. It is usually used to relinquish a claim. In certain sections of the country, quit claim deeds are used when there is a questionable interest, or to remove a cloud upon the title. In other areas it is more commonly used in ordinary transactions.

LEASES

A lease is both a contract and a conveyance between the owner of property (lessor) and the tenant (lessee) for possession and use of the property for a stipulated period of time, and in consideration for the payment of an agreed upon rent or services rendered. For a study of leases see page 123.

MORTGAGES

A mortgage is the pledge of property for the payment of a debt. In some states (title theory states[5]) it is the actual conveyance of land to the creditor until the terms of the mortgage are satisfied. In others (lien theory states[6]) it is regarded as just a lien and does not create an estate. In either instance, the mortgagor retains possession and use of the property during the term of the mortgage. For a study of mortgages see page 153.

OTHER LEGAL INSTRUMENTS

There are many other documents used in the practice of real estate. Some of those more frequently used are defined as follows:

An *assignment* is the transfer of title to, or interest in, a valuable right from one person or group to another. Assignments are concerned with the intangible rights an owner holds, such as contractual and personal ones in connection with the property, and not the property itself.

An assignment may be oral or written. When in writing it can take many forms. No consideration is needed to make it valid, but it must immediately convey that which is assigned. The assignee obtains only what the assignor has to convey and nothing more. The assignor generally remains liable for the performance of that which he assigned. To be recorded, an assignment must meet the requirements of local recording statutes. In New York, for example, an assignment of a mortgage cannot be recorded unless acknowledged before a notary. State and local jurisdic-

---

[5]Title theory states are Alabama, Arkansas, Connecticut, Delaware, Illinois, Maine, Maryland, Massachusetts, Mississippi, Missouri, New Hampshire, New Jersey, North Carolina, Ohio, Pennsylvania, Rhode Island, Tennessee, Vermont, Virginia, and West Virginia.

[6]Lien theory states are Alaska, Arizona, California, Colorado, Florida, Georgia, Hawaii, Idaho, Indiana, Iowa, Kansas, Kentucky, Louisiana, Michigan, Minnesota, Montana, Nebraska, Nevada, New Mexico, New York, North Dakota, Oklahoma, Oregon, South Carolina, South Dakota, Texas, Utah, Washington, Wisconsin, and Wyoming.

tion recording standards should be studied. In the absence of statements to the contrary, contracts, leases and mortgages can be assigned, as can be accounts receivable (to defray a debt), building loan contracts, chattels, businesses, option contracts, and almost any other asset one possesses.

A *bond* is a document, generally under seal, that creates evidence of an indebtedness. It obligates the maker, his heirs and assigns, to pay a stipulated sum to another at a specified time. In real estate, it is secured by a mortgage or other lien. In some jurisdictions, a bond is required to accompany the mortgage. This bond is not recorded. In the past, the penalty of the bond was often twice the amount of the money secured, but now it is usually the same amount. In New York State, a combined bond and mortgage is sometimes used. In other jurisdictions, such as Florida, the debt is evidenced by a promissory note instead of a bond. A properly drawn bond contains a promise to pay a specified amount, at a certain time, to the party named. The conditions, if any, and a testimonium clause (signed, sealed, witnessed, dated) follow.

An *easement* is a nonprofitable, limited right or privilege one is given for the use of land belonging to another. It can be permanent or temporary in nature. It is a right bestowed to travel on, over or through another's land or to use it for a specific purpose.

An easement must be created by a grant. To be valid or enforceable it cannot exist by merely an oral agreement. Unless prohibited by deed restrictions, easements generally transfer with the land when sold.

Easements can be categorized in various forms and distinctions. Those frequently encountered are the following:

An *Easement In Gross* is the granting of a personal interest in real property, rather than a right to the land itself. Such an easement is generally not assignable or inheritable. The right to use the outside wall of a building as a billboard is an example.

A *Negative Easement* is one that acts to curtail the complete use of the property. It relinquishes some valuable right or rights of the property. Building codes that limit the use of the land, and covenants preventing certain types of structures on a given lot, are examples.

Other types of easements include *Avigation Easements, permitting* aircraft to fly over one's land at certain elevations; *Sub-Surface Easements*, permitting use of land below the surface; and *Overflow Easements*, the right to backwater or submerge another's land. Also in modern real estate practice such grants as rights to party wall usage, light and view, and lateral support are in general use.

No specific wording is prescribed when preparing an easement agreement. The intentions of the parties, clearly and unambiguously stated, and an accurate description of the land are the basic requisites. Easements should be recorded so that future owners of the property are given constructive notice of their existence.

An *extension agreement* prolongs the term of a document. Such an agreement in a mortgage, for example, grants additional time to perform one or more of its provisions.

A *lien* is a charge or claim upon property which encumbers it until the obligation is satisfied. The property serves as the security, but it does not give the holder title to the property itself.

The most frequently used form of lien in real estate is the Mechanic's Lien. Its purpose is to establish a priority of payment for work and/or materials furnished a particular property. It attaches to the land as well as the improvements upon it.

Mechanic's Liens fall into two distinct categories: (a) Those in which the subcontractor's or materialman's lien is dependent upon and limited by the amount due the contractor. This is referred to as the "New York" system. (b) Mechanic's Liens in which the subcontractor's lien is not dependent upon the existence of any indebtedness due the contractor, but rather is a direct lien against the owner. This is known as the "Pennsylvania" system of liens.

Various jurisdictions in the United States require special wording to comply legally with local requirements. The right to acquire and enforce a lien depends almost wholly on these statutes. Therefore, specific area requirements should be carefully studied and proper reference made to them when preparing a lien.

An *option* is a right or privilege given by an owner to another person to purchase or lease property at some time in the future for a stated price and terms. The time that the option can be exercised must be stated, as an unlimited option violates the rule of law against perpetuities. In most jurisdictions a valuable consideration must accompany the agreement for it to be considered valid. The consideration is generally forfeited if the option is not exercised. This, however, is the optionee's only obligation. His loss of the consideration terminates the agreement. If the option is exercised, the amount of the consideration is frequently (but not necessarily) applied as a credit toward completing the transaction. If the option is not exercised, the payment is taxable as rental income received by the seller.

A contract may be in the form of an option, but in reality it is a sales contract with a provision for forfeiture. An option to purchase property is recordable if acknowledged and otherwise meets recording requirements.

A *promissory note* is written evidence of indebtedness in which the maker promises to pay a specified sum on demand to the party named, or at a stated time in the future. Its general form can be reduced to one simple sentence and still be valid, as follows:

> FOR VALUE RECEIVED, I (or we) promise to pay to the order of_____ the sum of $_____, with interest therein from_____the rate_____% per annum until paid, payable on_____and _____thereafter, and if not paid as it becomes due, to be added to the principal and become a part thereof bearing interest at the same rate.
>
> _____(Seal)
>
> _____(Seal)

Power of attorney is a written authorization for one to act as another's agent. The extent of the authority is limited to that stated in the document. A power of attorney is also known as an attorney in fact. One need not be a lawyer to act as a power of attorney.

A *release* is the discharge or relinquishment of a right, claim or privilege. It is the liberation of a person from any further legal obligation. As it is considered a contract, it must contain a valuable consideration.

A *satisfaction* indicates fulfillment or complete payment of an obligation, while a release just discharges the indebtedness without "satisfaction" necessarily taking place.

Releases and satisfactions should be acknowledged in proper form to meet the varied requirements of recording statutes. Each state's provisions should be consulted. When dealing with mortgages, upon the request of the mortgagor, the mortgagee (lender) or his assigns or successors in interest must execute an instrument in proper form for recording, showing satisfaction of the mortgage obligation. With release clauses in mortgages, partial releases of lots may be granted as payments are made. Releases and satisfactions need follow no specific form. There exists a wide variance among states. In Massachusetts, for example, the statutory form is only four lines long. In South Carolina, payment of the debt is acknowledged by writing across the face of the document, dating, signing and having the signature(s) witnessed by the recording officer.

LEGAL DESCRIPTIONS

There are four methods predominately in use today for legally identifying the location of land and defining its boundaries. They are: 1. Lot, Block and Subdivision. 2. Metes and Bounds. 3. Government Survey (variously called Section, Town and Range Description, Rectangular Survey, or U. S. Government Public Land Description). 4. Monuments.

In a *Lot, Block and Subdivision* description the tract is first assigned a name, and each block and lot within the subdivision is numbered or lettered. A map of the subdivision is then recorded with the proper governmental (usually county) authority. It then becomes officially recognized for use with legal instruments when describing property. A sample and illustration of such a description follows:

> Lot 10, Block 72, Wavecrest Estates Subdivision of the city of Seaside, as recorded in Plat Book 90, Page 37, of the records of Eastcoast County, Georgia.

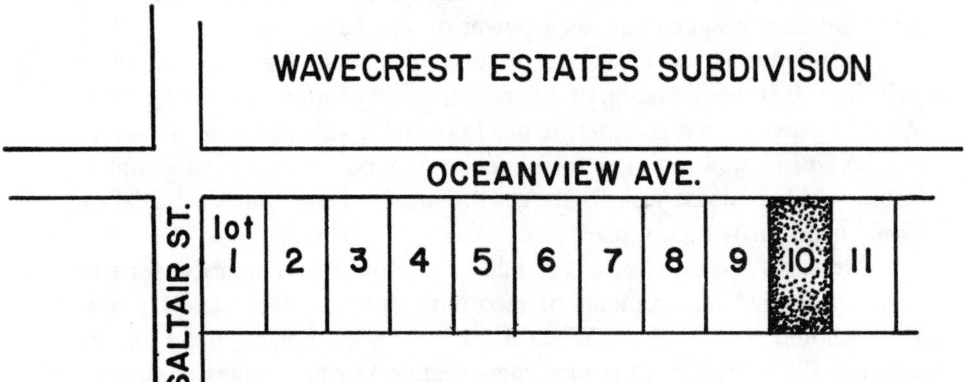

Figure 12-2.

When the highest degree of accuracy is required, particularly in or around urban areas, *Metes and Bounds* descriptions are used. Length (metes) and directions or boundaries (bounds) start at a known point of beginning and utilizing 360° of the compass for directions, with each degree further divided into minutes, 1/60th of a degree, and then seconds, 1/3600th of a degree, a pinpoint accurate description of land can be obtained.

The most practical description for rural areas where larger tracts of land are involved is the *Government* or *Rectangular Survey*. The federal government, in 1785, adopted this method of land description·and it is currently in use in 31 states. By this method acreage can be easily de‑ scribed and rapidly located. It employs a fixed, imaginary line running east and west across a state, called a Base Line and another, bisecting it and running north and south, called Prime or Principál Meridian. See map below showing the locations of the prime meridians and base lines in the California area.

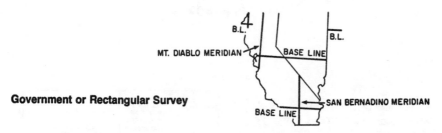

Government or Rectangular Survey

Figure 12-3.

Where the Prime Meridian and Base Line intersect as the point of origin, surveyors divide the land into squares, 24 miles by 24 miles, called "checks." The dividing lines, running east-west and forming the checks, are called Standard Parallels. The lines running north and south are called Guide Meridians.

The squares are further divided into smaller squares, six miles on each side, called Townships. The lines running east and west forming the townships are called Range Lines. The lines running north and south are referred to as Township Lines.

With slight corrections to allow for the earth's curvature, each town-ship is further divided into 36 sections one mile by one mile (640 acres).

Sections may be divided into still smaller half-, quarter-, eighth-, sixteenth-sections, and so on; thus providing an accurate description for even the smallest parcel. This method is also known as Section, Town-ship and Range Description, Rectangular Survey, and U.S. Government Public Land Description.

Checks and Townships

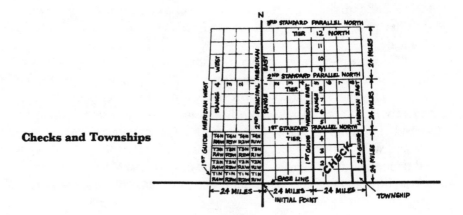

Figure 12-4.

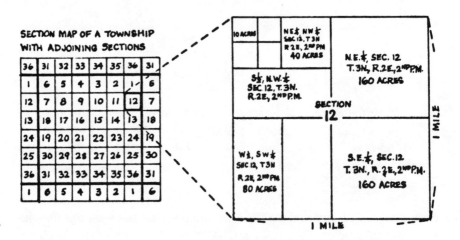

Figure 12-5.

Another, less-widely used, method of land description is by the use of *Monuments*. A monument description recognizes fixed boundary marks that identify the extent of the property. The monument can be man-made, such as a cement stake or slab, a mound of stones or a steel post. It can also be natural objects such as a boulder, a mountain peak, a prominent tree or the banks of a river.

FORMS OF VERIFICATION

Verifying facts and the proof of one's signature are continually required in the transacting of real estate. The methods of accomplishing this are by obtaining the appropriate acknowledgments, affidavits, affirmations, certificates, notarizations, seals and witnesses.

An *acknowledgment* is the certification of a signature by a properly authorized individual that a given document is his act and deed. See sample below.

GENERAL FORM OF ACKNOWLEDGMENT

State of _____

County of _____ } ss

Before me personally appeared _____ to me well known and known to me to be the person described in and who executed the foregoing instrument, and acknowledged to and before me that _____ executed said instrument for the purposes therein expressed.

WITNESS my hand and official seal, this _____ day of _____ A.D. 19__.

_____
Notary Public

(Notary Seal)

State of _____
My commission expires

An *affidavit* is a voluntary, written statement or declaration sworn to before a notary or other individual authorized to administer oaths. It often is accepted as proof when the maker of the affidavit (the affiant) cannot appear in person. Affidavits are frequently used in real estate to clarify a question of ownership or the status of a lien on property before title can be transferred.

An *affirmation* is a declaration or pledge in place of an oath. In law, it has the same significance as swearing to a supreme being, and is used when a person objects to taking an oath because of personal religious beliefs. Affirmations are accomplished by simply substituting the word "affirm" for "swear," as in the sentence, "I, Fred Smith, do solemnly affirm that . . . etc."

A *certificate* is a formal, written declaration. It can take a variety of forms, such as in acknowledgments, stock shares, or simply a letter. It need follow no prescribed pattern or phraseology. Its purpose is to certify to something, thereby authenticating or proving it as genuine.

Notarizing is the acknowledging, certifying or attesting to a document by a duly appointed, bonded public officer. It is the duty of a notary or notary public to testify to the authenticity of an instrument or signature. The signator must do so in his presence.

Notarization is required on many real estate documents. It generally appears at the end of the instrument in the form of a "jurat," which is the sentence used to evidence what is being authenticated. A typical jurat reads:

Subscribed and sworn to before me this _____ day of _____, 19___.

Notary Public, State of _____

My commission expires _____, 19___.
(Notary Seal)

The ancient custom of having documents signed "under *seal*" is no longer considered as significant in modern real estate law. It represents a formal attesting to. However, certain documents, notably deeds, are still required to be sealed in many states.

The antiquated custom of making a wax impression upon the document has long been supplanted by the word "Seal" or "L.S." at the end of the signature line. This is an abbreviation for the Latin "locus sigilli" meaning "the place of the seal," or "under seal." Sometimes these words appear in parenthesis, as shown:

_____ (Seal)

The embossed impression that serves to formalize a document, such as a corporate seal, or to verify a signature, as used by a notary public, is another way of assuring the authenticity of legal instruments.

Seal

Figure 12-6.

To *witness* is to observe and authenticate. In the execution of contracts as well as certain other real estate instruments, one, two, and in some jurisdictions, as many as three witnesses are required. Witnessing serves to verify the fact that the principals have signed the document of their own free will.

The witness should be a disinterested party to the agreement. His signature appears at the end of the document, on the left side of the page, opposite the signature(s) of the principal(s) he is witnessing.

13

SELECTED MODEL LETTERS

There are certain letter forms frequently used in real estate offices in the daily pursuit of business. While they are, for the most part, personalized in nature, the general content need not be composed anew each time one is needed. In the interest of good letter composition, as well as saving time and to facilitate office procedure, a secretary can prepare such a standard letter with a minimum of dictation and instruction. Brokers should find the selected model letters presented here both effective and readily adaptable to their needs.

LETTER SEEKING LISTINGS

Dear_____:

    We're not usually given to boasting, but we know we're top real estate pros, specializing in residential and investment properties, and can perform a valuable service for you!

    The fact of the matter is we have sold over 5,800 properties in the past twelve (12) years of serving the community, and we'd like to add your name to our ever-growing list of valued, satisfied clients.

    Our story is simple. We're competent Realtors not afraid of hard work, who can give you a personalized service and sell your property—

   *For The Best Price
   *Fast
     *With The Maximum Cash
       *Confidentially, and
         *At Standard Brokerage Fees

    If you really want to sell with a minimum of fuss and bother, and for the maximum cash possible, fill in and mail the below form today.

    We are at your service.

                       Sincerely yours,

---------------------- (cut here) ----------------------

Yes, I am interested in selling my property.

Name_____ Phone_____

Property Address_____

Selling Price $_____ Terms & Conditions_____

_____

_____

_____

LETTER SEEKING INCOME PROPERTY LISTINGS

Dear_____:

    We have a bona-fide investor interested in purchasing a motel[1] approximately the size of yours.

---

[1]This form letter can be used for other types of real estate such as apartments, office buildings, warehouses, shopping centers, etc., with only slight modifications in text.

Our buyer is an experienced, professional motel operator who has substantial cash and is in a position to close title immediately.

We are specialists in selling and leasing properties such as yours, and have an outstanding track record to prove it. Our elite, commercial property sales team consists of twelve (12) highly trained, experienced Realtors who *each* sell in excess of one million dollars in real estate *every* year. You can see that it is no accident that our office has come up with a highly qualified buyer such as we have.

Knowing of your long-established clientele and the many valued employees you have, please be assured that our discussions or correspondence will be held in strict confidence.

We are looking forward to hearing from you as soon as possible.

Very truly yours,

_____

LETTER SEEKING LISTINGS (Another Form)

Dear_____:

We have several qualified investors interested in obtaining ownership equities in_____(Type of Property)_____.

If you are considering offering your property for sale, please contact us giving sufficient details to make a presentation. We will need a description of the property, the sales price (including a_____% brokerage fee), terms, mortgages, income and expense figures, vacancy factor and any other information you consider pertinent. Also indicate whether or not you would be willing to dispose of less than a full interest (such as 50%) and remain on to operate the premises.

After analyzing the information you send, we will contact you to arrange for an inspection.

We are looking forward to hearing from you.

Sincerely yours,

_____

LETTER THANKING OWNER FOR LISTING

Dear Mr. and Mrs._____:

Please accept my thanks for the confidence and trust you have placed in our organization by listing your property with us. You may be assured that we will do everything possible to continue to merit this good relationship.

From the information you furnished, we have prepared a Fact Sheet for use by our sales associates. Color photos will be taken this week for brochure and newspaper advertising, and promotional purposes.

We will be advertising the property next Sunday in the classified sections of both newspapers. Before we show the premises, all prospects will first be carefully qualified by us. Whenever possible, we will endeavor to call you for an appointment prior to coming out.

If you have additional information to add to what you have given us, or if you are considering a price or other change, please let us know at once. Good communications between us can mean our doing a better, more direct and profitable job for you.

For our part, we will actively pursue the sale of your property and keep you informed of our progress.

Cordially yours,

_____ REALTY

_____
Broker

LETTER TO ATTORNEYS OFFERING SERVICES AS AN APPRAISER OR EXPERT WITNESS

Re: 1. Real Estate Appraisals
     2. Expert Witness Testimony

Dear Sir:

Save this letter! If you have no need for my services now, you may want my name on file for future reference.

My credentials as a *real estate appraiser* or as an *expert court witness* on real estate matters are as follows:

(Here list your educational background, years of experience, membership in real estate associations, appraisal societies, offices held, honors received, etc.)

Although I have handled every type of transaction, including homes, acreage, etc., I am currently specializing in the sale, leasing and management of commercial properties such as offices, apartment houses, shopping centers, warehouses and mobile home parks. My years of service as an active Realtor in every phase of the business qualify me both in a practical sense and technically to testify with complete creditability in any court of law.

At the risk of sounding self-serving, I pride myself in doing a highly competent, professional job. My fees are equitable.

My business and bank references are as follows:

(Here list one or two business and bank references.)

Please feel free to call if I can be of service to you or one of your clients.

Very truly yours,

LETTER TO INCOME PROPERTY PROSPECT

Dear_____ :

We have just exclusively listed an outstanding high-rise apartment house that makes sense!

It's a twelve-story, luxurious one-year young beauty that's now grossing over $485,000 annually and can do much better with aggressive management. The property is on the market for $3,700,000 (firm), with $650,000 cash required.

Because of location, quality construction and high rate of occupancy, the building will appraise well for refinancing purposes or condominium conversion.

The acquisition of this structure will give an investor a high tax shelter as well as a cash flow of approximately 11 percent.

We have the rent roll, CPA figures of income and expenses, as well as the mortgage information. If you are interested in further details, color photos, or an inspection of the premises, please call us today. PROPERTIES OF THIS CALIBER DO NOT REMAIN ON THE MARKET FOR LONG! I therefore urge you not to delay in responding. If you are out of town, call collect.

Sincerely yours,

FOLLOW-UP LETTER TO
INCOME PROPERTY PROSPECT

Dear_____:

Earlier this year you indicated an interest in acquiring investment properties.

We have since obtained a number of outstanding listings, including office buildings, shopping centers, warehouses, apartments and sale-leasebacks. Many of these we consider highly marketable and worth your time and effort to investigate.

May we suggest that you call us today. We would be particularly pleased to review any or all of them with you.

Sincerely yours,

_____

SUBMITTAL LETTER TO SELLER
REGISTERING PROSPECTS

Dear Mr._____:

Please be advised that today we offered your property located at _____ Avenue,_____ to the following prospects:_____

_____

_____

The price quoted was $_____.

We will endeavor to interest these prospects further. If they return for a further inspection of the premises, or telephone you, please notify us without delay. Your cooperation will greatly assist in the sale of your property.

Sincerely yours,

_____ Realty

_____

LETTER OF INTENTION

Offers to purchase real estate are made in a variety of forms. A letter or memorandum of intention is a frequently used, informal, yet valid, way of making a written offer. Even though in letter form and written in nonlegal terminology, when properly drawn and executed, it will contain all the elements of a valid agreement, and is binding upon both parties.

Dear_____:

This letter is to convey an offer to you for the purchase of your property at _____ Street, Town of _____, State of_____ ____. (A legal description is attached and made a part of this letter.)

The undersigned offers you the following price, terms and basic conditions of sale:

The selling price shall be $_____, of which $_____ is to be paid in cash at time of closing, which includes the trust account deposit below mentioned.

The purchase is subject to an existing first mortgage of $_____, payable $_____per month, including _____% interest per annum, until paid in full in 19__.

The balance of the purchase price is to be in the form of a purchase money second mortgage, payable in_____monthly installments of $_____, including_____% interest per annum.

The sale includes the following items of personal property:_____ _____ _____

As a show of good faith, we have today deposited in the trust account of _____, Realtor, the sum of $_____ .

This offer shall be declared null and void if not accepted by _____, 19__.

Yours truly,

Witnesses:

_____

_____   _____ Company

_____   _____

President

ACCEPTANCE

The above price, terms and conditions are accepted and agreed to.
Witnesses:

_____

_____   _____

OPTION LETTER

Brokers as well as other real estate practitioners are sometimes called
upon to prepare an option agreement. An example of a typical one in
letter form from the owner (optionor) is shown below, along with an
acceptance reply.

Dear Mr._____:

In consideration of_____dollars ($_____) paid to me, the
receipt of which is hereby acknowledged, I hereby give to you,_____
_____, your heirs and assigns, the exclusive option of buying, for the
price of_____dollars ($_____), the following described real
property, owned by me, along with the improvements thereon, situated
in the County of_____, Sate of_____, to-wit:

(Here include legal description and street address)

You have the right to close title on or before the_____day of
_____, 19__, at which time I will execute to you a good and sufficient
_____deed. Upon delivery of this deed, I am to be
paid the further sum of_____dollars ($_____), which shall
constitute payment in full for the above described property.

If the option is not exercised on or before the above specified date, I
am to retain the consideration as liquidated damages. If the option is closed
within the specified time, the consideration is to be applied toward the
purchase price.

Witness: Very truly yours,

_____   _____

_____

EXERCISE OF OPTION REPLY

Dear Mr._____:

You are hereby notified that I elect to exercise my option to purchase your property located at_____, in accordance with the terms and conditions of our option agreement dated _____, 19__. As we must close title on or before the_____ day of _____, 19__, I am prepared to do so on this date. Please let me know at what place and at what hour you wish to meet.

Very truly yours,

_____

Optionee

TELEGRAMS FROM SELLER ACCEPTING
OR CHANGING OFFER

An owner may be out of town when an offer is made. To expedite and facilitate the sale, a broker would best serve him by telephoning and reading the offer. If it is acceptable, the broker should have the wording ready for a suggested telegram or night letter that the seller would send confirming the transaction. All pertinent data such as dates, price, terms, property address, and the amount of commission need to be touched upon. The actual offer can be mailed to the seller for signature. Such a telegram might read:

DATE

TO: BRIGHT REALTY
    761 MAIN STREET
    CITY, STATE

I ACCEPT $80,000 FOR MY PROPERTY AT 646 JUNIPER DRIVE, CITY, INCLUDING A 7% COMMISSION. THE TERMS ARE $19,000 CASH OVER THE EXISTING $61,000 MORTGAGE. CLOSING TO BE WITHIN 60 DAYS.

SIMON OWNER

If the offer is not precisely acceptable, as frequently occurs, but is reasonably close, a telegram stating what *is* acceptable may still be used to expedite the matter.

DATE

TO: BRIGHT REALTY
     761 MAIN STREET
     CITY, STATE

THE OFFER OF $80,000 FOR MY PROPERTY AT 646 JUNIPER DRIVE, CITY, IS NOT ACCEPTABLE, BUT THE FOLLOWING PRICE AND TERMS ARE: $85,000 SELLING PRICE, $20,000 CASH OVER AN EXISTING $61,000 MORTGAGE. I WILL TAKE BACK A $4,000 SECOND MORTGAGE PAYABLE $64.36 PER MONTH INCLUDING 9% INTEREST FOR 7 YEARS. TITLE CLOSING SHALL BE IN 60 DAYS. THE FOREGOING INCLUDES YOUR 7% COMMISSION

SIMON OWNER

By having the owner commit himself via a telegram, there is no unnecessary time lapse, which experienced practitioners know is the danger point of any transaction. The written agreement can then be appropriately changed and mailed for the required signature(s).

COVERING LETTER TO ATTORNEY

Re: House Sale To Your Client
John C. Smith

Dear Mr._____:

Enclosed is a copy of a Binder Agreement for the purchase of a residence at 123 Broad Street entered into by your client John C. Smith.

The attorney for the seller is Raymond Bright, Esq., 4576 Main Street. Telephone 646-7616.

The abstract of title is with Fidelity Title Co., 62 Doe Ave. Telephone 646-8842.

Mr. Smith asked me to convey to you his desire to coordinate the closing of title of this property with the termination of his apartment house lease on July 1. If I can be of service to you in accomplishing this, or in any other matter regarding the transaction, please do not hesitate to call.

Very truly yours,

_____

LETTER REQUESTING ESTOPPEL LETTER

Re: Property at _____

Mortgage No. _____

Dear Sirs:

In reference to the above numbered mortgage, this office has sold the property that it encumbers and would greatly appreciate a reply from you stating the exact remaining balance of the loan, any funds held in escrow and through what date the interest is paid. Also, a confirmation of the term of this mortgage, the interest rate, and any other pertinent information you are able to furnish.

Thank you in advance for your attention to this matter.

Very truly yours,

_____

LETTER RELEASING ESCROW FUNDS

To free the broker of responsibility for holding escrow funds that could otherwise result in possible legal action, a release letter signed by all parties is sometimes necessary. One covering the pertinent points is shown.

TO WHOM IT MAY CONCERN

This release agreement is between the undersigned purchaser, seller

and real estate broker who are parties to a certain contract dated
_____ , 19___, covering the following described property:

(Here give legal and common known description)

It is hereby understood that in consideration of each of the parties
releasing the others from the aforesaid contract of all claims, actions or
demands whatsoever, which any of the parties may have up to the date of
this agreement, the funds held by the escrow agent will be forthwith distributed in the following manner:

$_____ TO _____

$_____ TO _____

$_____ TO _____

It is the express intention that any responsibility, obligation or rights
arising by virtue of said contract are, by this release, declared null and
void, and of no further effect whatsoever.

Witnesses:

_____   _____
                                Purchasers

_____   _____
                                Sellers

_____   _____
                                Broker

LETTERS TO REAL ESTATE EDITOR

Acting as your own publicity agent can result in a steady flow of free
newspaper space worth far more than paid advertisements. Here's how it
is done. A study of the Sunday Real Estate section will give you an idea
of what will prove of interest to the public. Most real estate editors are
constantly seeking photos and brief stories of properties recently sold.
The larger the commercial deal the better, but regular house sales, too,
have a tremendous, continual reader interest. It provides the home buyer
as well as the seller a clue to values. Your letter to the editor should be

crammed with facts and figures, and you should enclose a clear photo or two. Write the captions for the photos and one or more paragraphs as you envision them to appear. If he decides to use it, he may edit or embellish it to suit his needs. Three typical letters might read as follows:

#1

Dear Sir:

Please note the enclosed photo of a house our office sold earlier this week. The following write-up contains the facts—

Mr. & Mrs. Walter Jones have sold their three-bedroom, two-bath home with living room, dining room and two-car garage on a quarter-acre wooded parcel, located at 123 Parkview Lane. The purchasers were Mr. & Mrs. John Smith, formerly of Bakersville. The selling price was $64,750. There is an existing $41,000 mortgage bearing 9% interest. The house was listed and sold by Jane Brown of Acme Realty, Inc.

Thank you for any publicity you may give to this transaction.

Sincerely yours,

_____

For Acme Realty, Inc.

#2

Dear Sir:

Million dollar deals don't come along every day. It is for this reason that we believe the sale of the Camino Apartment high-rise would be of interest to your readers. Here is the story, along with two photos of the building that, we trust, are suitable for publication.

Three New Yorkers have purchased a high-rent apartment house, completed last year in the oceanfront section of Fort Lauderdale, from John Jones, the president of Camino Realty, Inc. The building, Camino Hall Apartments, is at 12345 Oceanside Drive. The buyers are Tom Smith, Margaret Close, and William C. Long, all of Rochester.

The purchase price was $7,150,000. Terms were $850,000 cash, subject to an existing first mortgage of $5.2 million, a second mortgage of $860,000 and a new third mortgage of $190,000. Bright

Realtors and Acme Realty, Inc. both of Ft. Lauderdale, were co-brokers in the transaction.

If further details are needed, please call. We will be pleased to furnish you with any additional facts you may desire.

Thank you for the publicity you deem this story warrants.

Sincerely yours,

_____

For Acme Realty, Inc.

#3

Dear Sir:

I am pleased to be able to report that our Commercial Department has been successful in negotiating the sale of Clearview Shopping Center on Overlook Drive. Title closed on Friday. Enclosed is a plot plan of this center along with aerial and ground photos. The details are as follows:

James Blanding, Realtor with Acme Realty, Inc. reported selling the Clearview Shopping Center on Overlook Drive and 10th Street to John Smith and Paul Jones, well-known real estate investors of this city. The seller was the ABC Construction Co., builders of the two-year-old, neighborhood center. Major tenants include Marks Department Store, Fast-Check SuperMarket, and Puro Gas Co. The selling price was $1,475,000, subject to an existing mortgage of $740,000. An adjoining acre was included with the sale and the new owners are reported planning to construct ten more stores on this land.

We appreciate the publicity you have given certain of our newsworthy sales in the past, and want to thank you in advance for any space you may give to this transaction.

Sincerely yours,

_____

for Acme Realty, Inc.

COOPERATIVE AGREEMENT BETWEEN BROKERS

Dear _____:

This will acknowledge receipt of information from your office regarding property known as _____, located at _____.

In cooperating with you, we agree to the following terms and conditions:

1. Only to solicit offers for the property from principals.
2. Not to advertise the property without written consent from you.
3. Not to negotiate with the owner directly, but rather submit all offers through you. In turn, it is understood that you will promptly submit all such offers to the owner.
4. Refrain from accepting authorization from the owner to sell, exchange or lease the property within one year of this date.
5. To follow your instructions as to the time and manner that the property can be shown, and to exercise consideration and courtesy when so doing.

It is understood that if we are successful in negotiating a sale of this property we shall divide the commission on a 50/50 basis.

Sincerely yours,

Witnesses: _____

_____

Cooperating Broker

_____

Acknowledged and Agreed to:

_____

Listing Broker

COMMISSION RECEIPT

DATE _____

SELLER _____

PURCHASER _____

PROPERTY _____

TO WHOM IT MAY CONCERN:

We acknowledge receipt of the amount of $_____ from the sellers as commission in connection with the subject transaction.

Co-op Realtor (if any)_____.

Co-op Realtor's amount of commission $_____.

Thank you very much.

By_____

COMMISSION AGREEMENT

Dear Sirs:

The purpose of this letter is to confirm the commission agreement regarding the sale of your property located at

It is understood that the commission shall be_____% of the selling price, payable in full at time of closing, if we are successful in bringing about a sale.

Very truly yours,

_____
for_____Realty Corp.

Agreed to and accepted this
_____day of_____, 19___.

_____
for_____Company

COMBINED
COMMISSION AND COOPERATIVE
LISTING AGREEMENT

In consideration of procuring ____(Name of buyer)____, or assigns, purchaser for the property known as_____(Here include name and location of property)_____, the seller_____(Name of seller)_____agrees to pay the sum of $_____to be di-

vided evenly between _____(Real estate firm A)_____ and
_____(Real estate firm B)_____. The said commission is to be paid
in cash at time of closing.

_____   _____
Seller   Real Estate Firm A

                                                _____
                                                Real Estate Firm B

COMMISSION STATEMENT

When a real estate transaction is completed, the party paying the
broker's commission will require a statement for his records indicating
the amount of the fee and an acknowledgment of its having been paid. A
broker should prepare such a statement on his letterhead.

                    BLANK REALTY COMPANY
                         1 Main Street
                         Centerville

                                        Date_____

To:_____
   _____
   _____

                                Re: The Sale Of The Following
                                    Described Property:_____
                                    _____
                                    _____
FOR SERVICES in bringing about the above captioned transaction.

                         $_____

                         Received Payment

                         _____

14

ZONING

People who are actively engaged in real estate should have a thorough, working knowledge of local zoning laws and regulations, and be aware of any changes that are taking place, as well as the types of variances being granted. Real property values directly stem from the manner in which land is permitted to be used. Thus, zoning plays a vitally important part in land values and sales. The restrictions imposed upon land usage, when properly applied, nevertheless, work for its ultimate benefit. While they limit the size, height, type of structure, population density, etc., they also help create harmonious surroundings, which in turn enhance values.

POLICE POWERS

A municipality or county has the inherent legal right to impose zoning regulations by its police powers—the control that a government possesses over the life and property of its citizens. The exercising of police power, however, must be in the best interest of the general public to be lawful. If not, it is in conflict with the Fourteenth Amendment of the U.S. Constitution, which safeguards the civil rights and freedom of the people.

PURPOSE OF ZONING

The purpose of zoning is to control the manner in which an area develops. When zoning laws are administered with wisdom, they can be a positive force for community betterment. When abused, deteriorating real estate values inevitably (and rapidly) follow.

Zoning boards and the courts decide zoning issues on an individual case basis. Good zoning practices occur when logic and fairness are applied in making decisions. In the interest of maintaining equitable zoning regulations, authorities take into consideration the following factors:

1. Will the interest of the public be best served?
2. Is the property under study being unfairly discriminated against?
3. Will the decision create a serious hardship to the owner?
4. Will the good created by a zoning ordinance or variance offset its harmful effects?

ZONING ORDINANCE AIMS

Good zoning ordinances safeguard the peace, tranquility and economy of a community. They work toward enhancing real estate values, and should be restrictive only when serving the best interest of the public. The intent and purposes of a large southeastern city's zoning ordinance is repeated here in part, as it exemplifies good zoning aims and practices.[1]

---

[1]The city is Miami, Florida, which has been cited as one of the cleanest and most pollution-free municipalities in the country. Its comprehensive zoning ordinances serve as a model for other communities.

"The comprehensive plan of this ordinance is created for the purpose of promoting public health, safety, morals, convenience, comfort, amenities, prosperity and general welfare of the community and of a wholesome, serviceable and attractive municipality, by having regulations and restrictions that increase the safety and security of home life; that preserve and create a more favorable environment in which to rear children; that develop permanent good citizenship; that stabilize and enhance property and civic values; that provide for a uniform, just land-use pattern and tax-assessment basis; that facilitate adequate provisions for increased safety in traffic and for transportation, vehicular parking, parks, parkways, recreation, schools, public buildings, housing, light, air, water supply, sewerage, sanitation, and other public requirements; that lessen congestion, disorder and danger which often inhere in unregulated municipal development; that prevent overcrowding of land and undue congestion of population; and that provide more reasonable and serviceable means and methods of protecting and safeguarding the economic structure upon which the good of all depend."

ZONING CLASSIFICATIONS

Most communities have basic zoning classifications that include the following:

Residential

Commercial

Industrial

Agricultural

Recreational

Within these broad classifications are further divisions of land usage. They will be categorized in the outline below simply to give the reader a general idea of what the various classifications cover. The list is by no means complete.

Residential zoning is the use of property for any form of dwelling unit. Within this classification may be found—

One-family Dwellings—Private homes.

Low Density Multiple Dwellings—Duplex homes to one-story garden apartments.

Rooming Houses—Other than high-rise structures.[2]

Hotels and Motels—Other than high-rise structures.

Medium Density Multiple Dwellings—Hospitals, sanitariums, university dormitories,. private clubs, bungalow courts, mobile home parks, planned unit developments (PUD's), and medium-rise garden apartments.

High Density Multiple Dwellings—All high-rise residential structures.

Commercial zoning covers business and plants of a widely varied nature. The following divisions will serve as a guide.

Community Commercial—Retail stores, restaurants, taverns, clubs or lodges, professional offices, laboratories, educational institutions.

Medium Commercial—Bus terminals, parking lots and garages, night clubs, printing establishments, heliports, sports arenas.

General Commercial—Gas stations and auto repairs, automobile sales and service, boat sales and service, drive-in theaters, race tracks, mortuaries, wholesale distributors, storage warehouses, laundry and dry cleaning establishments.

Liberal Commercial—Bottling plants, machinery sales and services, lumber yards, freight and truck terminals, tire recapping, woodworking plants.

Industrial zoning covers manufacturing in all its aspects. Some "clean" production processes do not cause air, noise or water pollution. Others create fallout, odors or are otherwise objectionable to a neighborhood.

---

[2]The terms high-rise, medium-rise and low-rise are variously interpreted in different areas of the country. For this study, a high-rise building refers to one over seven stories; a medium-rise, four to seven stories; and a low-rise, up to three stories.

Light Industry—Bakery, food processing, ice manufacturing, yacht repair, milk distribution, motion picture production, cleaning and dying plants.

Medium Industry—Gas manufacturing, brick manufacturing, railroad repair, rock, sand or gravel distribution, paper and pulp manufacturing, tanneries.

Heavy Industry—Foundries, oil refineries, ship building, chemical manufacturing, cement plants.

Agricultural zoning restricts the land use to the production of vegetables, plants, trees, shrubs, flowers and livesotck, as well as the necessary structures (silos, barns, greenhouses, storehouses, etc.) to operate such farming and horticultural enterprises.

Recreational zoning covers publicly owned parks, camp grounds, beaches, and such recreational facilities as tennis courts, golf courses, ball fields of all kinds, marinas, etc. The municipality generally reserves the right to construct the necessary buildings to operate and maintain these facilities. Such structures should be in harmony with the land and water usage of the recreational area.

ZONING CONTROLS

Zoning dictates how a property may be used. There are three ways that this is accomplished.

1. Controlling the population density of an area by limiting the number of separate living units per acre. It may also be accomplished by "open space" requirements:—the necessity of providing ample walkways, roadways and plantings between structures.
2. Size of buildings. A structure's front, side and rear set-back requirement, as well as the height that it can be built, limits the amount of people the building can house or serve.
3. Usage. Restricting the type of activity to which a building can be put. Some buildings are strictly for residential purposes, others are utilized just for factories, assembly plants, office buildings, retail stores, warehouses, etc.

VARIANCES

A variance is the granting of a special request to utilize property which creates an exception to the prevailing zoning laws. It is a change from that which is in existence. A special zoning Board Of Appeals (sometimes called a Board Of Adjustment) hears such requests for changes. Variances are ordinarily granted only when it can be shown that a logical reason exists for the change; and when such a variance, if granted, would not act as a detrimental factor within the neighborhood or community.

An owner must show that undue and unfair hardship would be caused him if the variance is not granted, as may occur, for example, when an irregular lot could not be built upon if the set-back requirements were complied with. Or to correct inequitable situations, as when the lots on each side of a property have already been granted variances.

NONCONFORMING USES

Every community that has zoning laws has properties that were in use for special purposes before the laws were put into effect.[3] Though they do not comply, they are lawfully allowed to remain and operate as they have been in existence before zoning was enacted. This situation is referred to as a "Grandfather Clause." It is an exemption based on circumstances that previously existed. Generally, by ordinance, such properties cannot be enlarged, replaced or remodeled. The only repairs permitted would be to conform to safety regulations. And if the property is destroyed by fire, storm, or other occurrence, it cannot be rebuilt, except to a conforming use. In this manner, with the passage of time, such properties become obsolete and are forced to close down.

CITY PLANNING

City planning is an attempt to direct the natural growth of a commun-

---

[3]Zoning ordinances came into being in many cities throughout the country in the 1920's. Prior to that time there was very limited city planning as we know it today.

ity for its best social and economic good. City planning administrators seek to look into the future of an area, and then to devise an orderly expansion plan in order that the land can be put to its highest and best use. Administrators have come up with Master or Comprehensive plans that project ten, 20 and more years into the future. These plans chart the real estate course of a community. Zoning ordinances for the inner city as well as for outlying areas are enacted. Experts are in agreement, however, that long-range plans for a city, no matter how well conceived, need to be flexible in nature. Real estate is an ever-changing, viable commodity. Long-range, planned zoning cannot stay static for long if it is to prosper.

EXTENT OF ZONING

Over 98 percent of all United States municipalities with a population of 10,000 or more have enacted zoning laws. While zoning ordinances are not infallible, good zoning practices result in sound real estate economics. Properly-enacted ordinances serve to protect property owners and inhabitants against undesirable influences. Zoning is a vital, positive force that helps promote lasting, ever-appreciating real estate values.

Appendix I

GLOSSARY OF

REAL ESTATE TERMS

A grasp of the language of real estate is a prime requisite to succeed today. One must have a thorough knowledge of its technical terms, as well as the jargon words and phrases that are constantly used in transacting real estate. The definitions that follow were selected from the author's book on real estate terminology,[1] as well as from a compilation of numerous new words that have found their way into everyday real estate practice.

A

ABANDONMENT—Voluntary renunciation of ownership. Relinquishing any claim or rights to property. Giving up entirely without any intention of regaining possession or interest at a later time. Permanently leave or desert.

ABATE—To decrease; make less; diminish or reduce. Used in real estate phrases such as *abatement of taxes* (a tax rebate), *abatement of-rent-clause* (a clause releasing a tenant from paying rent in the event the premises are made uninhabitable.)

---

[1]*Illustrated Encyclopedic Dictionary Of Real Estate Terms*, by Jerome S. Gross (Prentice-Hall, Inc., Englewood Cliffs, N. J., 1969).

ABLE—Capable; qualified; competent. Financially able, as in the term *ready, willing and able*.

ABROGATE—To annul or nullify. Eliminate by the act of an authority. Abolish or otherwise put to an end.

ABSTRACT: ABSTRACT OF TITLE—A summarized, chronological compilation of all the recorded instruments and a history of ownership that has affected the title to a specific piece of land. A synopsis of its recorded documents.

ABUTTING—Property contiguous to another. Bordering; joining; adjacent; touching.

ACCELERATION CLAUSE—A clause generally found in a mortgage or installment contract stipulating that the payment of the indebtedness must be made in full in the event of a default of any of its covenants. Certain other instruments, such as bonds, leases, and notes may also contain acceleration clauses.

ACCESS RIGHT—The vested right of an owner to pass over adjoining public property in order to enter and leave his land.

ACCRETION—The gradual acquisition of additional land by the forces of nature, such as occurs when wind or tides add sand deposits to waterfront properties, or when a watercourse is altered by the action of floods.

ACCRUE—An increase or addition. Something that is periodically accumulated. A natural process of growth. To come into existence. *Accrued interest*, for example, is interest that has already been earned. *Accruing depreciation* is accumulating depreciation.

ACKNOWLEDGMENT—The formal certification of a signature on a document before an authorized officer, such as a Notary or County Clerk. A verification that the document which has been signed is that person's willful act and deed.

ACRE—Land measuring 43,560 square feet. 4,840 square yards. 1/640th of a square mile. An acre measures 208.75' × 208.75'.

ACT OF GOD—An event occurring through the unexpected force of nature, as a hurricane, flood, or earthquake. An act not created or able to be controlled by human activity.

ADEMPTION—The disposal of specific property by a living person who has bequeathed the property in his will. Upon the death of that person, the portion of the will that is unable to be fulfilled is automatically revoked.

ADJUSTMENTS—As applied to real estate, the credits and debits of a closing statement including such matters as taxes, insurance, rent prorations, escrowed funds, etc. when property is sold.

AD VALOREM—Latin. According to value.

ADVERSE POSSESSION—The acquiring of property by one who does not have title, or who has defective title, to it. That person must be in "actual, open, notorious, exclusive, and continuous" occupancy for a prescribed statutory period.

AFFIDAVIT—A voluntary statement, testimony, or declaration in writing, that is sworn to be affirmed before a Notary, County Clerk or other person authorized by law to administer oaths. An affidavit is often required as proof in the absence of other verifying facts or documents.

AGRARIAN—Matters relating to the land and soil; its use, ownership, distribution, and acquisition.

AIR RIGHTS—The rights to the use of the open space above a property, as occurs in the leasing of air space over existing buildings, highways, or railroad tracks. Also, the right to control the air space by *not* building, thereby assuring that light and air will not be blocked out.

ALLIGATOR—A jargon expression meaning property difficult to hold on to due to high taxes, upkeep or other expenses.

AMENITIES—The pleasantness and satisfaction gained from one's surroundings. Features both hidden and visible that enhance and add to the desirability of real estate. Frequently used when referring to residential properties, the word embraces the personal, human aspect of livability and pride of ownership.

AMORTIZE—The gradual payment of a debt in periodic amounts until the total amount along with interest, if any, is paid.

ANCHOR TENANT—A major tenant such as a large department store, or a nationally known chain store that forms the nucleus of a shopping center. The anchor tenant is the one that draws the public and stabilizes the center, thereby helping to create a profitable operation for the other tenants.

APPURTENANCE—That which goes with or pertains to the land, but is not necessarily a part of it. An adjunct. Examples include a right of way or an easement, as well as physical improvements such as buildings, roads, power lines, fences, etc. Appurtenances pass with the land when sold.

ARM'S LENGTH—A term which clearly implies that a person should approach all business and real estate transactions with due caution. When two parties, each with uncommon interests, undertake an open market transaction, they should proceed with caution.

AS IS—When these words are inserted in a contract, they mean that no guarantees whatsoever are given regarding the subject property. It is being conveyed in exactly the condition in which it is found.

ASSESSMENT—1. The act of evaluating a property for the purpose of levying a property tax. 2. A charge levied against property in the form of a tax.

ASSIGNMENT—Transfer of title or interest in writing from one person or group to another.

ASSUMPTION OF MORTGAGE—Taking title to property that has an existing mortgage, and being personally liable for its payments.

ATTACHMENT—The taking of a debtor's property into legal custody. This usually occurs when a person lives in another part of the country and his property is within the jurisdiction of a specified court. Property may also be attached if it is feared that a person is anticipating leaving an area to avoid payment or responsibility for an obligation.

ATTORNEY IN FACT—One who has the written authority of another to act in his place. This authority is limited by the extent of the written instrument appointing him. One need not be a lawyer to be an attorney in fact. Also called a power of attorney.

AVULSION—A noticeable shifting of land area from one property to another caused by floods, currents or other movements of a body of water. For example, when a river changes its course.

B

BALLOON MORTGAGE—A mortgage that provides for periodic payments which do not completely amortize the loan at the time of its termination. As a consequence, a larger final payment becomes due. Some states require that a balloon mortgage be clearly identified as such on the mortgage instrument in order for it to be valid.

BILATERAL CONTRACT—A term used to indicate that both principals have mutually agreed upon and have fully executed a contract, and are bound to fulfill its terms and conditions.

BILL OF SALE—An instrument used in a real estate transaction when items other than real property are included in a sale. Furniture, fixtures, appliances, merchandise, motor vehicles and similar items of personalty are found in a bill of sale. The document certifies that ownership has been transferred.

BINDER—1. A preliminary agreement in writing, with a valuable consideration given, as evidence of good faith by the offerer. It is an offer to purchase; a unilateral contract. Upon acceptance, it becomes a bilateral contract. Though it contains all the elements of a valid contract, in some areas it is considered to be temporary in nature until a more formal contract can be drawn. 2. A written instrument giving immediate insurance coverage until a regular policy can be issued.

BIRD DOG—An expression referring to a salesman whose sole function is to "flush out" prospects or listings. Once he has obtained a good lead, he turns everything over to his broker, or to another salesman who is more experienced in transacting real estate.

BLOCK BUSTING—The highly unethical real estate practice of creating fear and unrest by moving one or more families of another race or creed into a neighborhood, then exploiting the situation by urging residents to sell their homes at deflated prices.

BLUE SKY LAWS—Laws designed to regulate companies for the protection of the public. Fly-by-night firms selling securities, land, gold mines, etc. are prevented by these laws from making wild and fraudulent claims.

BONA FIDE—Latin. Made with sincere, good intentions. Honestly and openly done. Without fraud, as when an authentic offer is tended as a show of good faith.

BOONDOCKS—A colloquial term for remote, outlying areas offering few, if any, advantages.

BOOT—A term used in the exchange of realty when the properties being traded are not exactly equal. Cash, other properties, or services are included in order to bring the transaction to par. That which is given in addition is referred to as being "to boot." It serves to compensate for any difference in value.

BREACH OF CONTRACT—Not living up to the terms and conditions of a contract; refusal to carry out the provisions therein. Failure to perform without legal justification.

BUILT-INS—Certain stationary equipment, such as kitchen appliances (wall-oven, counter-top range, garbage disposal, dishwasher), book case, furniture, wall safe, etc.) Something permanently affixed to a house and understood to be included with it when sold. Also, a garage that is under the same roof as the structure it serves.

BUNDLE OF RIGHTS—All the legal rights that go with ownership of property. The rights to sell, lease, mine, build, mortgage, improve, will to another, etc. that one possesses with ownership of real estate. Rights within the framework of the law to control one's property.

BURN-OFF—A jargon expression used when someone ceases to make payments on an installment sales contract, and the sale is "burned-off," or terminated. The property reverts to the deedholder.

BUSINESS TRUST—An unincorporated business association in which title to property is given to trustees to hold, manage, or sell. It is similar to the usual corporate organization in that a transferable certificate is issued to a shareholder, but unlike a corporation, the trustees must be principals and hold office in the trust on a permanent basis. In real estate, this type of business structure is sometimes used when a tract of land is subdivided, improved, and sold. It is also referred to as a Massachusetts Trust or Common Law Trust.

C

CAPITAL GAIN—1. Profit gained from the sale of a capital asset in excess of its cost or appraised value. The amount of the selling price above the acquisition cost. 2. Appreciation in value over a period of time on money invested in an asset.

CARRYOVER CLAUSE—The clause, found in an exclusive listing, that protects the broker for a specified time (beyond the expiration date of the listing). By this clause a broker would still be considered the procuring cause of a transaction, if someone, who was shown the property when the exclusive listing was in force, later should decide to purchase.

CASH FLOW—The net income. The usable cash after all expenses are paid.

CAVEAT EMPTOR—Latin. "Let the buyer beware!" Under the theory of this legal maxim, the buyer is expected to judge and evaluate property carefully before purchasing. As long as there is no misrepresentation, a person buys at his own risk.

CAVEAT VENDOR—Latin. "Let the seller beware!"

CERTIFICATE OF OCCUPANCY—A certificate or permit issued by a building department verifying that all work on the project complies with local zoning ordinances and is completed (or so nearly completed) that people may occupy it.

CERTIFICATE OF TITLE—A document issued by a title company or an opinion rendered by an attorney that the seller has good, marketable and/or insurable title to the property. If a title company has issued such a certificate and a defect in the title is later found, the title company will cure the defect or indemnify the title holder.

CERTIORARI—Latin. The proceedings of a higher court reviewing actions of a lower one or those of a board (such as a real estate commission or industrial commission) acting in its judicial capacity.

CHAIN OF TITLE—The history of ownership, conveyances and encumbrances, both recorded and unrecorded, that have affected the title of a specific parcel of land. (See *Abstract: Abstract Of Title*.)

CHATTEL—Personal property. Tangible property other than real estate. Furniture, automobiles, goods, leases, money, livestock, etc. are chattels. Chattels are classified as either personal or real: Chattels *personal* include property that can be transported (jewelry, domestic animals, merchandise); Chattels *real* are any possessory interests in real property such as leases, estates for life, for years, at will, etc.

CLAIM OF LIEN—A legal claim for payment, made by one who performed labor, services or furnished material. A mechanic's lien.

CLOSED-END MORTGAGE—A mortgage that has no provisions for increasing the balance. This is the opposite of an open-end mortgage which permits the mortgagor to continue borrowing from it, it amounts up to the original sum.

COMPLETION BOND—A performance bond posted by a contractor as a guarantee that he will satisfactorily complete a project and that it will be free of any liens. It is also called a performance bond.

CONDEMNATION—1. The taking of private property for public use. There must be a need for the government to acquire it, and that need must be in the general interest of the public. The owner is entitled to just compensation for that which is taken, and if it is determined that loss in value in the remaining property was sustained, he will likewise receive an equitable payment for it. Condemnation is exercising the power of *eminent domain*. 2. A government's right under its police powers to declare a structure unsafe or unfit for use or for human habitation when it is a menace to public safety.

CONSIDERATION—Something of value given to influence a person to enter into a contract. It usually is money, but need not be. Personal services, merchandise, or simply love and affection can be the inducement or consideration.

CONSTRUCTIVE—A legal declaration or interpretation. *Constructive notice*, for example, is notification by recording documents in public records. *Constructive possession* is having legal possession by virtue of title, but not necessarily occupying the property. *Constructive fraud* is fraud relating to a breach of fiduciary relationship, as when a person who has gained another's confidence takes an unconscionable advantage of this relationship. *Constructive eviction* occurs when a landlord renders a property unfit for its intended use.

CONTIGUOUS—Physically adjoining, as between two or more properties. Touching along a boundary line.

CONTINUANCE—The up-dating of an abstract, noting changes in ownership, new liens and encumbrances, etc. The abstract is *continued* to the present time.

CONVENTIONAL LOAN—The type of mortgage loan that is customarily granted by a bank or savings and loan association. A loan based on real estate as security, as distinguished from one guaranteed or insured by an agency of the government.

CONVEYANCE—An instrument, in writing, used to transfer title to property from one to another. A contract and deed are two familiar forms of conveyances.

CORPORATE VEIL—The legal shield or curtain that protects a corporation where an individual would be liable. Because of this protection, individuals sometimes choose the corporate structure when going into a business venture, so that in the event of bankruptcy or legal action, they will not be personally accountable.

CORPOREAL PROPERTY—Real or personal property having body or form; relating to or having physical substance such as a house, furniture, fixtures or land. Something tangible; a material body. It is the opposite of incorporeal property such as franchises, stocks, bonds, accounts receivable, rents, etc.

COVENANT—An agreement between parties, written into legal instruments, promising to do or refrain from doing certain acts.

CREAM-PUFF—In real estate parlance, an expression meaning property easy to sell. It is usually applied to a house, but may be used when referring to any type of real property that has many desirable features.

CURTESY—A husband's interest for the duration of his life in his wife's estate. As with dower (the wife's interest), state laws vary as to the right of curtesy. Most states have abolished this form of estate.

CUSHION—A term used in business, meaning a financial margin of safety against hidden or unforeseen costs. A reserve fund or contingency allowance for a sudden loss in revenue or a sharp increase in expenses.

D

DEALER—In real estate, an individual who buys property with the prime objective of reselling it for profit as soon as possible, rather than retaining it as an investment for the future.

DEBT SERVICE—The amount of money required periodically to make the payments necessary to amortize a debt and interest charges; the principal and interest payments.

DECLARATORY JUDGMENT—1. A binding legal decree. 2. In real estate it is the court ruling sought by a third party holding money in trust, when a dispute concerning it arises between the principals. When so doing, the third party does not relinquish his interest, but is held responsible for court costs.

DE FACTO—Latin. In actual fact. In reality; actually.

DEFICIENCY JUDGMENT—A judgment issued when the security for a loan is insufficient to satisfy the debt upon its going into default. It is the awarding of the amount still due on a foreclosed mortgage, after applying the sum received for the sale of the property.

DE JURE—Latin. Lawful title. Under authority of law. By right.

DEPONENT—One who gives evidence in writing under oath. A witness.

DEPOSITION—Testimony of a witness, usually in writing, as ordered by a court. A formal declaration. A deposition is used primarily when a court appearance is not necessary, such as for a witness residing out of the area or a person who is not able or available to testify in court.

DEPRECIATION—1. A lowering of value. A reduction; lessening. The decline in value of property. Loss in market value. Deterioration over a period of time. The opposite of appreciation. 2. In appraising, depreciation is the reduction in value of a property as measured from the cost to replace it. It is the difference between the replacement cost and the market value. 3. In accounting, it is a writeoff (usually computed annually) of a portion of an asset on the records.

DESCENT—To obtain something by inheritance. To receive from one's ancestors. The passing on of property to an heir or heirs. The transfer of property by inheritance. Receiving an estate by succession.

DIRECT REDUCTION MORTGAGE—A mortgage loan in which the periodic payments are applied to the outstanding principal balance. Only when this sum is completely satisfied, is interest or other charges deducted.

DISBURSEMENTS—1. Money paid out. Expenditures. 2. At a real estate closing, the necessary moneys expended by buyer and seller in order to transfer ownership.

DISCRIMINATORY COVENANTS—Agreements made for reasons other than individual merit. Unfair covenants, running with the land, created to bar a particular group or race of people. Discrimination by category rather than on an individual basis. Discriminatory covenants have been declared unconstitutional by the United States Supreme Court.

DISPOSSESS—Forcing an individual to vacate property. Putting one out of possession or occupancy.

DISSEISIN—The loss of possession of property by one claiming ownership. Dispossession; forcible explusion of an owner from his land.

DISTRAIN—To seize another's property as security or a pledge for an unfulfilled obligation.

DOCUMENTARY STAMPS—A state tax, in the form of stamps, required on deeds and mortgages when real estate title passes from one owner to another. The amount of stamps required varies with each state.

DOUBLE-DECKING—The illegal act of selling the same property twice. A practice familiar to disreputable land operators.

DOWER—The legal rights that a widow possesses to her husband's estate. In some states, she holds an estate for life in his property. State laws vary as to dower rights, with many of them having abolished this form of interest entirely. In some states, under common law, a wife owns 1/3 of her deceased husband's real estate.

DUAL EMPLOYMENT—Employment of a broker by both a buyer and a seller. As long as both parties are made aware of this double employment, there is nothing illegal or unethical about such an arrangement. Both principals pay a brokerage commission. One serving in such a dual capacity is sometimes called a Middleman.

E

EARNEST MONEY—A purchaser's partial payment, as a show of good faith, to make a contract binding. A deposit; a down payment.

EARNING-PRICE RATIO—A ratio of the net income of property to the selling price. As an example, if a building nets $100,000 profit and is sold for $800,000, the earning-price ratio is 8 (8 times the income). In computing earning-price ratio, net income refers to the sum remaining after all expenses except mortgage payments are deducted.

EASEMENT—A limited right to use another's property in a specified manner. The right given to travel on, over, or through adjoining land, or to use it for a specific purpose. An easement can be permanent or temporary. Utility right-of-ways, pole easements and party walls are examples of permanent easements. The temporary right to cross a neighbor's land to reach one's own, until roads are repaired, is a temporary easement. Generally, easements pass with the land when it is sold, unless prohibited by deed restrictions.

EGRESS—A passageway leading from property. The means of exiting. The opposite of *Ingress*.

EMINENT DOMAIN—The right or power of the state or a public utility to expropriate private property for public use, upon paying just compensation. For this right to be exercised, it must be in the best interest and security of the general public (as in times of war the government may take over privately held lands). In peacetime, the government can obtain private property for roadways, right-of-ways, railroads, channels or similar public benefits.

ENCROACHMENT—An intrusion or infringement upon the property of another without his consent. As an example, a portion of a building that protrudes beyond its property line and onto another. Encroachments that continue for a great length of time may without objection be adjudged an implied easement. Encroachments can be written into a contract of sale with the buyer aware of, and accepting, the risk. If, however, an encroachment is not known and a further study reveals that one exists, it may render the title unmarketable.

ENCUMBRANCE—A legal right or interest in land that diminishes its value. It can take numerous forms, such as zoning restrictions, easements, claims, mortgages, liens, charges, a pending legal action, unpaid taxes or in the form of restrictive covenants. It does not prevent transfer of the property to another.

EQUITY—1. The difference between the current market value of a property and the liens that exist against it. Equity can also refer to the difference between the cost of the property and the liens against it. 2. In law, equity refers to natural justice. Something that is fair, just and morally right, after all facts are carefully considered. The law of equity is different from, and generally overrides, statute law. It covers reason, natural rights and ethics, rather than a strict interpretation of the written law.

ESTATE AT SUFFERANCE—This type of estate exists when one who was rightfully in possession or had lawful title, keeps it beyond the termination period of the agreement or after title was vested in another.

ESTATE AT WILL—An estate of indefinite duration allowing the lessee possession as long as both lessor and lessee mutually agree to it. If this reciprocal agreement is changed by either party, the estate at will may be terminated. A month-to-month tenancy is an example of this type of estate.

ESTATE BY THE ENTIRETY—A single estate held by both husband and wife jointly. An estate in which husband and wife are as one. They are each in possession of the entire estate and when one dies the surviving spouse does not inherit the other's interest, but automatically comes into sole ownership and use.

ESTATE FOR YEARS—An estate established for a definite period of time, longer than a person's lifetime, for a year, or even less.

ET AL—Latin. The term means "and another" or "and others." It is used in legal documents when a list of names are given that has to be repeated later in the instrument. Rather than state again the entire roster, the first name or two on the list is given followed by et al.

ET UXOR—Latin. It means "and wife." It is frequently abbreviated et ux.

EVICTION—The act of dispossessing a person from property. Forcing out; ejection, expulsion. Eviction can take three forms: actual, constructive or partial. Actual or total eviction is physical expulsion from the premises. Constructive eviction occurs when a landlord's acts render the property unfit for use, such as by shutting off water, heat or electricity. Partial eviction takes place when one in possession is deprived of a portion of the leased or occupied premises.

EXECUTOR—A man appointed under the terms of a will to execute its provisions and dispose of the property as written or implied.

F

FAÇADE—The exterior face or front side of a building. The front of a structure that often has an imposing or distinctive architectural design or flair.

FANNIE MAE—A common name for the Federal National Mortgage Association.

FEE: FEE SIMPLE: FEE SIMPLE ABSOLUTE—All three terms are synonymous and mean that the owner has absolute, good and marketable title to the property conveyed to him. It is complete ownership without condition. Fee simple is the largest and highest possible estate one can possess in real estate. The owner of an estate in fee simple has every legal possession with unconditional power and right to dispose of it in his lifetime or retain it for his heirs.

FIDUCIARY—A position of trust and confidence. One who transacts business for another and by so doing establishes a relationship of great faith. A broker is automatically put in such a position when he is employed to act for another in real estate. A person performs in a fiduciary capacity when he is given authorization to act for the best interests of another.

FINDER'S FEE—As applied to real estate brokerage it is generally understood to mean a fee paid to another for furnishing a buyer or a property listing. As an example, it is not uncommon for a broker specializing in one phase of real estate to have prospects referred to him. If a sale results, the specializing broker would pay the referring broker a fee for "finding" the customer for him.

FLYSPECKING—A jargon word referring to the careful scrutiny of a document, particularly in reference to an abstract of title, to uncover every technical defect; the inference being that even a flyspeck will be detected and examined by the diligent searcher.

FRAUD—Deceiving; misrepresenting. An untruth in order to obtain an illegal advantage of or something of value from another. Willful deceit to deprive someone of his rights or otherwise to injure him. Fraud can follow three forms: 1. Actual fraud, which has to do with an intentional untruth, direct deceit or cunning and outright trickery; 2. Constructive fraud, which is less direct and relates to a person's conscience or to a breach of fiduciary relationship; and 3. Legal fraud, which refers to a misrepresentation made without knowingly doing so.

FREEHOLD—A real estate interest in fee simple or one that is not less than an estate for life. For an estate to be a freehold, it must have (a) the qualities of immobility, meaning land or an interest that is derived from land, and (b) ownership of indeterminate duration; that is, the length of time for the estate to endure cannot be fixed.

FRONT MONEY—Money required to get a project underway. Funds used for such matters as the down payment, feasibility study, preliminary plans, appraisal, survey, test borings, etc.

G

GRACE PERIOD—A period when a mortgage payment or other debt becomes due, and before it goes into default. Most mortgages provide for a specified period of time when it can be paid without penalty or default.

GROUND RENT—Rent for the possession and use of the land, often with a lease of long duration. The length can be for any span of time, but ground on which buildings are erected customarily have 49-year leases, 99-year leases, or longer.

H

HARD MONEY—Earnest money; down payment; good faith money. Hand money; deposit.

HEREDITAMENT—Property that can be inherited. It may be real, personal, tangible or intangible property, or the combination of these.

HOLDOVER TENANT—One who remains in possession of the premises after the term of his lease has expired. Also called a Tenant At Sufferance.

HOLOGRAPHIC INSTRUMENT—An instrument, such as a will, contract or deed completely written in the testator's own hand.

HYPOTHECATE—The pledge of property as security for a debt, without giving up possession of it.

I

INCURABLE TITLE—A cloud or other encumbrance on the title to property that cannot be removed, consequently preventing the transfer of ownership.

INGRESS—Entrance or access to property. The ability to enter upon land. The opposite of *egress*, which means going out.

IN INVITUM—Latin. Something uninvited and done against another's will. Proceedings or taxes imposed against one who does not consent to them.

IN PERSONAM—Latin. An action directed against a specific person. The opposite of *In Rem*.

INTERIM FINANCING—Short term, temporary financing that is generally in effect during a building's construction or until a permanent, long-term loan can be obtained.

INTERPLEADER—In real estate, the filing in the proper court, by a third party holding disputed funds in trust. By so doing, the third party divests himself of liability. The funds in trust are turned over to the court. The purpose of a Bill of Interpleader is to force the conflicting principals to litigate the dispute between themselves and not the third party. The third party relinquishes any claim to the money and in turn is relieved of any court costs or fees. If the third party desires to lay claim to all or part of the money in his trust, he should file for a Declaratory Judgment.

INTER-VIVOS TRUST—Latin. A trust formed by living people. It is the opposite of one that is created upon death.

INTESTATE—A person who dies without having made a will. Also, one who dies leaving an invalid will. His estate is given to administrators for settlement.

J

JOG—An irregular change in direction of a property line creating a small corner or pocket of land.

JOINT TENANCY—See *Tenancy*.

JUNIOR MORTGAGE—A second or third mortgage (or any other) that is subordinated to the first or prior mortgage.

JURAT—Latin. A clause found at the end of an affidavit, acknowledgment or any other legal instrument stating when, before whom, and where the document was sworn to. A sample jurat reads as follows:

        Witness my hand and official seal at_____,
        County of_____, State of_____, this_____day of
        _____, A.D. 19__.

JURISPRUDENCE—The study and philosophy of common law and its practice. A civilized state's body of laws and their application.

K

KEY LOT—1. A lot that is strategically located and thus has added market value. 2. A lot adjoining a corner lot at the corner lot's rear property line and fronting on the secondary street. Also referred to as a Butt Lot.

KICK-BACK—The unauthorized, secret payment of money to an individual or group in return for a favorable decision, information or assistance.

L

LACHES—Neglect or an undue lapse of time in bringing about a legal claim or asserting a right. As a long delay can change conditions and cloud memories, a court often dismisses an action that is not pursued with at least reasonable diligence.

LAND GRANT—A gift of government land to a university, public utility, railroad or the like that would be in the best interest and benefit of the general public.

LEGALITY OF OBJECT—Having a legal purpose. It is an essential element of every contract. If the purpose is not legal, a contract is automatically void.

LEVERAGE—In real estate, the word means effective use of money. It is usually accomplished by investing the least amount of capital possible when acquiring property in order that it may bring the maximum percentage of return. This can be done by mortgaging to the highest amount that is practical. As long as the mortgage payments and operating expenses are not prohibitively high, the greatest percentage of return on capital invested can generally be obtained in this manner.

LIGHT AND AIR EASEMENT—An easement that provides for open space in a specified area. For example, an owner of a building might obtain an easement from the owner of adjoining property that another building will not be erected on the property line, thereby assuring him light and air that otherwise would have been blocked out.

LIS PENDENS—Latin. A pending legal action.

LITTORAL LAND—Land bounded by a large body of water such as an ocean, sea or large lake. Property lines for littoral land are usually determined by the high water mark of the tide.

LOCUS SIGILLI—Latin. Abbreviated "L.S." and found at the end of signature lines on legal documents, it means "under seal" or "place of the seal" and appears as follows:

_____ L.S.

LOVE AND AFFECTION—The good or valuable consideration sometimes used when real estate is conveyed between members of a family with no money being exchanged. The law recognizes this as being legally as good as any other form of consideration.

M

MARKETABLE TITLE—Good title; clear title. Title to property that is free of significant defects and which a purchaser will accept without objections. Title under which an owner can be assured of quiet and peaceful enjoyment and that he can convey to others. It is marketable title in the sense that it is good enough not to present a valid objection to the sale of the property; merchantable title.

MASTER PLAN—A long-range, overall concept of an area's development generally proposed by the planning department of a city or other community. By projecting population changes and growth trends, it becomes possible to prepare plans for adequate highways, parks, housing and the overall highest and best usage of the land. A well prepared master plan can do much toward eliminating blighted and slum areas, inadequate public transportation facilities, insufficient and improper housing, over-crowded and congested business and residential areas. Proper master planning can result in important and lasting improvements made to America's cities and towns, thereby permanently enriching our standard of living.

MEANDER LINE—The uneven, winding property line formed by the natural turning of streams, rivers, brooks and other water courses.

MEETING OF THE MINDS—When two or more parties are in complete agreement as to price, terms and conditions of a sale, a common under-standing or meeting of the minds is said to take place. It comes about as a result of their expressed purpose and intentions.

MILLAGE—In conjunction with property taxes, it is the factor generally used to state the rate of taxation and compute the taxes. One mill per thousand is equivalent to $1 of taxes per thousand of assessed value. Thus, the assessed value multiplied by the millage rate will equal the tax rate. A mill is one-tenth part of one cent.

MORATORIUM—An authorized postponement in meeting an agreed obligation during a period of financial distress; temporary suspension of payments. A legal delay in paying an obligation; an officially granted waiting period.

MORTGAGEE—The one who holds the mortgage as security for the money he has loaned on property. The lender or creditor.

MORTGAGOR—The giver of a mortgage as security for money he bor-rows on his property.

MULTIPLE LISTING—An exclusive listing, for the sale or lease of real estate, given to one broker for distribution to others. Many local real estate boards have a central clearing house where multiple listings are submitted by member brokers. Photos and brochures are printed and sent to participating agents for cooperative sales. In this way, a client is assured his property will receive wide market exposure.

N

NAKED CONTRACT—A contract in which there is no consideration given, and is, therefore, uninforceable. Also called a Nude Contract.

NET INCOME—The money remaining after expenses are subtracted from the income. The profit.

NONBEARING WALL—A wall that does not help support the structure. The opposite of a Bearing Wall, which is built to hold the weight of the floors above. Also referred to as a Nonload Bearing wall.

NONCONFORMING USE—The lawful use of land or improvements upon it that do not comply with current zoning regulations. It is allowed to remain as it was before the zoning ordinance was passed. Generally, such properties cannot be replaced, remodeled or enlarged.

NOTORIOUS POSSESSION—Possession of land that is obvious and common knowledge to the neighbors or the public in general. It is a legal requirement before one can obtain property by Adverse Posssession.

NOVATION—The exchange or substitution of a new obligation or debt for an old one by mutual agreement.

O

OBLIGEE—A party to whom something is owed; the creditor. One to whom another has an obligation to perform.

OBLIGOR—One who has an obligation to fulfill; the debtor.

OPEN-END MORTGAGE—A mortgage which permits the borrower to reborrow the money paid on the principal, usually up to the original amount.

OPEN LISTING—A listing made available to more than one broker. The first one who procures a buyer, Ready, Willing and Able for the price and terms of the listing, is the one who receives the commission. The listing is then automatically terminated.

OPEN LOT—A parcel of land having all sides fronting on streets.

OPEN MORTGAGE—1. A mortgage that can be paid off at any time before maturity without penalty. 2. When mortgage payments are overdue, it is sometimes referred to as an "open mortgage," in that it is open for a foreclosure action.

OPINION OF TITLE—An attorney's opinion as to how good the title to a specified piece of property is after he studies the abstract. He renders a judgment as to whether the seller has good and marketable title, defective title or any title at all.

ORAL CONTRACT—A contract that may be partly in writing and partly verbal, or one that is completely verbal; a Parol Contract. Though oral contracts are said to be binding, they are considered virtually unenforceable.

ORDINANCE—A law or rule of order established by a recognized, authoritative agency. A local government's code, regulation or statute.

ORIGINATION FEE—In reference to mortgaging, it is a charge for establishing and processing a new mortgage loan.

OVERAGE—Retail store leases are sometimes established at a minimum figure with a percentage of the volume of business the store does over a specified amount going to the landlord as additional rent. This amount is referred to as overage.

P

PAPER—A jargon reference to the taking of a note or mortgage in lieu of cash. When there is limited money being put down in a real estate transaction, the seller may agree to take the balance in "paper."

PARTY WALL—A wall built between two adjoining parcels. One built on the property line as a common part of two structures separately owned. Each owner has an equal interest in the wall, which may not be disturbed without their joint consent.

PASSING TITLE—The change in ownership of real property. The actual handing over of title to the new owner. A closing.

PENDENS—Latin. Pending. *Lis Pendens* is a notice of a pending legal action.

PERPETUITY—Endless; the quality of being perpetual. An estate is said to be willed in perpetuity.

P.I.T.I.—Abbreviation of Principal, Interest, Taxes and Insurance when stating the monthly carrying charges of a mortgage.

PLANNED UNIT DEVELOPMENT (PUD)—Complete community development, including an area's housing needs, stores, recreation facilities, industrial space, etc.

POINT—1. A "point" represents 1 percent of the principal amount. The term is most frequently used when referring to mortgage premiums. It is a method used by lenders to obtain additional revenue over the interest rate. 2. As used in legal descriptions, it is the extreme end of a boundary line.

POLICE POWER—The control that a government has over the life and property of its citizens. The exercising of police power should be in the best interest of the general public, and not in conflict with the Fourteenth Amendment to the United States Constitution, which protects the civil rights and freedom of the individual.

POSSESSORY INTEREST—The rights and interest one has in possessing property: the use, benefits and enjoyment of it.

POWER OF ATTORNEY—A written authority for one to act as another's agent. The extent of the authority is limited to that stated in the instrument. A power of attorney is also known as an attorney-in-fact.

PREPAYMENT CLAUSE—A clause in a mortgage permitting the mortgagee to pay all or part of the unpaid balance before it becomes due, thereby saving the interest or clearing the way for a new mortgage. A typical prepayment clause reads as follows: "The purchaser shall have the privilege at any time of paying any sum or sums in addition to the payments herein required upon the consideration, and it is understood and agreed that no such prepayment, except payment in full, shall stop the accrual of interest on the amount so paid until the next succeeding semiannual computation of interest after such payment is made as herein provided." A short form of this clause reads: "This mortgage may be prepaid in full or part at any time without penalty."

PRIMA FACIE—Latin. On the face of it; an obvious fact; on the surface. Evidence at first hand; presumably.

PRIVITY—A mutual relationship of people having the same legal interest in a right or in property.

PROBATE COURT—A court dealing with wills, estate settlements, intestate succession and guardianships. It is also referred to as a Surrogate Court or County Judges Court.

PRO FORMA—Latin. According to a prescribed form; as a matter of form.

PRORATE—Proportion according to one's interest. In real estate contracts, for example, taxes, insurance, rents, interest and certain other annual expenses of the property are generally prorated at the time of closing or when the sale is recorded. A proportionate amount of these fixed expenses is charged to the seller and buyer.

PUD—Abbreviation for *Planned Unit development*. See that term.

PUFF—The superlative, sometimes exaggerated buildup a salesman or the seller may give to property. It is recognized in law as an opinion and not necessarily representing the facts.

PURCHASE MONEY MORTGAGE—A mortgage which is taken at the time of closing by the seller in lieu of part or all of the money required to make up the purchase price.

Q

QUALITY OF ESTATE—The manner in which an estate is to be owned as to type of possession (sole, jointly, tenancy-in-common, etc.) and time (present or future). The term does not allude to value or physical characteristics of the estate.

QUASI—Latin. "As if." Having a limited legal status. Sufficiently similar but not actual; in some degree; almost. A combination form, familiar to the real estate field, with such words as quasi-contract; quasi-possession; quasi-corporation; quasi-official; quasi-judicial, etc.

QUIET ENJOYMENT—The right an owner or tenant has to enjoy property in peace and without disturbance. When referring to ownership, quiet enjoyment means freedom from being disturbed by title defects. Applied to a tenant, it takes on the added meaning of his right of privacy and his not being unnecessarily disturbed.

QUIT-CLAIM DEED—The instrument used to remove any and all claims or interest in ownership that an individual may have without his warranting the quality or validity of the title. In some sections of the country, quit-claim deeds are used when there is a questionable interest in the property or to remove a cloud upon the title. In other areas, they are more commonly used in ordinary transactions to transfer title without warranting it.

R

RATIFICATION—Confirmation; affirmation. Making something binding by formally approving it. Validation.

READY, WILLING AND ABLE—The phrase means that a buyer is completely agreeable and fully qualified to enter into and consummate a transaction. "Ready" means that he is prepared at this time to enter into a contract. "Willing" refers to a person's own free choice and that he is of a mind to buy. "Able" has to do with his ability to meet the financial requirements of the agreement.

REAL ESTATE INVESTMENT TRUST (REIT)—A group of real estate investors consisting of one or more trustees who hold title to the assets for the trust, and control its acquisitions, management and sale. Though unincorporated, the trust must be owned in the form of shares by one hundred or more people (no five of whom are to possess over 50 percent interest). The major advantage of a business structure of this nature is the tax benefit, as no corporation tax need be paid. A disadvantage are the strict federal and state regulatory requirements as to the type of investments that can be made. When a real estate investments trust has shareholders in more than one state, they are also subject to Security and Exchange Commission regulations.

REALTOR—"A professional in real estate who subscribes to a strict Code of Ethics as a member of the local and state boards and of the National Association of Realtors." The term Realtor is a service mark registered in the United States Patent Office. Only members of the National Association of Realtors and its state and local affiliates may use it and display its seal.

RECAPTURE CLAUSE—1. A clause in leases giving the landlord the right to terminate the lease if certain conditions or standards are not maintained, such as may occur in a percentage lease, where the landlord has the right to cancel if a specified minimum volume of business is not maintained. 2. A clause found in ground leases providing an option for the outright purchase of the land for a specific price and at a specified time in the future.

RECASTING A MORTGAGE—The act of reconstructing an existing mortgage by increasing its amount, interest rate or length of time.

RECONVEYANCE—To convey or return ownership of real estate to one who previously had title to it. The transfer of title back to its former owner.

RECORD—1. A written statement; to officially commit to writing; to transcribe for future use or reference. 2. Placing a document on the public records by recording it in the proper county office where the general public may examine it.

REDDENDUM CLAUSE—A clause in a conveyance that reserves something to the grantor out of what he has granted. In a lease, for example, it reserves the periodic rent payments to the lessor. It may also cause a future interest in land to be retained, as occurs in the granting of a life estate. It is the clause that first renders or yields, then reserves something out of it to be returned.

RELICTION—Land uncovered by the permanent receding of a water line. This can occur when a river changes course or a build-up of sand deposits takes place on sea or oceanfront properties. The new land thus formed becomes the property of the riparian owner. Also referred to as Dereliction.

REMAINDER ESTATE—An estate that comes into being upon the termination of a prior estate, such as when an owner grants a life estate to one party. Upon completion of the life estate, the property either reverts to the owner or goes to another (generally an heir). If the owner does not take it back, a remainder estate is created. The holder of such an estate is called a Remainderman.

RENUNCIATION—The unilateral act of relinquishing a right to or interest in property, usually without consideration and without transferring title. Abandonment.

REPLEVIN—Legal proceedings referred to as a possessory action to recover personal belongings that have been unlawfully taken (usually for nonpayment of rent).

RESTRICTIVE COVENANTS—Agreements written into instruments that curtail the full use of the property. As for example, imposing limitations on the density of buildings per acre, permitting only certain sizes and styles of structures to be erected, preventing particular businesses from operating or barring minority groups from owning or occupying homes in a given area. (This latter discriminatory covenant has been declared unconstitutional by the United States Supreme Court.) Also referred to as Protective Covenants.

REVERSIONARY INTEREST—The future interest a person has in property that is presently in another's possession.

REVERTER—That which reverts; reversion. That portion of an estate which returns to an owner or his heirs at the end of an Estate in Reversion.

RIGHT(S)—1. That which is just, proper and lawful. 2. The democratic concept that power, privilege and free action are born to all men. 3. An interest in or title to property. A well founded, established legal claim.

The word is in continual use in connection with real estate in such terms as Exclusive Right, Riparian Rights, Vested Rights, Right of Privacy, Right of Possession, Right of Property, Right of Redemption, Right of Survivorship, Right, Title and Interest, Right of Way, Squatter's Rights, and so on.

RIPARIAN RIGHTS—An owner's natural rights in regard to the banks of a river, stream or other watercourse, including access rights, accretion rights, abutting rights, reasonable use of the water and the right to the soil under the water. The rights of owners in connection wtih ocean and sea-front property, though sometimes referred to as riparian rights, should more accurately be called Littoral Rights.

RISK CAPITAL—Invested capital that is speculative in nature and the least secured, consequently offering the greatest chance of loss.

RULE AGAINST PERPETUITIES—A rule of law that disallows the granting of a future estate if it is not vested within the life or lives then in being, plus 21 years and the gestation period (9 months) from the time the estate was created.

S

SCILICET—Latin. To wit; that is to say. It is abbreviated as "SS."

SECTION OF LAND—As used in the Government Survey of public lands, it is an area one mile square containing 640 acres. A section is 1/36th of a township.

SETBACK LINE—A zoning regulation prohibiting the construction of a building, beyond a prescribed distance from the property line. Most local zoning ordinances require structures to be set back specified distances from the street, as well as from rear and side lines.

SETTLEMENT—1. The process of making adjustments in a business transaction, an estate or in a legal dispute. 2. In real estate, it is the transfer of title with the resulting financial prorations and adjustments. A Closing.

SEVERALTY—Sole ownership. An estate held by one person only; no other individual has any part or interest in the estate.

SEXTERY LANDS—Property given to and maintained by a church.

SHELTER—Protection; refuge. Certain types of income property, for example, offer great tax savings by allowing the owner to deduct depreciation of the improvements from otherwise taxable income. This is referred to as a Tax Shelter.

SHORT FORM—Legal instruments that do not actually contain the usually lengthy statute laws, although they are implied, and have the same effect as if they were included.

SIMPLE INTEREST—Interest that is computed on the principal amount of a loan only. No amount need be paid for amassing interest, as occurs with a loan containing Compound Interest.

SPECIFICATIONS—Detailed information covering exact measurements, elevations, type of materials, workmanship, and other elements that go into a structure.

SPECIFIC PERFORMANCE—1. Performing exactly, or as reasonably so as possible, the terms of a contract. Fulfilling specifically as agreed. 2. In the event of a default by one of the parties, it is the name given the lawsuit brought for failure to perform as stated in the agreement.

SQUATTER'S RIGHTS—A squatter may begin to obtain rights when his occupancy is considered in adverse possession. Occupancy must be in "actual, open, notorious, exclusive and continuous" possession for a prescribed statutory period. State laws vary as to the amount of time; some require as short a period as five or seven years, with others up to 20.

STATUTE—1. A written law of a government's legislative body. 2. An act of a corporation, university, society, etc. setting forth its rules, bylaws or regulations.

STATUTE OF FRAUDS—All states recognize the early English statute (enacted in the year 1677) which provides that real estate contracts must be in writing and duly signed to be enforceable. In general, oral contracts pertaining to real property are not enforceable by law. This statute was founded to prevent frauds and perjuries, and has been enlarged to become a basic concept and foundation of real estate and contract law.

STATUTE OF LIMITATIONS—A statute placing a time limit on the right of action in certain cases where a remedy is sought in a court of law.

STRAIGHT LOAN—A flat loan.

SUBORDINATION—When a lien holder agrees to place his interest in lesser rank than another. This frequently occurs when the seller of vacant land, in order to make the sale, takes back a mortgage and agrees to lower its rank to second position behind a construction or permanent loan.

SUBROGATION—Replacing one person with another in regard to a legal right, interest or obligation. Substitution, such as a mortgage holder's selling his rights and interest to another.

SYNDICATE—An association of investors who undertake to success-fully transact business for a limited period of time. A short-term partner-ship. A group of individuals who combine abilities and finances in a business venture. Similar to a joint venture.

T

TAXPAYER—1. A property owner who pays taxes. 2. A one-story building, typically a store, originally so called because the revenue from it was sufficient only to pay the taxes on the property. Though still called taxpayers, stores as income-producing real estate are now often highly profitable forms of investment, bringing far greater return to the owner than merely the taxes.

TAX SHELTER—Tax protection. See SHELTER.

TENANCY—1. The act of occupying property belonging to another. Possession by any of numerous forms of title, such as:

Joint Tenancy—An estate held by two or more people with equal and undivided interest and ownership. Upon the death of one, his interest automatically passes to the survivor(s).

Tenancy at Will—A tenant who is legally occupying property but has no fixed term or lease.

Tenancy by the Entirety—A joint estate equally owned by husband and wife, with the survivor receiving the entire estate.

Tenancy in Common—A tenancy where two or more people own property with each possessing a separate, undivided interest.

Tenancy in Partnership—One created when property is purchased with funds of a business partnership.

Tenant at Sufferance—A tenant who originally lawfully occupied but remained in possession after the tenancy has expired.

Tenant for Life—One who possesses property for the term of his life, or during the life or lives of others.

Tenant in Severalty—A tenancy held by one person only. No other person has any part or interest.

TENEMENT—1. An apartment house; any structure being occupied as a dwelling; a residence. The term's common meaning refers to older, run-down, city apartment buildings. 2. Land or corporeal and incorporeal property being held by one person though owned by another. Tenement refers to everything of a permanent nature.

TENENDUM—Latin. That portion of a deed that is united with the *habendum clause*, indicating that the grantee is "to have and to hold" the subject land.

TESTIMONY CLAUSE—A clause at the end of a document that reads, "In witness whereof, I hereunto set my hand and official seal at said County and State, this_____ day   of_____, A.D. 19__."

THROW-OFF—A slang reference to the income that a property will bring.

TIME IS THE ESSENCE CLAUSE—The clause in a contract that places great importance on completing the terms and conditions exactly when specified. It means the specific date is an essential element of the agreement.

U

UNEARNED INCREMENT—An increase in property value that came about because of outside factors and not necessarily through any knowledgeable acts of the owner. It is often due to an increase in population and the normal economic growth and real estate appreciation that follow.

UNILATERAL CONTRACT—A contract in which only one party expressly agrees to something. Unlike a fully executed (bilateral) contract, just one principal is bound by the terms of the agreement. As an example, a contract that has been signed by the purchaser but not as yet by the seller. It can be recalled and declared void at any time prior to it becoming a bilateral agreement.

URBAN RENEWAL—The acquisition of slum or run-down city areas for purposes of redevelopment. Federal, state and local governments are working cooperatively to eliminate blighted sections throughout some of our most heavily populated communities. The Department of Housing and Urban Development (HUD) has instituted programs of redevelopment in certain major cities throughout the country to clear and replace slum areas with low-rent, public housing. It is called the Model Cities program.

USURY—The charging of excessively high or unlawful interest rates for the use of money.

V

VENDEE—A buyer; purchaser. In a contract, he is usually called the party of the second part.

VENDOR—A seller. In a contract, he is usually referred to as the party of the first part.

VENTURE CAPITAL—Risk capital. Money invested that is unsecured. Because of the risks involved it usually offers the highest percentage of return for the investment.

VISIBLE AMENITIES—The visual, apparent attractiveness, pleasantness and desirability that a property possesses. Its outward appearance.

VIZ—Latin. An abbreviation of *videlicet* meaning "to wit," "that is to say," "namely."

W

WILLING—Consenting of one's own free choice and without reluctance.

WITH PREJUDICE—In law, when an adverse decision is made "with prejudice," it means that the court has issued a final decision and no further appeal to that court will be heard, nor will the opinion rendered be altered. The judge's decision is final.

WITHOUT PREJUDICE—In law, when a decision is handed down "without prejudice," it means that an individual's right to amend his appeal or seek a different verdict has not been jeopardized.

WITHOUT RECOURSE—This term is most frequently found in endorsements of negotiable instruments, and means that the endorser does not assume responsibility or liability for its collection.

WRIT—A court order, under seal, directing a person or group to do or refrain from doing something.

X

X—In signing legal documents, individuals who cannot write should affix an "X" where the signature would ordinarily go. A witness writes the person's name around the mark as follows:

his
Robert (X) Jones
mark

Y

YIELD—1. That which an investment or property will return; the profit or income. The money derived from any given business venture. 2. To turn over or surrender possession.

Z

ZONING—The division of an area into separate districts reserved for different real property usages such as business, residential, light, medium or heavy industry, etc., as well as regulating the type and density of the improvements upon it.

Appendix II

TABLES AND CHARTS

Measurement Tables . . . Section of Land Showing Area and Distances . . . Determining the Number of Acres in a Field . . . Table of Square Foot Land Values . . . Monthly Payments to Amortize a Loan for Each $1,000 of Loan . . . Constant Annual Percent Table . . . Mortgage Pay-Off Table . . . Even Total Percentage . . . Present Value of $1 Due at Various Times in Future and at Various Interest Rates . . . Percentage of Principal Unpaid at End of 5-10-15 Years by Interest Rate.

A good real estate broker is expected to possess a storehouse of information. Facts and figures must either be in his head or at his fingertips. This is part of his stock in trade, and every successful real estate professional knows where to find what he can not possibly keep in mind.

The tables and charts reproduced here have been carefully selected for their overall usefulness to the general real estate practitioner.

MEASUREMENT TABLES

Linear Measure

1 foot equals 12 inches
1 yard equals 3 feet
1 meter equals 3 feet 3.7 inches
1 rod equals 16½ feet, 5½ yards or 25 links

1 chain is 66 feet or 4 rods or 100 links
1 furlong is 660 feet or 40 rods
1 mile is 8 furlongs, 320 rods, 80 chains or 5,280 feet

Square Measure

144 square inches equal 1 square foot
  9 square feet equal 1 square yard
 30¼ square yards equal 1 square rod
 40 square rods equal 1 rood
  4 roods equal 1 acre
640 acres equal 1 square mile

Surveyor's Linear Measure

7.92 inches equal 1 link
25 links equal 1 rod
 4 rods equal 1 chain
80 chains equal 1 mile

Surveyor's Square Measure

625 square links equal 1 pole
 16 poles equal 1 square chain
 10 square chains equal 1 acre
640 acres equal 1 square mile
 36 square miles equal 1 township

SECTION OF LAND SHOWING
AREA AND DISTANCES

A section of land contains 1 square mile or 640 acres

20 CHAINS-80 RODS	20 CHAINS-80 RODS	40 CHAINS - 160 RODS			
W½ N.W¼ 80 ACRES	E½ N.W¼ 80 ACRES	N.E¼ 160 ACRES			
1320 FT	1320 FT	2640 FT			
N.W¼ S.W¼ 40 ACRES	N.E¼ S W¼ 40 ACRES	N½ N.W¼ S.E¼ 20 ACRES		W½ N.E¼ S.E¼ 20 ACRES	E½ N.E¼ S.E¼ 20 ACRES
		S½ N.W¼ S.E¼ 20 ACRES 20 CHAINS		10-CHAINS	10-CHAINS
S W¼ S.W¼ 40 ACRES 80-RODS	S.E¼ S.W¼ 40 ACRES 440 YARDS	N.W¼ S.W¼ S.E¼ 10 ACRES	N.E¼ S.W¼ S.E¼ 10 ACRES	5 ACRES 5-ACRES 1-FURLONG	5 ACRES 5 CHS.
					5 ACRES 20 RDS
		S.W¼ S.W¼ S.E¼ 10 ACRES 660 FT.	S.E¼ S.W¼ S.E¼ 10 ACRES 660 FT.	2½ ACRS 2½ ACRS 330 FT	2½ ACRS 2½ ACRS 330 FT	10 ACRES MAY BE SUBDIVIDED INTO ABOUT 80 LOTS OF 50 x125 EACH

⇐ONE MILE - 320 RODS - 80 CHAINS OR 5280 FT.⇒

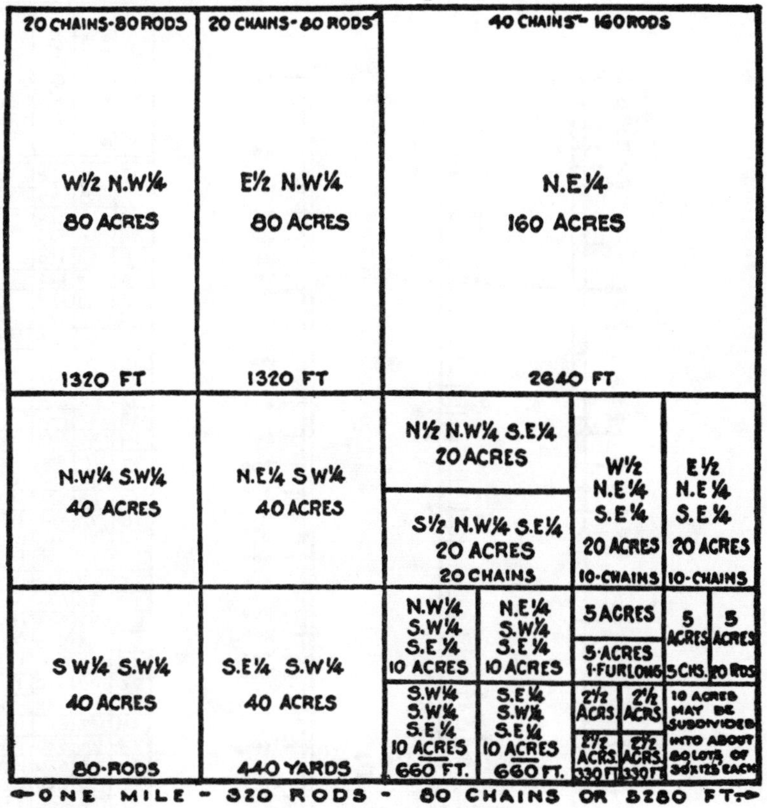

Measurements Relating to Section and Township

1 acre contains 43,560 square feet
1 acre contains 160 square rods
1 acre is about 8 rods by 20 rods long, or any two numbers (of rods)
   whose product is 160
1 acre may be divided into about 4 lots 60 × 125 feet
1 hectare contains 2.47 acres
1 section of land contains 1 square mile or 640 acres
1 township (6 miles × 6 miles) equals 36 square miles
1 check (24 miles × 24 miles) equals 576 square miles

DETERMINING THE NUMBER OF
ACRES IN A FIELD

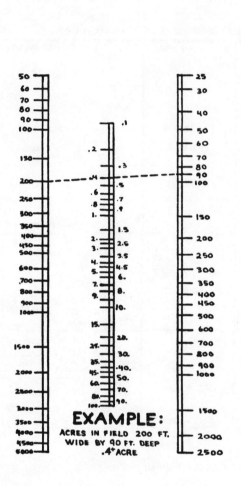

CHAINS	RODS, POLES PERCHES	YARDS	FEET
		EQUIVALENTS	
1	4	22	66
2	8	44	132
3	12	66	198
4	16	88	264
5	20	110	330
6	24	132	396
7	28	154	462
8	32	176	528
9	36	198	594
10	40	220	660
11	44	242	726
12	48	264	792
13	52	286	858
14	56	308	924
15	60	330	990
16	64	352	1056
17	68	374	1122
18	72	396	1188
19	76	418	1254
20	80	440	1320
21	84	462	1386
22	88	484	1452
23	92	506	1518
24	96	528	1584
25	100	550	1650
26	104	572	1716
27	108	594	1782
28	112	616	1848
29	116	638	1914
30	120	660	1980
31	124	682	2046
32	128	704	2112
33	132	726	2178
34	136	748	2244
35	140	770	2310
36	144	792	2376
37	148	814	2442
38	152	836	2508
39	156	858	2574
40	160	880	2640

EXAMPLE:
ACRES IN FIELD 200 FT.
WIDE BY 90 FT. DEEP
.4⁺ ACRE

TABLE OF SQUARE FOOT LAND VALUES

Land, particularly in urban areas, is frequently quoted by the square foot. This table shows both the value of a lot 25' × 100' and that of an acre.

Value per Sq. Ft. of Land	Value of a Lot 25 x 100	Value of an Acre	Value per Sq. Ft. of Land	Value of a Lot 25 x 100	Value of an Acre
$ .01	$ 25.00	$ 435.60	$ .51	$ 1,275.00	$ 22,215.60
.02	50.00	871.20	.52	1,300.00	22,651.20
.03	75.00	1,306.80	.53	1,325.00	23,086.80
.04	100.00	1,742.40	.54	1,350.00	23,522.40
.05	125.00	2,178.00	.55	1,375.00	23,958.00
.06	150.00	2,613.60	.56	1,400.00	24,393.60
.07	175.00	3,049.20	.57	1,425.00	24,829.20
.08	200.00	3,484.80	.58	1,450.00	25,264.80
.09	225.00	3,920.40	.59	1,475.00	25,700.40
.10	250.00	4,356.00	.60	1,500.00	26,136.00
.11	275.00	4,791.60	.61	1,525.00	26,571.60
.12	300.00	5,227.20	.62	1,550.00	27,007.20
.13	325.00	5,662.80	.63	1,575.00	27,442.80
.14	350.00	6,098.40	.64	1,600.00	27,878.40
.15	375.00	6,534.00	.65	1,625.00	28,314.00
.16	400.00	6,969.60	.66	1,650.00	28,749.60
.17	425.00	7,405.20	.67	1,675.00	29,185.20
.18	450.00	7,840.80	.68	1,700.00	29,620.80
.19	475.00	8,276.40	.69	1,725.00	30,056.40
.20	500.00	8,712.00	.70	1,750.00	30,492.00
.21	525.00	9,147.60	.71	1,775.00	30,927.60
.22	550.00	9,583.20	.72	1,800.00	31,363.20
.23	575.00	10,018.80	.73	1,825.00	31,798.80
.24	600.00	10,454.40	.74	1,850.00	32,234.40
.25	625.00	10,890.00	.75	1,875.00	32,670.00
.26	650.00	11,325.60	.76	1,900.00	33,105.60
.27	675.00	11,761.20	.77	1,925.00	33,541.20
.28	700.60	12,196.80	.78	1,950.00	33,976.80
.29	725.00	12,632.40	.79	1,975.00	34,412.40
.30	750.00	13,068.00	.80	2,000.00	34,848.00
.31	775.00	13,503.60	.81	2,025.00	35,283.60
.32	800.00	13,939.20	.82	2,050.00	35,719.20
.33	825.00	14,374.80	.83	2,075.00	36,154.80
.34	850.00	14,810.40	.84	2,100.00	36,590.40
.35	875.00	15,246.00	.85	2,125.00	37,026.00
.36	900.00	15,681.60	.86	2,150.00	37,461.60
.37	925.00	16,117.20	.87	2,175.00	37,897.20
.38	950.00	16,552.80	.88	2,200.00	38,332.80
.39	975.00	16,988.40	.89	2,225.00	38,768.40
.40	1,000.00	17,424.00	.90	2,250.00	39,204.00
.41	1,025.00	17,859.60	.91	2,275.00	39,639.60
.42	1,050.00	18,295.20	.92	2,300.00	40,075.20
.43	1,075.00	18,730.80	.93	2,325.00	40,510.80
.44	1,100.00	19,166.40	.94	2,350.00	40,946.40
.45	1,125.00	19,602.00	.95	2,375.00	41,382.00
.46	1,150.00	20,037.60	.96	2,400.00	41,817.60
.47	1,175.00	20,473.20	.97	2,425.00	42,253.20
.48	1,200.00	20,908.80	.98	2,450.00	42,688.80
.49	1,225.00	21,344.40	.99	2,475.00	43,124.40
.50	1,250.00	21,780.00	1.00	2,500.00	43,560.00

MONTHLY PAYMENTS NECESSARY TO AMORTIZE
A LOAN FOR EACH $1,000 OF LOAN (*)

Yrs	4½%	4¾%	5%	5¼%	5½%	5¾%	6%	6½%	7%	8%	9%	10%
1	85.38	85.50	85.61	85.73	85.84	85.96	86.07	86.30	86.53	86.99	87.46	87.92
2	43.65	43.76	43.88	43.99	44.10	44.21	44.33	44.55	44.78	45.23	45.69	46.15
3	29.75	29.86	29.88	30.09	30.20	30.31	30.43	30.65	30.88	31.34	31.80	32.27
4	22.81	22.92	23.03	23.15	23.26	23.38	23.49	23.72	23.95	24.42	24.89	25.37
5	18.65	18.76	18.88	18.99	19.11	19.22	19.34	19.57	19.81	20.28	20.76	21.25
6	15.88	15.99	16.11	16.23	16.34	16.46	16.58	16.81	17.05	17.54	18.03	18.53
7	13.91	14.02	14.14	14.26	14.38	14.49	14.61	14.85	15.10	15.59	16.09	16.61
8	12.43	12.55	12.66	12.78	12.90	13.03	13.15	13.39	13.64	14.14	14.66	15.18
9	11.28	11.40	11.52	11.64	11.76	11.89	12.01	12.26	12.51	13.02	13.55	14.08
10	10.37	10.49	10.61	10.73	10.86	10.98	11.11	11.36	11.62	12.14	12.67	13.22
11	9.62	9.75	9.87	9.99	10.12	10.25	10.37	10.63	10.89	11.42	11.97	12.52
12	9.01	9.13	9.25	9.38	9.51	9.63	9.76	10.02	10.29	10.83	11.39	11.96
13	8.48	8.61	8.74	8.86	8.99	9.12	9.25	9.52	9.79	10.34	10.90	11.48
14	8.04	8.17	8.29	8.42	8.55	8.68	8.82	9.09	9.36	9.92	10.49	11.09
15	7.65	7.78	7.91	8.04	8.18	8.31	8.44	8.72	8.99	9.56	10.15	10.75
16	7.32	7.45	7.58	7.71	7.85	7.98	8.12	8.40	8.68	9.25	9.85	10.46
17	7.03	7.16	7.29	7.43	7.56	7.70	7.84	8.12	8.40	8.99	9.59	10.22
18	6.77	6.90	7.04	7.17	7.31	7.45	7.59	7.87	8.16	8.75	9.37	10.00
19	6.54	6.67	6.81	6.95	7.08	7.22	7.37	7.65	7.95	8.55	9.17	9.82
20	6.33	6.47	6.60	6.74	6.88	7.03	7.17	7.46	7.76	8.37	9.00	9.66
21	6.15	6.28	6.42	6.56	6.70	6.85	6.99	7.29	7.59	8.21	8.85	9.51
22	5.98	6.12	6.26	6.40	6.54	6.69	6.84	7.13	7.44	8.07	8.72	9.39
23	5.83	5.97	6.11	6.25	6.40	6.54	6.69	7.00	7.30	7.94	8.60	9.28
24	5.69	5.83	5.97	6.12	6.27	6.41	6.56	6.87	7.18	7.83	8.49	9.18
25	5.56	5.71	5.85	6.00	6.15	6.30	6.45	6.76	7.07	7.72	8.40	9.09
26	5.45	5.59	5.74	5.89	6.04	6.19	6.34	6.65	6.97			
27	5.34	5.49	5.64	5.78	5.94	6.09	6.24	6.56	6.88			
28	5.24	5.39	5.54	5.69	5.84	6.00	6.16	6.48	6.80			
29	5.15	5.30	5.45	5.61	5.76	5.92	6.08	6.40	6.73			
30	5.07	5.22	5.37	5.53	5.68	5.84	6.00	6.33	6.66			

* (All payments shown hereon represent principal & interest only)

CONSTANT ÀNNUAL PERCENT TABLE

Select the interest rate and the term of the mortgage and read the annual *percent* to amortize.

CONSTANT ANNUAL PERCENT TO AMORTIZE

INTEREST RATE

YEARS	6 1/2	6 5/8	6 3/4	6 7/8	7	7 1/8	7 1/4	7 3/8
5	23.48	23.55	23.63	23.70	23.77	23.84	23.91	23.98
6	20.18	20.25	20.32	20.39	20.46	20.54	20.61	20.68
7	17.82	17.90	17.97	18.04	18.12	18.19	18.26	18.34
8	16.07	16.14	16.22	16.29	16.37	16.44	16.52	16.59
9	14.71	14.79	14.86	14.94	15.01	15.09	15.16	15.24
10	13.63	13.71	13.78	13.86	13.94	14.02	14.09	14.17
11	12.75	12.83	12.91	12.99	13.07	13.14	13.22	13.30
12	12.03	12.11	12.19	12.27	12.35	12.43	12.51	12.59
13	11.42	11.50	11.58	11.66	11.74	11.82	11.91	11.99
14	10.90	10.98	11.07	11.15	11.23	11.31	11.40	11.48
15	10.46	10.54	10.62	10.71	10.79	10.87	10.96	11.04
16	10.07	10.16	10.24	10.33	10.41	10.50	10.58	10.67
17	9.74	9.82	9.91	9.99	10.08	10.17	10.25	10.34
18	9.44	9.53	9.62	9.70	9.79	9.88	9.97	10.06
19	9.18	9.27	9.36	9.45	9.54	9.62	9.71	9.80
20	8.95	9.04	9.13	9.22	9.31	9.40	9.49	9.58
21	8.75	8.84	8.93	9.02	9.11	9.20	9.29	9.38
22	8.56	8.65	8.74	8.83	8.93	9.02	9.11	9.21
23	8.39	8.49	8.58	8.67	8.76	8.86	8.95	9.05
24	8.24	8.34	8.43	8.52	8.62	8.71	8.81	8.90
25	8.11	8.20	8.30	8.39	8.49	8.58	8.68	8.78
26	7.98	8.08	8.17	8.27	8.37	8.46	8.56	8.66
27	7.87	7.97	8.06	8.16	8.26	8.36	8.46	8.55
28	7.77	7.87	7.96	8.06	8.16	8.26	8.36	8.46
29	7.68	7.77	7.87	7.97	8.07	8.17	8.27	8.37
30	7.59	7.69	7.79	7.89	7.99	8.09	8.19	8.29
31	7.51	7.61	7.71	7.81	7.91	8.02	8.12	8.22
32	7.44	7.54	7.64	7.74	7.85	7.95	8.05	8.16
33	7.37	7.47	7.58	7.68	7.78	7.89	7.99	8.09
34	7.31	7.41	7.52	7.62	7.72	7.83	7.93	8.04
35	7.25	7.36	7.46	7.57	7.67	7.78	7.88	7.99
36	7.20	7.31	7.41	7.52	7.62	7.73	7.84	7.94
37	7.15	7.26	7.36	7.47	7.58	7.68	7.79	7.90
38	7.11	7.22	7.32	7.43	7.54	7.64	7.75	7.86
39	7.07	7.18	7.28	7.39	7.50	7.61	7.72	7.82
40	7.03	7.14	7.25	7.35	7.46	7.57	7.68	7.79
41	7.00	7.10	7.21	7.32	7.43	7.54	7.65	7.76
42	6.96	7.07	7.18	7.29	7.40	7.51	7.62	7.73
43	6.93	7.04	7.15	7.26	7.37	7.48	7.59	7.71
44	6.90	7.01	7.12	7.23	7.35	7.46	7.57	7.68
45	6.88	6.99	7.10	7.21	7.32	7.43	7.55	7.66
46	6.85	6.96	7.07	7.19	7.30	7.41	7.53	7.64
47	6.83	6.94	7.05	7.17	7.28	7.39	7.51	7.62
48	6.81	6.92	7.03	7.15	7.26	7.37	7.49	7.60
49	6.79	6.90	7.01	7.13	7.24	7.36	7.47	7.59
50	6.77	6.88	7.00	7.11	7.23	7.34	7.46	7.57

CONSTANT ANNUAL PERCENT TO AMORTIZE

INTEREST RATE

YEARS	7 1/2	7 5/8	7 3/4	7 7/8	8	8 1/8	8 1/4	8 3/8
5	24.05	24.12	24.19	24.26	24.34	24.41	24.48	24.55
6	20.75	20.83	20.90	20.97	21.04	21.12	21.19	21.27
7	18.41	18.49	18.56	18.63	18.71	18.78	18.86	18.93
8	16.67	16.74	16.82	16.89	16.97	17.05	17.12	17.20
9	15.32	15.40	15.47	15.55	15.63	15.71	15.78	15.86
10	14.25	14.33	14.41	14.49	14.56	14.64	14.72	14.80
11	13.38	13.46	13.54	13.62	13.70	13.78	13.87	13.95
12	12.67	12.75	12.83	12.91	12.99	13.08	13.16	13.24
13	12.07	12.15	12.24	12.32	12.40	12.49	12.57	12.65
14	11.56	11.65	11.73	11.82	11.90	11.99	12.07	12.16
15	11.13	11.21	11.30	11.39	11.47	11.56	11.65	11.73
16	10.75	10.84	10.93	11.02	11.10	11.19	11.28	11.37
17	10.43	10.52	10.61	10.69	10.78	10.87	10.96	11.05
18	10.14	10.23	10.32	10.41	10.50	10.60	10.69	10.78
19	9.89	9.98	10.08	10.17	10.26	10.35	10.44	10.54
20	9.67	9.76	9.86	9.95	10.04	10.14	10.23	10.32
21	9.47	9.57	9.66	9.76	9.85	9.94	10.04	10.14
22	9.30	9.39	9.49	9.58	9.68	9.78	9.87	9.97
23	9.14	9.24	9.33	9.43	9.53	9.62	9.72	9.82
24	9.00	9.10	9.19	9.29	9.39	9.49	9.59	9.69
25	8.87	8.97	9.07	9.17	9.27	9.37	9.47	9.57
26	8.76	8.86	8.96	9.06	9.16	9.26	9.36	9.46
27	8.65	8.75	8.85	8.96	9.06	9.16	9.26	9.36
28	8.56	8.66	8.76	8.86	8.97	9.07	9.17	9.28
29	8.47	8.58	8.68	8.78	8.88	8.99	9.09	9.20
30	8.40	8.50	8.60	8.71	8.81	8.91	9.02	9.13
31	8.32	8.43	8.53	8.64	8.74	8.85	8.95	9.06
32	8.26	8.36	8.47	8.58	8.68	8.79	8.90	9.00
33	8.20	8.31	8.41	8.52	8.63	8.73	8.84	8.95
34	8.15	8.25	8.36	8.47	8.57	8.68	8.79	8.90
35	8.10	8.20	8.31	8.42	8.53	8.64	8.75	8.86
36	8.05	8.16	8.27	8.38	8.49	8.60	8.71	8.82
37	8.01	8.12	8.23	8.34	8.45	8.56	8.67	8.78
38	7.97	8.08	8.19	8.30	8.41	8.52	8.63	8.75
39	7.93	8.04	8.16	8.27	8.38	8.49	8.60	8.72
40	7.90	8.01	8.12	8.24	8.35	8.46	8.57	8.69
41	7.87	7.98	8.10	8.21	8.32	8.43	8.55	8.66
42	7.84	7.96	8.07	8.18	8.30	8.41	8.52	8.64
43	7.82	7.93	8.05	8.16	8.27	8.39	8.50	8.62
44	7.80	7.91	8.02	8.14	8.25	8.37	8.48	8.60
45	7.77	7.89	8.00	8.12	8.23	8.35	8.46	8.58
46	7.75	7.87	7.98	8.10	8.21	8.33	8.45	8.56
47	7.74	7.85	7.97	8.08	8.20	8.31	8.43	8.55
48	7.72	7.83	7.95	8.07	8.18	8.30	8.42	8.54
49	7.70	7.82	7.94	8.05	8.17	8.29	8.40	8.52
50	7.69	7.80	7.92	8.04	8.16	8.27	8.39	8.51

CONSTANT ANNUAL PERCENT TABLE

Select the interest rate and the term of the mortgage and read the annual *percent* to amortize.

CONSTANT ANNUAL PERCENT TO AMORTIZE

INTEREST RATE

YEARS	8 1/2	8 5/8	8 3/4	8 7/8	9	9 1/8	9 1/4	9 3/8
5	24.62	24.70	24.77	24.84	24.92	24.99	25.06	25.13
6	21.34	21.41	21.49	21.56	21.64	21.71	21.78	21.86
7	19.01	19.08	19.16	19.24	19.31	19.39	19.46	19.54
8	17.28	17.35	17.43	17.51	17.59	17.66	17.74	17.82
9	15.94	16.02	16.10	16.18	16.26	16.34	16.42	16.50
10	14.88	14.96	15.04	15.13	15.21	15.29	15.37	15.45
11	14.03	14.11	14.19	14.28	14.36	14.44	14.52	14.61
12	13.33	13.41	13.49	13.58	13.66	13.75	13.83	13.92
13	12.74	12.82	12.91	13.00	13.08	13.17	13.25	13.34
14	12.24	12.33	12.42	12.50	12.59	12.68	12.77	12.86
15	11.82	11.91	12.00	12.09	12.18	12.27	12.36	12.45
16	11.46	11.55	11.64	11.73	11.82	11.91	12.00	12.09
17	11.14	11.24	11.33	11.42	11.51	11.60	11.70	11.79
18	10.87	10.96	11.06	11.15	11.24	11.34	11.43	11.53
19	10.63	10.72	10.82	10.91	11.01	11.10	11.20	11.29
20	10.42	10.51	10.61	10.71	10.80	10.90	11.00	11.09
21	10.23	10.33	10.43	10.52	10.62	10.72	10.82	10.92
22	10.07	10.16	10.26	10.36	10.46	10.56	10.66	10.76
23	9.92	10.02	10.12	10.22	10.32	10.42	10.52	10.62
24	9.79	9.89	9.99	10.09	10.19	10.29	10.39	10.50
25	9.67	9.77	9.87	9.97	10.08	10.18	10.28	10.39
26	9.56	9.66	9.77	9.87	9.97	10.08	10.18	10.29
27	9.47	9.57	9.67	9.78	9.88	9.99	10.09	10.20
28	9.38	9.48	9.59	9.69	9.80	9.91	10.01	10.12
29	9.30	9.41	9.51	9.62	9.73	9.83	9.94	10.05
30	9.23	9.34	9.45	9.55	9.66	9.77	9.88	9.99
31	9.17	9.28	9.38	9.49	9.60	9.71	9.82	9.93
32	9.11	9.22	9.33	9.44	9.55	9.66	9.77	9.88
33	9.06	9.17	9.28	9.39	9.50	9.61	9.72	9.83
34	9.01	9.12	9.23	9.34	9.45	9.56	9.68	9.79
35	8.97	9.08	9.19	9.30	9.41	9.53	9.64	9.75
36	8.93	9.04	9.15	9.26	9.38	9.49	9.60	9.72
37	8.89	9.00	9.12	9.23	9.34	9.46	9.57	9.69
38	8.86	8.97	9.09	9.20	9.31	9.43	9.54	9.66
39	8.83	8.94	9.06	9.17	9.29	9.40	9.52	9.63
40	8.80	8.92	9.03	9.15	9.26	9.38	9.49	9.61
41	8.78	8.89	9.01	9.12	9.24	9.35	9.47	9.59
42	8.75	8.87	8.99	9.10	9.22	9.33	9.45	9.57
43	8.73	8.85	8.97	9.08	9.20	9.32	9.43	9.55
44	8.71	8.83	8.95	9.07	9.18	9.30	9.42	9.54
45	8.70	8.81	8.93	9.05	9.17	9.29	9.40	9.52
46	8.68	8.80	8.92	9.03	9.15	9.27	9.39	9.51
47	8.67	8.78	8.90	9.02	9.14	9.26	9.38	9.50
48	8.65	8.77	8.89	9.01	9.13	9.25	9.37	9.49
49	8.64	8.76	8.88	9.00	9.12	9.24	9.36	9.48
50	8.63	8.75	8.87	8.99	9.11	9.23	9.35	9.47

CONSTANT ANNUAL PERCENT TO AMORTIZE

INTEREST RATE

YEARS	9 1/2	9 5/8	9 3/4	9 7/8	10	10 1/8	10 1/4	10 3/8
5	25.21	25.28	25.35	25.43	25.50	25.58	25.65	25.72
6	21.93	22.01	22.09	22.16	22.24	22.31	22.39	22.46
7	19.62	19.69	19.77	19.85	19.93	20.00	20.08	20.16
8	17.90	17.98	18.06	18.13	18.21	18.29	18.37	18.45
9	16.58	16.66	16.74	16.82	16.90	16.98	17.06	17.14
10	15.53	15.61	15.70	15.78	15.86	15.95	16.03	16.11
11	14.69	14.78	14.86	14.94	15.03	15.11	15.20	15.28
12	14.00	14.09	14.17	14.26	14.35	14.43	14.52	14.61
13	13.43	13.52	13.60	13.69	13.78	13.87	13.96	14.05
14	12.95	13.03	13.12	13.21	13.30	13.39	13.48	13.58
15	12.54	12.63	12.72	12.81	12.90	12.99	13.08	13.18
16	12.18	12.28	12.37	12.46	12.56	12.65	12.74	12.84
17	11.88	11.98	12.07	12.16	12.26	12.35	12.45	12.55
18	11.62	11.72	11.81	11.91	12.00	12.10	12.20	12.29
19	11.39	11.49	11.58	11.68	11.78	11.88	11.98	12.08
20	11.19	11.29	11.39	11.49	11.59	11.68	11.78	11.88
21	11.01	11.11	11.21	11.31	11.41	11.52	11.62	11.72
22	10.86	10.96	11.06	11.16	11.26	11.37	11.47	11.57
23	10.72	10.82	10.93	11.03	11.13	11.23	11.34	11.44
24	10.60	10.70	10.81	10.91	11.01	11.12	11.22	11.33
25	10.49	10.59	10.70	10.80	10.91	11.02	11.12	11.23
26	10.39	10.50	10.60	10.71	10.82	10.92	11.03	11.14
27	10.31	10.41	10.52	10.63	10.73	10.84	10.95	11.06
28	10.23	10.34	10.44	10.55	10.66	10.77	10.88	10.99
29	10.16	10.27	10.38	10.48	10.59	10.70	10.82	10.93
30	10.10	10.20	10.31	10.43	10.54	10.65	10.76	10.87
31	10.04	10.15	10.26	10.37	10.48	10.60	10.71	10.82
32	9.99	10.10	10.21	10.32	10.44	10.55	10.66	10.77
33	9.94	10.05	10.17	10.28	10.39	10.51	10.62	10.73
34	9.90	10.01	10.13	10.24	10.36	10.47	10.58	10.70
35	9.86	9.98	10.09	10.21	10.32	10.44	10.55	10.67
36	9.83	9.95	10.06	10.17	10.29	10.41	10.52	10.64
37	9.80	9.92	10.03	10.15	10.26	10.38	10.50	10.61
38	9.77	9.89	10.00	10.12	10.24	10.35	10.47	10.59
39	9.75	9.86	9.98	10.10	10.22	10.33	10.45	10.57
40	9.73	9.84	9.96	10.08	10.19	10.31	10.43	10.55
41	9.71	9.82	9.94	10.06	10.18	10.29	10.41	10.53
42	9.69	9.80	9.92	10.04	10.16	10.28	10.40	10.52
43	9.67	9.79	9.91	10.03	10.15	10.26	10.38	10.50
44	9.66	9.77	9.89	10.01	10.13	10.25	10.37	10.49
45	9.64	9.76	9.88	10.00	10.12	10.24	10.36	10.48
46	9.63	9.75	9.87	9.99	10.11	10.23	10.35	10.47
47	9.62	9.74	9.86	9.98	10.10	10.22	10.34	10.46
48	9.61	9.73	9.85	9.97	10.09	10.21	10.33	10.45
49	9.60	9.72	9.84	9.96	10.08	10.20	10.32	10.45
50	9.59	9.71	9.83	9.95	10.07	10.20	10.32	10.44

CONSTANT ANNUAL PERCENT TABLE

Select the interest rate and the term of the mortgage and read the
annual *percent* to amortize.

CONSTANT ANNUAL PERCENT TO AMORTIZE

YEARS	10 1/2	10 5/8	10 3/4	10 7/8	11	11 1/8	11 1/4	11 3/8
5	25.80	25.87	25.95	26.02	26.10	26.17	26.25	26.32
6	22.54	22.62	22.69	22.77	22.85	22.92	23.00	23.08
7	20.24	20.32	20.39	20.47	20.55	20.63	20.71	20.79
8	18.53	18.61	18.69	18.77	18.86	18.94	19.02	19.10
9	17.23	17.31	17.39	17.47	17.56	17.64	17.72	17.81
10	16.20	16.28	16.37	16.45	16.54	16.62	16.71	16.79
11	15.37	15.46	15.54	15.63	15.72	15.80	15.89	15.98
12	14.69	14.78	14.87	14.96	15.05	15.14	15.23	15.32
13	14.14	14.22	14.31	14.40	14.50	14.59	14.68	14.77
14	13.67	13.76	13.85	13.94	14.03	14.13	14.22	14.31
15	13.27	13.36	13.46	13.55	13.64	13.74	13.83	13.93
16	12.93	13.03	13.12	13.22	13.31	13.41	13.51	13.60
17	12.64	12.74	12.84	12.93	13.03	13.13	13.23	13.32
18	12.39	12.49	12.59	12.69	12.79	12.88	12.98	13.08
19	12.17	12.27	12.37	12.47	12.57	12.68	12.78	12.88
20	11.99	12.09	12.19	12.29	12.39	12.49	12.60	12.70
21	11.82	11.92	12.03	12.13	12.23	12.34	12.44	12.54
22	11.68	11.78	11.88	11.99	12.09	12.20	12.30	12.41
23	11.55	11.65	11.76	11.86	11.97	12.08	12.18	12.29
24	11.43	11.54	11.65	11.75	11.86	11.97	12.08	12.18
25	11.34	11.44	11.55	11.66	11.77	11.87	11.98	12.09
26	11.25	11.36	11.46	11.57	11.68	11.79	11.90	12.01
27	11.17	11.28	11.39	11.50	11.61	11.72	11.83	11.94
28	11.10	11.21	11.32	11.43	11.54	11.65	11.77	11.88
29	11.04	11.15	11.26	11.37	11.48	11.60	11.71	11.82
30	10.98	11.09	11.21	11.32	11.43	11.55	11.66	11.77
31	10.93	11.05	11.16	11.27	11.39	11.50	11.62	11.73
32	10.89	11.00	11.12	11.23	11.35	11.46	11.58	11.69
33	10.85	10.96	11.08	11.19	11.31	11.43	11.54	11.66
34	10.81	10.93	11.05	11.16	11.28	11.39	11.51	11.63
35	10.78	10.90	11.02	11.13	11.25	11.37	11.48	11.60
36	10.75	10.87	10.99	11.11	11.22	11.34	11.46	11.58
37	10.73	10.85	10.96	11.08	11.20	11.32	11.44	11.56
38	10.71	10.82	10.94	11.06	11.18	11.30	11.42	11.54
39	10.69	10.80	10.92	11.04	11.16	11.28	11.40	11.52
40	10.67	10.79	10.91	11.03	11.14	11.26	11.38	11.50
41	10.65	10.77	10.89	11.01	11.13	11.25	11.37	11.49
42	10.64	10.76	10.88	11.00	11.12	11.24	11.36	11.48
43	10.62	10.74	10.86	10.98	11.11	11.23	11.35	11.47
44	10.61	10.73	10.85	10.97	11.09	11.22	11.34	11.46
45	10.60	10.72	10.84	10.96	11.09	11.21	11.33	11.45
46	10.59	10.71	10.83	10.96	11.08	11.20	11.32	11.44
47	10.58	10.70	10.83	10.95	11.07	11.19	11.31	11.44
48	10.57	10.70	10.82	10.94	11.06	11.18	11.31	11.43
49	10.57	10.69	10.81	10.93	11.06	11.18	11.30	11.42
50	10.56	10.68	10.81	10.93	11.05	11.17	11.30	11.42

MORTGAGE PAY-OFF TABLE

Select the interest rate and the term of the mortgage and read the percent paid off at any stage along the way.

PAY-OFF TABLE—*shows % paid off*

10 YEAR LOAN—% paid off

INT	3YR	5YR	7YR	8YR	9YR	10YR
6 1/2	23.53	41.96	62.95	74.51	86.84	
7	23.06	41.36	62.39	74.06	86.58	
7 1/2	22.61	40.76	61.83	73.62	86.31	
7 3/4	22.38	40.46	61.56	73.39	86.18	
8	22.15	40.16	61.28	73.17	86.05	
8 1/4	21.93	39.86	61.00	72.94	85.91	
8 1/2	21.70	39.56	60.72	72.72	85.78	
8 3/4	21.48	39.27	60.44	72.49	85.64	
9	21.26	38.97	60.16	72.27	85.51	
9 1/4	21.04	38.68	59.88	72.04	85.37	
9 1/2	20.82	38.38	59.60	71.81	85.24	
9 3/4	20.61	38.09	59.32	71.58	85.10	
9 7/8	20.50	37.94	59.18	71.47	85.03	
10	20.39	37.80	59.04	71.36	84.96	
10 1/8	20.28	37.65	58.90	71.24	84.89	
10 1/4	20.18	37.51	58.76	71.13	84.83	
10 3/8	20.07	37.36	58.62	71.01	84.76	
10 1/2	19.97	37.22	58.48	70.90	84.69	
10 5/8	19.86	37.07	58.34	70.78	84.62	
10 3/4	19.75	36.93	58.20	70.67	84.55	
10 7/8	19.65	36.78	58.06	70.55	84.48	
11	19.54	36.64	57.92	70.44	84.41	
11 1/8	19.44	36.50	57.78	70.32	84.34	
11 1/4	19.34	36.35	57.64	70.21	84.27	
11 3/8	19.23	36.21	57.50	70.09	84.20	

11 YEAR LOAN—% paid off

INT	3YR	5YR	7YR	8YR	9YR	10YR
6 1/2	20.63	36.80	55.20	65.33	76.15	87.68
7	20.16	36.15	54.54	64.75	75.69	87.42
7 1/2	19.70	35.52	53.89	64.16	75.22	87.15
7 3/4	19.47	35.20	53.56	63.86	74.99	87.01
8	19.24	34.89	53.24	63.57	74.75	86.87
8 1/4	19.02	34.57	52.91	63.27	74.52	86.73
8 1/2	18.80	34.26	52.58	62.97	74.29	86.60
8 3/4	18.57	33.95	52.26	62.68	74.05	86.46
9	18.35	33.64	51.93	62.38	73.81	86.32
9 1/4	18.13	33.33	51.61	62.09	73.58	86.18
9 1/2	17.92	33.02	51.28	61.79	73.34	86.04
9 3/4	17.70	32.72	50.96	61.49	73.10	85.90
9 7/8	17.59	32.57	50.79	61.34	72.98	85.83
10	17.49	32.41	50.63	61.19	72.86	85.75
10 1/8	17.38	32.26	50.47	61.05	72.74	85.68
10 1/4	17.28	32.11	50.31	60.90	72.62	85.61
10 3/8	17.17	31.96	50.15	60.75	72.50	85.54
10 1/2	17.06	31.81	49.98	60.60	72.38	85.47
10 5/8	16.96	31.66	49.82	60.45	72.27	85.40
10 3/4	16.86	31.51	49.66	60.30	72.14	85.33
10 7/8	16.75	31.36	49.50	60.15	72.02	85.25
11	16.65	31.21	49.34	60.00	71.90	85.18
11 1/8	16.55	31.06	49.18	59.86	71.78	85.11
11 1/4	16.44	30.91	49.02	59.71	71.66	85.04
11 3/8	16.34	30.77	48.86	59.56	71.54	84.96

PAY-OFF TABLE—*shows % paid off*

12 YEAR LOAN—% paid off

INT	3YR	5YR	7YR	8YR	9YR	10YR
6 1/2	18.24	32.52	48.79	57.75	67.30	77.50
7	17.77	31.86	48.06	57.05	66.69	77.03
7 1/2	17.30	31.20	47.33	56.35	66.07	76.55
7 3/4	17.08	30.87	46.97	56.00	65.76	76.30
8	16.85	30.55	46.61	55.66	65.45	76.06
8 1/4	16.62	30.22	46.25	55.31	65.14	75.82
8 1/2	16.40	29.90	45.89	54.96	64.83	75.57
8 3/4	16.18	29.58	45.53	54.61	64.52	75.33
9	15.96	29.26	45.17	54.26	64.21	75.08
9 1/4	15.75	28.95	44.81	53.92	63.90	74.84
9 1/2	15.53	28.63	44.46	53.57	63.58	74.59
9 3/4	15.32	28.32	44.10	53.22	63.27	74.34
9 7/8	15.21	28.16	43.93	53.05	63.11	74.22
10	15.11	28.01	43.75	52.88	62.96	74.10
10 1/8	15.00	27.85	43.57	52.70	62.80	73.97
10 1/4	14.90	27.70	43.39	52.53	62.65	73.85
10 3/8	14.80	27.54	43.22	52.36	62.49	73.72
10 1/2	14.69	27.39	43.04	52.18	62.33	73.60
10 5/8	14.59	27.24	42.87	52.01	62.18	73.47
10 3/4	14.49	27.09	42.69	51.84	62.02	73.35
10 7/8	14.39	26.93	42.52	51.67	61.86	73.22
11	14.29	26.78	42.34	51.49	61.70	73.10
11 1/8	14.19	26.63	42.17	51.32	61.55	72.97
11 1/4	14.09	26.48	41.99	51.15	61.39	72.85
11 3/8	13.99	26.33	41.82	50.98	61.24	72.72

13 YEAR LOAN—% paid off

INT	3YR	5YR	7YR	8YR	10YR	12YR
6 1/2	16.23	28.94	43.41	51.38	68.96	88.97
7	15.76	28.26	42.63	50.60	68.32	88.69
7 1/2	15.30	27.58	41.85	49.82	67.67	88.41
7 3/4	15.07	27.25	41.46	49.44	67.35	88.26
8	14.85	26.92	41.07	49.05	67.03	88.12
8 1/4	14.63	26.59	40.69	48.66	66.70	87.97
8 1/2	14.41	26.26	40.31	48.27	66.38	87.83
8 3/4	14.19	25.94	39.92	47.89	66.05	87.68
9	13.97	25.62	39.54	47.50	65.73	87.53
9 1/4	13.76	25.30	39.16	47.12	65.40	87.39
9 1/2	13.55	24.98	38.79	46.73	65.08	87.24
9 3/4	13.34	24.66	38.41	46.35	64.75	87.09
9 7/8	13.24	24.51	38.22	46.16	64.59	87.01
10	13.14	24.35	38.04	45.97	64.42	86.94
10 1/8	13.03	24.19	37.85	45.78	64.26	86.86
10 1/4	12.93	24.04	37.66	45.59	64.09	86.79
10 3/8	12.83	23.89	37.48	45.40	63.93	86.71
10 1/2	12.73	23.73	37.29	45.21	63.77	86.64
10 5/8	12.63	23.58	37.11	45.02	63.60	86.56
10 3/4	12.53	23.43	36.92	44.83	63.44	86.48
10 7/8	12.43	23.27	36.74	44.65	63.28	86.41
11	12.33	23.12	36.55	44.46	63.11	86.33
11 1/8	12.24	22.97	36.37	44.27	62.95	86.26
11 1/4	12.14	22.82	36.19	44.08	62.78	86.18
11 3/8	12.04	22.67	36.01	43.89	62.62	86.10

MORTGAGE PAY-OFF TABLE

Select the interest rate and the term of the mortgage and read the percent paid off at any stage along the way.

PAY-OFF TABLE—*shows % paid off*

14 YEAR LOAN—*% paid off*

INT	3YR	5YR	7YR	8YR	10YR	12YR
6 1/2	14.52	25.89	38.84	45.97	61.70	79.61
7	14.05	25.20	38.02	45.13	60.93	79.10
7 1/2	13.60	24.52	37.20	44.29	60.16	78.59
7 3/4	13.38	24.18	36.80	43.87	59.77	78.33
8	13.15	23.85	36.39	43.46	59.39	78.08
8 1/4	12.94	23.52	35.99	43.04	59.00	77.82
8 1/2	12.72	23.19	35.59	42.63	58.62	77.56
8 3/4	12.51	22.86	35.19	42.21	58.23	77.30
9	12.30	22.54	34.80	41.80	57.84	77.03
9 1/4	12.09	22.22	34.41	41.39	57.46	76.77
9 1/2	11.88	21.91	34.02	40.99	57.07	76.51
9 3/4	11.68	21.59	33.63	40.58	56.69	76.24
9 7/8	11.58	21.44	33.43	40.38	56.49	76.11
10	11.48	21.28	33.24	40.18	56.30	75.98
10 1/8	11.38	21.13	33.05	39.97	56.11	75.85
10 1/4	11.28	20.97	32.86	39.77	55.92	75.71
10 3/8	11.18	20.82	32.67	39.57	55.72	75.58
10 1/2	11.09	20.67	32.47	39.37	55.53	75.45
10 5/8	10.99	20.51	32.28	39.17	55.34	75.31
10 3/4	10.89	20.36	32.10	38.97	55.15	75.18
10 7/8	10.80	20.21	31.91	38.77	54.95	75.05
11	10.70	20.06	31.72	38.58	54.76	74.91
11 1/8	10.61	19.92	31.53	38.38	54.57	74.78
11 1/4	10.51	19.77	31.34	38.18	54.38	74.64
11 3/8	10.42	19.62	31.16	37.98	54.19	74.51

15 YEAR LOAN—*% paid off*

INT	5YR	10YR	11YR	12YR	13YR	14YR
6 1/2	23.28	55.47	63.26	71.57	80.44	89.90
7	22.58	54.60	62.46	70.89	79.92	89.61
7 1/2	21.90	53.73	61.66	70.19	79.39	89.31
7 3/4	21.56	53.30	61.25	69.85	79.13	89.16
8	21.23	52.86	60.85	69.50	78.87	89.01
8 1/4	20.90	52.43	60.45	69.15	78.60	88.86
8 1/2	20.57	52.00	60.04	68.80	78.33	88.70
8 3/4	20.25	51.57	59.64	68.45	78.06	88.55
9	19.93	51.13	59.24	68.10	77.79	88.40
9 1/4	19.61	50.70	58.83	67.75	77.52	88.24
9 1/2	19.30	50.27	58.43	67.40	77.25	88.09
9 3/4	18.99	49.85	58.03	67.04	76.98	87.93
9 7/8	18.83	49.63	57.83	66.87	76.84	87.85
10	18.68	49.42	57.63	66.69	76.71	87.77
10 1/8	18.53	49.20	57.42	66.52	76.57	87.69
10 1/4	18.37	48.99	57.22	66.34	76.43	87.61
10 3/8	18.22	48.78	57.02	66.16	76.30	87.53
10 1/2	18.07	48.57	56.82	65.99	76.16	87.45
10 5/8	17.93	48.35	56.62	65.81	76.02	87.38
10 3/4	17.78	48.14	56.42	65.63	75.88	87.30
10 7/8	17.63	47.93	56.22	65.45	75.75	87.22
11	17.48	47.72	56.02	65.28	75.61	87.13
11 1/8	17.34	47.51	55.82	65.10	75.47	87.05
11 1/4	17.19	47.30	55.62	64.92	75.33	86.97
11 3/8	17.05	47.09	55.42	64.75	75.19	86.89

PAY-OFF TABLE—*shows % paid off*

16 YEAR LOAN—*% paid off*

INT	5YR	10YR	11YR	12YR	13YR	14YR
6 1/2	21.01	50.08	57.11	64.61	72.62	81.16
7	20.32	49.13	56.20	63.78	71.91	80.63
7 1/2	19.64	48.18	55.29	62.95	71.20	80.09
7 3/4	19.30	47.71	54.83	62.53	70.84	79.82
8	18.97	47.24	54.38	62.11	70.48	79.54
8 1/4	18.64	46.77	53.93	61.69	70.12	79.27
8 1/2	18.32	46.31	53.47	61.27	69.76	79.00
8 3/4	18.00	45.84	53.02	60.85	69.40	78.72
9	17.68	45.38	52.57	60.43	69.04	78.44
9 1/4	17.37	44.91	52.12	60.01	68.67	78.17
9 1/2	17.06	44.45	51.67	59.59	68.31	77.89
9 3/4	16.76	44.00	51.22	59.18	67.95	77.61
9 7/8	16.61	43.77	50.99	58.97	67.76	77.47
10	16.46	43.54	50.77	58.76	67.58	77.33
10 1/8	16.31	43.31	50.55	58.55	67.40	77.19
10 1/4	16.16	43.08	50.32	58.34	67.22	77.05
10 3/8	16.01	42.86	50.10	58.13	67.03	76.91
10 1/2	15.86	42.63	49.88	57.92	66.85	76.77
10 5/8	15.72	42.40	49.65	57.71	66.67	76.63
10 3/4	15.57	42.18	49.43	57.50	66.49	76.48
10 7/8	15.43	41.96	49.21	57.29	66.30	76.34
11	15.29	41.73	48.99	57.09	66.12	76.20
11 1/8	15.15	41.51	48.77	56.88	65.94	76.06
11 1/4	15.01	41.28	48.55	56.67	65.75	75.92
11 3/8	14.87	41.06	48.33	56.46	65.57	75.77

17 YEAR LOAN—*% paid off*

INT	5YR	10YR	11YR	12YR	13YR	15YR
6 1/2	19.04	45.37	51.74	58.54	65.79	81.79
7	18.35	44.36	50.75	57.59	64.93	81.24
7 1/2	17.67	43.36	49.75	56.64	64.07	80.69
7 3/4	17.34	42.86	49.26	56.17	63.63	80.41
8	17.01	42.36	48.76	55.69	63.20	80.13
8 1/4	16.69	41.87	48.27	55.22	62.77	79.85
8 1/2	16.37	41.38	47.78	54.75	62.33	79.57
8 3/4	16.05	40.89	47.29	54.28	61.90	79.29
9	15.74	40.40	46.80	53.81	61.47	79.01
9 1/4	15.44	39.92	46.32	53.34	61.03	78.72
9 1/2	15.14	39.44	45.83	52.87	60.60	78.44
9 3/4	14.84	38.96	45.35	52.40	60.16	78.15
9 7/8	14.69	38.72	45.11	52.16	59.95	78.01
10	14.54	38.48	44.87	51.93	59.73	77.86
10 1/8	14.40	38.24	44.63	51.70	59.51	77.72
10 1/4	14.25	38.01	44.39	51.47	59.30	77.58
10 3/8	14.11	37.77	44.16	51.23	59.08	77.43
10 1/2	13.97	37.54	43.92	51.00	58.86	77.29
10 5/8	13.83	37.30	43.68	50.77	58.65	77.14
10 3/4	13.69	37.07	43.44	50.54	58.43	77.00
10 7/8	13.55	36.84	43.21	50.31	58.22	76.85
11	13.41	36.61	42.97	50.08	58.00	76.71
11 1/8	13.27	36.37	42.74	49.84	57.78	76.56
11 1/4	13.14	36.14	42.50	49.61	57.57	76.42
11 3/8	13.00	35.92	42.27	49.38	57.35	76.27

MORTGAGE PAY-OFF TABLE

Select the interest rate and the term of the mortgage and read the percent paid off at any stage along the way.

PAY-OFF TABLE—*shows % paid off*

18 YEAR LOAN—% paid off

INT	5YR	10YR	11YR	12YR	13YR	15YR
6 1/2	17.30	41.24	47.03	53.20	59.79	74.33
7	16.62	40.18	45.96	52.16	58.81	73.58
7 1/2	15.95	39.13	44.91	51.12	57.83	72.83
7 3/4	15.62	38.62	44.38	50.61	57.33	72.45
8	15.30	38.10	43.86	50.09	56.84	72.07
8 1/4	14.98	37.59	43.34	49.58	56.35	71.69
8 1/2	14.67	37.08	42.82	49.06	55.86	71.31
8 3/4	14.36	36.58	42.30	48.55	55.37	70.93
9	14.06	36.07	41.79	48.04	54.88	70.55
9 1/4	13.76	35.58	41.28	47.54	54.40	70.16
9 1/2	13.46	35.08	40.77	47.03	53.91	69.78
9 3/4	13.17	34.59	40.27	46.53	53.42	69.39
9 7/8	13.03	34.35	40.02	46.28	53.18	69.20
10	12.89	34.10	39.77	46.02	52.94	69.01
10 1/8	12.75	33.86	39.52	45.77	52.69	68.82
10 1/4	12.61	33.62	39.27	45.53	52.45	68.62
10 3/8	12.47	33.38	39.02	45.28	52.21	68.43
10 1/2	12.33	33.14	38.77	45.03	51.97	68.24
10 5/8	12.20	32.90	38.53	44.78	51.73	68.04
10 3/4	12.06	32.67	38.28	44.53	51.49	67.85
10 7/8	11.93	32.43	38.04	44.29	51.25	67.66
11	11.79	32.19	37.79	44.04	51.01	67.46
11 1/8	11.66	31.96	37.55	43.79	50.77	67.27
11 1/4	11.53	31.73	37.31	43.55	50.53	67.08
11 3/8	11.40	31.49	37.07	43.31	50.29	66.88

19 YEAR LOAN—% paid off

INT	5YR	10YR	11YR	12YR	15YR	18YR
6 1/2	15.77	37.58	42.86	48.49	67.74	91.13
7	15.09	36.49	41.74	47.37	66.83	90.82
7 1/2	14.43	35.42	40.64	46.27	65.91	90.50
7 3/4	14.11	34.89	40.09	45.72	65.45	90.33
8	13.80	34.36	39.55	45.17	64.99	90.17
8 1/4	13.49	33.84	39.01	44.63	64.53	90.01
8 1/2	13.18	33.32	38.47	44.08	64.07	89.84
8 3/4	12.88	32.80	37.94	43.54	63.61	89.68
9	12.58	32.29	37.41	43.01	63.15	89.51
9 1/4	12.29	31.79	36.88	42.47	62.69	89.34
9 1/2	12.01	31.29	36.36	41.94	62.23	89.17
9 3/4	11.73	30.79	35.84	41.41	61.77	89.00
9 7/8	11.59	30.54	35.59	41.15	61.54	88.92
10	11.45	30.30	35.33	40.89	61.31	88.83
10 1/8	11.31	30.05	35.07	40.63	61.08	88.75
10 1/4	11.18	29.81	34.82	40.37	60.85	88.66
10 3/8	11.05	29.57	34.56	40.11	60.62	88.58
10 1/2	10.91	29.33	34.31	39.85	60.39	88.49
10 5/8	10.78	29.09	34.06	39.59	60.16	88.40
10 3/4	10.65	28.85	33.81	39.33	59.93	88.32
10 7/8	10.52	28.61	33.56	39.08	59.70	88.23
11	10.40	28.38	33.31	38.82	59.47	88.14
11 1/8	10.27	28.14	33.07	38.57	59.24	88.06
11 1/4	10.14	27.91	32.82	38.31	59.01	87.97
11 3/8	10.02	27.68	32.58	38.06	58.78	87.88

PAY-OFF TABLE—*shows % paid off*

20 YEAR LOAN—% paid off

INT	5YR	10YR	11YR	12YR	15YR	18YR
6 1/2	14.41	34.33	39.15	44.30	61.89	83.26
7	13.74	33.22	38.00	43.13	60.84	82.68
7 1/2	13.09	32.13	36.87	41.97	59.79	82.09
7 3/4	12.78	31.59	36.30	41.40	59.27	81.80
8	12.47	31.05	35.75	40.83	58.74	81.50
8 1/4	12.17	30.53	35.19	40.26	58.22	81.20
8 1/2	11.87	30.00	34.64	39.70	57.70	80.90
8 3/4	11.58	29.48	34.10	39.14	57.17	80.60
9	11.29	28.97	33.56	38.58	56.65	80.30
9 1/4	11.01	28.46	33.02	38.03	56.13	80.00
9 1/2	10.73	27.96	32.50	37.48	55.61	79.69
9 3/4	10.46	27.46	31.97	36.94	55.09	79.39
9 7/8	10.32	27.22	31.71	36.67	54.83	79.24
10	10.19	26.97	31.45	36.40	54.57	79.09
10 1/8	10.06	26.73	31.19	36.13	54.32	78.93
10 1/4	9.93	26.49	30.94	35.86	54.06	78.78
10 3/8	9.80	26.24	30.68	35.60	53.80	78.62
10 1/2	9.68	26.01	30.43	35.33	53.55	78.47
10 5/8	9.55	25.77	30.17	35.07	53.29	78.31
10 3/4	9.43	25.53	29.92	34.81	53.03	78.16
10 7/8	9.30	25.30	29.67	34.55	52.78	78.00
11	9.18	25.06	29.42	34.29	52.52	77.85
11 1/8	9.06	24.83	29.17	34.03	52.27	77.69
11 1/4	8.94	24.60	28.93	33.77	52.01	77.54
11 3/8	8.82	24.37	28.68	33.51	51.76	77.38

21 YEAR LOAN—% paid off

INT	5YR	10YR	12YR	15YR	18YR	20YR
6 1/2	13.19	31.44	40.56	56.67	76.23	91.55
7	12.53	30.31	39.35	55.51	75.43	91.23
7 1/2	11.90	29.21	38.15	54.35	74.62	90.90
7 3/4	11.59	28.66	37.56	53.78	74.22	90.73
8	11.29	28.13	36.98	53.20	73.81	90.56
8 1/4	11.00	27.59	36.39	52.63	73.41	90.39
8 1/2	10.71	27.07	35.82	52.06	73.00	90.22
8 3/4	10.42	26.55	35.25	51.49	72.59	90.05
9	10.15	26.04	34.68	50.92	72.18	89.88
9 1/4	9.87	25.53	34.12	50.36	71.77	89.71
9 1/2	9.61	25.03	33.56	49.79	71.35	89.53
9 3/4	9.35	24.54	33.01	49.23	70.94	89.36
9 7/8	9.22	24.30	32.73	48.95	70.74	89.27
10	9.09	24.05	32.46	48.67	70.53	89.18
10 1/8	8.96	23.81	32.19	48.39	70.32	89.09
10 1/4	8.84	23.57	31.92	48.12	70.12	89.00
10 3/8	8.72	23.34	31.65	47.84	69.91	88.91
10 1/2	8.60	23.10	31.39	47.56	69.70	88.83
10 5/8	8.47	22.87	31.12	47.29	69.49	88.74
10 3/4	8.36	22.63	30.86	47.01	69.29	88.65
10 7/8	8.24	22.40	30.59	46.74	69.08	88.56
11	8.12	22.17	30.33	46.47	68.87	88.47
11 1/8	8.01	21.95	30.07	46.19	68.67	88.38
11 1/4	7.89	21.72	29.81	45.92	68.46	88.29
11 3/8	7.78	21.50	29.56	45.65	68.25	88.20

MORTGAGE PAY-OFF TABLE

Select the interest rate and the term of the mortgage and read the percent paid off at any stage along the way.

PAY-OFF TABLE—*shows % paid off*

22 YEAR LOAN—% paid off

INT	5YR	10YR	12YR	15YR	18YR	20YR
6 1/2	12.10	28.84	37.21	51.98	69.93	83.99
7	11.46	27.70	35.97	50.74	68.95	83.39
7 1/2	10.84	26.60	34.75	49.50	67.96	82.78
7 3/4	10.54	26.05	34.14	48.88	67.47	82.48
8	10.25	25.52	33.55	48.27	66.97	82.17
8 1/4	9.96	24.99	32.96	47.66	66.48	81.86
8 1/2	9.68	24.47	32.37	47.05	65.98	81.55
8 3/4	9.40	23.95	31.80	46.45	65.48	81.24
9	9.13	23.44	31.22	45.85	64.99	80.93
9 1/4	8.87	22.94	30.66	45.25	64.49	80.61
9 1/2	8.62	22.45	30.10	44.66	63.99	80.30
9 3/4	8.36	21.96	29.54	44.07	63.50	79.98
9 7/8	8.24	21.72	29.27	43.77	63.25	79.82
10	8.12	21.49	29.00	43.48	63.00	79.66
10 1/8	8.00	21.25	28.73	43.19	62.75	79.50
10 1/4	7.88	21.01	28.46	42.90	62.51	79.34
10 3/8	7.76	20.78	28.19	42.61	62.26	79.18
10 1/2	7.65	20.55	27.92	42.32	62.01	79.02
10 5/8	7.53	20.32	27.66	42.03	61.76	78.87
10 3/4	7.42	20.09	27.40	41.74	61.52	78.71
10 7/8	7.31	19.87	27.13	41.46	61.27	78.54
11	7.20	19.65	26.88	41.17	61.02	78.38
11 1/8	7.09	19.42	26.62	40.89	60.78	78.22
11 1/4	6.98	19.20	26.36	40.60	60.53	78.06
11 3/8	6.87	18.99	26.11	40.32	60.29	77.90

23 YEAR LOAN—% paid off

INT	5YR	10YR	15YR	18YR	20YR	22YR
6 1/2	11.12	26.50	47.77	64.27	77.19	91.89
7	10.49	25.37	46.46	63.13	76.36	91.56
7 1/2	9.89	24.26	45.16	62.00	75.52	91.22
7 3/4	9.60	23.72	44.51	61.43	75.10	91.05
8	9.31	23.19	43.87	60.86	74.67	90.87
8 1/4	9.03	22.67	43.23	60.30	74.25	90.70
8 1/2	8.76	22.15	42.60	59.73	73.83	90.52
8 3/4	8.50	21.64	41.97	59.17	73.40	90.35
9	8.24	21.14	41.34	58.60	72.97	90.17
9 1/4	7.98	20.65	40.72	58.04	72.55	89.99
9 1/2	7.74	20.16	40.11	57.48	72.12	89.81
9 3/4	7.50	19.69	39.50	56.92	71.69	89.63
9 7/8	7.38	19.45	39.19	56.64	71.48	89.54
10	7.26	19.22	38.89	56.36	71.26	89.45
10 1/8	7.15	18.99	38.59	56.08	71.05	89.36
10 1/4	7.03	18.76	38.29	55.80	70.83	89.27
10 3/8	6.92	18.53	37.99	55.52	70.62	89.17
10 1/2	6.81	18.31	37.70	55.24	70.40	89.08
10 5/8	6.70	18.09	37.40	54.97	70.19	88.99
10 3/4	6.59	17.86	37.11	54.69	69.97	88.90
10 7/8	6.49	17.65	36.82	54.41	69.76	88.81
11	6.38	17.43	36.53	54.14	69.54	88.71
11 1/8	6.28	17.21	36.24	53.86	69.33	88.62
11 1/4	6.18	17.00	35.95	53.59	69.11	88.53
11 3/8	6.08	16.79	35.66	53.32	68.90	88.44

PAY-OFF TABLE—*shows % paid off*

24 YEAR LOAN—% paid off

INT	5YR	10YR	15YR	18YR	20YR	22YR
6 1/2	10.23	24.39	43.97	59.15	71.05	84.58
7	9.62	23.26	42.60	57.90	70.02	83.96
7 1/2	9.03	22.17	41.25	56.64	68.99	83.34
7 3/4	8.75	21.63	40.59	56.01	68.48	83.02
8	8.47	21.10	39.92	55.39	67.96	82.70
8 1/4	8.20	20.59	39.27	54.77	67.44	82.38
8 1/2	7.94	20.08	38.62	54.15	66.93	82.06
8 3/4	7.69	19.58	37.97	53.53	66.41	81.74
9	7.44	19.09	37.33	52.91	65.89	81.42
9 1/4	7.19	18.61	36.70	52.30	65.37	81.09
9 1/2	6.96	18.13	36.07	51.69	64.86	80.77
9 3/4	6.73	17.67	35.45	51.08	64.34	80.44
9 7/8	6.62	17.44	35.14	50.78	64.08	80.28
10	6.50	17.21	34.83	50.48	63.82	80.11
10 1/8	6.39	16.99	34.53	50.17	63.57	79.95
10 1/4	6.29	16.77	34.23	49.87	63.31	79.79
10 3/8	6.18	16.55	33.92	49.57	63.05	79.62
10 1/2	6.07	16.33	33.62	49.27	62.79	79.46
10 5/8	5.97	16.11	33.33	48.98	62.54	79.29
10 3/4	5.87	15.90	33.03	48.68	62.28	79.13
10 7/8	5.77	15.69	32.73	48.38	62.02	78.96
11	5.67	15.48	32.44	48.09	61.77	78.80
11 1/8	5.57	15.27	32.14	47.80	61.51	78.63
11 1/4	5.48	15.07	31.86	47.50	61.26	78.47
11 3/8	5.38	14.87	31.57	47.21	61.00	78.30

25 YEAR LOAN—% paid off

INT	5YR	10YR	15YR	18YR	20YR	22YR
6 1/2	9.43	22.48	40.53	54.52	65.49	77.96
7	8.83	21.36	39.12	53.17	64.30	77.10
7 1/2	8.26	20.28	37.74	51.82	63.12	76.24
7 3/4	7.99	19.75	37.06	51.14	62.52	75.80
8	7.72	19.23	36.38	50.48	61.93	75.36
8 1/4	7.46	18.72	35.71	49.81	61.34	74.93
8 1/2	7.21	18.22	35.05	49.15	60.75	74.49
8 3/4	6.96	17.74	34.39	48.49	60.16	74.05
9	6.72	17.26	33.75	47.84	59.57	73.60
9 1/4	6.49	16.79	33.11	47.18	58.98	73.16
9 1/2	6.26	16.33	32.47	46.54	58.39	72.72
9 3/4	6.04	15.87	31.85	45.90	57.81	72.28
9 7/8	5.94	15.65	31.54	45.58	57.52	72.06
10	5.83	15.43	31.23	45.26	57.23	71.83
10 1/8	5.73	15.22	30.93	44.94	56.94	71.61
10 1/4	5.62	15.00	30.62	44.62	56.65	71.39
10 3/8	5.52	14.79	30.32	44.31	56.36	71.17
10 1/2	5.42	14.58	30.02	44.00	56.07	70.95
10 5/8	5.33	14.37	29.72	43.68	55.78	70.72
10 3/4	5.23	14.17	29.43	43.37	55.49	70.50
10 7/8	5.13	13.96	29.14	43.06	55.20	70.28
11	5.04	13.76	28.84	42.75	54.92	70.06
11 1/8	4.95	13.56	28.55	42.45	54.63	69.84
11 1/4	4.86	13.37	28.27	42.14	54.35	69.61
11 3/8	4.77	13.17	27.98	41.84	54.06	69.39

MORTGAGE PAY-OFF TABLE

Select the interest rate and the term of the mortgage and read the percent paid off at any stage along the way.

PAY-OFF TABLE—*shows % paid off*

26 YEAR LOAN—% paid off

INT	5YR	10YR	15YR	18YR	20YR	22YR
6 1/2	8.71	20.75	37.41	50.32	60.44	71.96
7	8.12	19.64	35.97	48.88	59.12	70.89
7 1/2	7.57	18.57	34.57	47.46	57.81	69.83
7 3/4	7.30	18.05	33.87	46.75	57.15	69.29
8	7.04	17.55	33.19	46.05	56.50	68.76
8 1/4	6.79	17.05	32.52	45.35	55.85	68.22
8 1/2	6.55	16.56	31.85	44.66	55.20	67.69
8 3/4	6.31	16.08	31.19	43.97	54.55	67.15
9	6.08	15.62	30.54	43.29	53.91	66.61
9 1/4	5.86	15.16	29.90	42.61	53.27	66.08
9 1/2	5.65	14.71	29.27	41.94	52.63	65.54
9 3/4	5.44	14.28	28.65	41.28	51.99	65.01
9 7/8	5.33	14.06	28.34	40.95	51.68	64.74
10	5.23	13.85	28.03	40.62	51.36	64.47
10 1/8	5.13	13.64	27.73	40.29	51.05	64.20
10 1/4	5.04	13.44	27.43	39.97	50.73	63.94
10 3/8	4.94	13.23	27.13	39.64	50.42	63.67
10 1/2	4.85	13.03	26.83	39.32	50.11	63.40
10 5/8	4.75	12.83	26.54	39.00	49.80	63.14
10 3/4	4.66	12.63	26.24	38.68	49.49	62.87
10 7/8	4.57	12.44	25.95	38.36	49.18	62.61
11	4.48	12.25	25.67	38.05	48.87	62.34
11 1/8	4.40	12.06	25.38	37.73	48.56	62.08
11 1/4	4.31	11.87	25.10	37.42	48.26	61.81
11 3/8	4.23	11.69	24.82	37.11	47.95	61.55

27 YEAR LOAN—% paid off

INT	5YR	10YR	15YR	20YR	22YR	25YR
6 1/2	8.04	19.17	34.57	55.85	66.49	85.28
7	7.48	18.08	33.11	54.42	65.26	84.63
7 1/2	6.94	17.03	31.69	53.01	64.03	83.98
7 3/4	6.68	16.52	31.00	52.30	63.41	83.65
8	6.43	16.02	30.31	51.60	62.80	83.32
8 1/4	6.19	15.54	29.64	50.90	62.18	82.98
8 1/2	5.96	15.06	28.97	50.21	61.57	82.65
8 3/4	5.73	14.60	28.31	49.52	60.95	82.31
9	5.51	14.15	27.67	48.83	60.34	81.98
9 1/4	5.30	13.70	27.03	48.15	59.73	81.64
9 1/2	5.09	13.27	26.40	47.48	59.12	81.30
9 3/4	4.89	12.85	25.79	46.80	58.52	80.96
9 7/8	4.80	12.65	25.48	46.47	58.22	80.79
10	4.70	12.44	25.18	46.14	57.91	80.62
10 1/8	4.61	12.24	24.88	45.81	57.61	80.45
10 1/4	4.51	12.04	24.58	45.48	57.31	80.28
10 3/8	4.42	11.85	24.29	45.15	57.01	80.11
10 1/2	4.33	11.65	24.00	44.82	56.71	79.93
10 5/8	4.25	11.46	23.71	44.49	56.41	79.76
10 3/4	4.16	11.28	23.42	44.17	56.11	79.59
10 7/8	4.08	11.09	23.14	43.84	55.82	79.42
11	3.99	10.91	22.86	43.52	55.52	79.25
11 1/8	3.91	10.73	22.58	43.20	55.23	79.08
11 1/4	3.83	10.55	22.30	42.88	54.93	78.90
11 3/8	3.75	10.37	22.03	42.56	54.64	78.73

PAY-OFF TABLE—*shows % paid off*

28 YEAR LOAN—% paid off

INT	5YR	10YR	15YR	20YR	22YR	25YR
6 1/2	7.44	17.74	31.97	51.66	61.50	78.88
7	6.89	16.66	30.51	50.15	60.13	77.98
7 1/2	6.37	15.63	29.09	48.65	58.77	77.08
7 3/4	6.12	15.13	28.39	47.91	58.08	76.62
8	5.88	14.65	27.71	47.17	57.40	76.16
8 1/4	5.65	14.17	27.04	46.44	56.73	75.71
8 1/2	5.42	13.71	26.37	45.71	56.05	75.25
8 3/4	5.21	13.26	25.72	44.99	55.38	74.79
9	5.00	12.82	25.08	44.28	54.71	74.32
9 1/4	4.79	12.40	24.45	43.57	54.04	73.86
9 1/2	4.60	11.98	23.84	42.86	53.38	73.40
9 3/4	4.41	11.58	23.23	42.17	52.72	72.94
9 7/8	4.32	11.38	22.93	41.82	52.39	72.71
10	4.23	11.19	22.64	41.48	52.06	72.48
10 1/8	4.14	10.99	22.34	41.13	51.74	72.24
10 1/4	4.05	10.80	22.05	40.79	51.41	72.01
10 3/8	3.96	10.62	21.77	40.46	51.09	71.78
10 1/2	3.88	10.43	21.48	40.12	50.76	71.55
10 5/8	3.80	10.25	21.20	39.78	50.44	71.32
10 3/4	3.72	10.07	20.92	39.45	50.12	71.09
10 7/8	3.64	9.89	20.64	39.12	49.80	70.86
11	3.56	9.72	20.37	38.79	49.48	70.63
11 1/8	3.48	9.55	20.10	38.46	49.16	70.40
11 1/4	3.41	9.38	19.83	38.13	48.85	70.17
11 3/8	3.33	9.21	19.57	37.81	48.53	69.93

29 YEAR LOAN—% paid off

INT	5YR	10YR	15YR	20YR	25YR	28YR
6 1/2	6.89	16.42	29.60	47.83	73.04	92.59
7	6.35	15.36	28.14	46.25	71.93	92.23
7 1/2	5.85	14.36	26.72	44.69	70.81	91.86
7 3/4	5.61	13.87	26.03	43.92	70.25	91.68
8	5.38	13.40	25.35	43.16	69.69	91.49
8 1/4	5.16	12.94	24.69	42.40	69.12	91.30
8 1/2	4.94	12.49	24.03	41.65	68.56	91.11
8 3/4	4.73	12.06	23.39	40.91	68.00	90.92
9	4.53	11.64	22.76	40.17	67.44	90.73
9 1/4	4.34	11.23	22.14	39.45	66.88	90.54
9 1/2	4.15	10.83	21.54	38.73	66.32	90.35
9 3/4	3.97	10.44	20.94	38.02	65.76	90.15
9 7/8	3.89	10.25	20.65	37.66	65.48	90.05
10	3.80	10.06	20.36	37.31	65.20	89.96
10 1/8	3.72	9.88	20.08	36.97	64.92	89.86
10 1/4	3.63	9.70	19.80	36.62	64.64	89.76
10 3/8	3.55	9.52	19.52	36.28	64.37	89.66
10 1/2	3.47	9.34	19.24	35.93	64.09	89.57
10 5/8	3.40	9.17	18.97	35.59	63.81	89.47
10 3/4	3.32	9.00	18.70	35.26	63.53	89.37
10 7/8	3.25	8.83	18.43	34.92	63.26	89.27
11	3.17	8.67	18.17	34.59	62.98	89.17
11 1/8	3.10	8.50	17.90	34.26	62.71	89.07
11 1/4	3.03	8.34	17.65	33.93	62.43	88.97
11 3/8	2.96	8.19	17.39	33.60	62.16	88.87

MORTGAGE PAY-OFF TABLE

Select the interest rate and the term of the mortgage and read the percent paid off at any stage along the way.

PAY-OFF TABLE—*shows % paid off*

30 YEAR LOAN—*% paid off*

INT	5YR	10YR	15YR	20YR	25YR	28YR
6 1/2	6.38	15.22	27.44	44.33	67.69	85.81
7	5.86	14.18	25.98	42.69	66.40	85.14
7 1/2	5.38	13.20	24.57	41.09	65.10	84.46
7 3/4	5.15	12.73	23.88	40.30	64.45	84.11
8	4.93	12.27	23.21	39.52	63.81	83.77
8 1/4	4.71	11.82	22.56	38.74	63.16	83.43
8 1/2	4.50	11.39	21.91	37.98	62.52	83.08
8 3/4	4.31	10.97	21.28	37.22	61.87	82.73
9	4.11	10.57	20.66	36.48	61.23	82.38
9 1/4	3.93	10.17	20.06	35.74	60.59	82.03
9 1/2	3.75	9.79	19.47	35.01	59.96	81.68
9 3/4	3.58	9.42	18.89	34.30	59.32	81.33
9 7/8	3.50	9.24	18.61	33.94	59.01	81.15
10	3.42	9.06	18.33	33.59	58.69	80.98
10 1/8	3.34	8.88	18.05	33.24	58.38	80.80
10 1/4	3.26	8.71	17.78	32.89	58.06	80.62
10 3/8	3.19	8.54	17.51	32.55	57.75	80.45
10 1/2	3.11	8.37	17.24	32.20	57.44	80.27
10 5/8	3.04	8.21	16.98	31.86	57.13	80.09
10 3/4	2.97	8.05	16.72	31.53	56.81	79.92
10 7/8	2.90	7.89	16.46	31.19	56.50	79.74
11	2.83	7.73	16.21	30.86	56.19	79.56
11 1/8	2.76	7.58	15.96	30.53	55.89	79.39
11 1/4	2.70	7.43	15.71	30.20	55.58	79.21
11 3/8	2.63	7.28	15.46	29.88	55.27	79.03

32 YEAR LOAN—*% paid off*

INT	5YR	10YR	15YR	20YR	25YR	28YR
6 1/2	5.50	13.10	23.62	38.16	58.28	73.87
7	5.01	12.11	22.18	36.46	56.71	72.71
7 1/2	4.55	11.18	20.81	34.81	55.15	71.55
7 3/4	4.34	10.74	20.15	34.00	54.37	70.96
8	4.14	10.31	19.50	33.20	53.61	70.38
8 1/4	3.94	9.89	18.87	32.41	52.84	69.79
8 1/2	3.75	9.49	18.25	31.64	52.08	69.21
8 3/4	3.57	9.10	17.65	30.88	51.33	68.63
9	3.40	8.73	17.07	30.13	50.58	68.04
9 1/4	3.23	8.36	16.50	29.39	49.83	67.46
9 1/2	3.07	8.01	15.94	28.67	49.09	66.88
9 3/4	2.92	7.68	15.40	27.96	48.36	66.30
9 7/8	2.85	7.51	15.14	27.61	48.00	66.01
10	2.78	7.35	14.88	27.26	47.63	65.72
10 1/8	2.71	7.19	14.62	26.92	47.27	65.43
10 1/4	2.64	7.04	14.37	26.58	46.92	65.15
10 3/8	2.57	6.88	14.12	26.24	46.56	64.86
10 1/2	2.50	6.73	13.87	25.90	46.20	64.57
10 5/8	2.44	6.59	13.63	25.57	45.85	64.28
10 3/4	2.38	6.44	13.39	25.25	45.50	64.00
10 7/8	2.32	6.30	13.15	24.92	45.15	63.71
11	2.26	6.16	12.92	24.60	44.80	63.43
11 1/8	2.20	6.03	12.69	24.28	44.45	63.14
11 1/4	2.14	5.89	12.47	23.97	44.11	62.86
11 3/8	2.08	5.76	12.24	23.66	43.76	62.58

EVEN TOTAL CONSTANT PERCENTAGE

Select an interest rate and the total constant payment, and read the term and the percent paid off along the way.

EVEN TOTAL CONSTANT PERCENT

TOTAL CONSTANT RATE	INT-EREST RATE	PERCENT PAID OFF IN				FULL TERM	
		5YR	10YR	15YR	20YR	YRS	MOS
8%	6 1/2	8.83	21.05	37.94	61.30	25	10
	6 5/8	8.12	19.43	35.16	57.04	26	8
	6 3/4	7.41	17.78	32.31	52.65	27	7
	6 7/8	6.69	16.12	29.39	48.10	28	8
	7	5.97	14.42	26.41	43.41	29	10
8½%	6 1/2	11.78	28.07	50.59	81.74	22	4
	6 5/8	11.08	26.49	47.94	77.79	22	11
	6 3/4	10.37	24.90	45.23	73.70	23	6
	6 7/8	9.66	23.28	42.46	69.48	24	2
	7	8.95	21.64	39.62	65.12	24	11
	7 1/8	8.23	19.97	36.72	60.60	25	8
	7 1/4	7.51	18.28	33.74	55.94	26	7
	7 3/8	6.78	16.57	30.70	51.12	27	7
	7 1/2	6.04	14.83	27.59	46.14	28	8
9%	6 1/2	14.72	35.08	63.24		19	10
	6 5/8	14.03	33.56	60.73	98.53	20	2
	6 3/4	13.34	32.01	58.16	94.76	20	8
	6 7/8	12.64	30.44	55.52	90.86	21	1
	7	11.93	28.85	52.83	86.82	21	7
	7 1/8	11.22	27.23	50.07	82.64	22	1
	7 1/4	10.51	25.59	47.24	78.32	22	8
	7 3/8	9.79	23.93	44.35	73.84	23	4
	7 1/2	9.07	22.24	41.39	69.22	24	0
	7 5/8	8.34	20.53	38.36	64.43	24	9
	7 3/4	7.60	18.79	35.26	59.48	25	7
	7 7/8	6.87	17.03	32.08	54.37	26	6
	8	6.12	15.25	28.84	49.09	27	7

EVEN TOTAL CONSTANT PERCENT

TOTAL CONSTANT RATE	INT-EREST RATE	PERCENT PAID OFF IN				FULL TERM	
		5YR	10YR	15YR	20YR	YRS	MOS
9½%	6 1/2	17.67	42.10	75.89		17	10
	6 5/8	16.99	40.62	73.51		18	2
	6 3/4	16.30	39.12	71.08		18	6
	6 7/8	15.61	37.60	68.59		18	10
	7	14.92	36.06	66.03		19	2
	7 1/8	14.22	34.49	63.42		19	7
	7 1/4	13.51	32.90	60.74		20	0
	7 3/8	12.80	31.29	58.00	96.56	20	5
	7 1/2	12.09	29.66	55.19	92.29	20	11
	7 5/8	11.37	28.00	52.31	87.86	21	5
	7 3/4	10.65	26.31	49.36	83.28	21	11
	7 7/8	9.92	24.60	46.34	78.54	22	6
	8	9.18	22.87	43.25	73.63	23	2
	8 1/8	8.45	21.11	40.09	68.55	23	11
	8 1/4	7.70	19.32	36.85	63.30	24	9
	8 3/8	6.96	17.51	33.54	57.87	25	7
	8 1/2	6.20	15.68	30.15	52.25	26	7
	8 5/8	5.45	13.82	26.68	46.44	27	9
	8 3/4	4.68	11.93	23.12	40.44	29	2
	8 7/8	3.92	10.01	19.49	34.24	30	10
	9	3.14	8.06	15.77	27.83	32	11
10%	6 1/2	20.61	49.12	88.53		16	3
	6 5/8	19.94	47.69	86.30		16	6
	6 3/4	19.26	46.24	84.00		16	9
	6 7/8	18.58	44.77	81.65		17	0
	7	17.90	43.27	79.24		17	3
	7 1/8	17.21	41.75	76.77		17	7
	7 1/4	16.51	40.22	74.24		17	11
	7 3/8	15.81	38.65	71.64		18	3
	7 1/2	15.11	37.07	68.98		18	7
	7 5/8	14.40	35.46	66.26		18	11
	7 3/4	13.69	33.83	63.46		19	4
	7 7/8	12.97	32.17	60.60		19	9
	8	12.25	30.49	57.67	98.17	20	3
	8 1/8	11.52	28.79	54.67	93.48	20	9
	8 1/4	10.79	27.05	51.60	88.62	21	3
	8 3/8	10.05	25.30	48.45	83.58	21	10
	8 1/2	9.31	23.52	45.22	78.37	22	5
	8 5/8	8.56	21.71	41.92	72.98	23	2
	8 3/4	7.81	19.88	38.54	67.40	23	11
	8 7/8	7.05	18.01	35.08	61.63	24	9
	9	6.29	16.13	31.53	55.66	25	9
	9 1/8	5.52	14.21	27.91	49.48	26	10
	9 1/4	4.75	12.27	24.19	43.09	28	2
	9 3/8	3.97	10.30	20.39	36.49	29	9
	9 1/2	3.18	8.30	16.50	29.66	31	8

EVEN TOTAL CONSTANT PERCENTAGE

Select an interest rate and the total constant payment, and read the term and the percent paid off along the way.

EVEN TOTAL CONSTANT PERCENT

TOTAL CONSTANT RATE	INT- EREST RATE	PERCENT PAID OFF IN 5YR	10YR	15YR	20YR	FULL TERM YRS	MOS
	6 1/2	23.56	56.13			14	11
	6 3/4	22.23	53.35	96.93		15	4
	7	20.88	50.48	92.45		15	9
	7 1/8	20.20	49.02	90.12		16	0
	7 1/4	19.52	47.53	87.73		16	3
	7 3/8	18.83	46.02	85.29		16	6
	7 1/2	18.13	44.48	82.78		16	10
	7 5/8	17.43	42.93	80.21		17	1
	7 3/4	16.73	41.35	77.57		17	5
	7 7/8	16.02	39.74	74.86		17	8
10½%	8	15.31	38.11	72.09		18	0
	8 1/8	14.59	36.46	69.25		18	5
	8 1/4	13.87	34.78	66.34		18	9
	8 3/8	13.14	33.08	63.36		19	2
	8 1/2	12.41	31.36	60.30		19	7
	8 5/8	11.67	29.60	57.17	99.52	20	1
	8 3/4	10.93	27.83	53.96	94.36	20	7
	8 7/8	10.18	26.02	50.67	89.02	21	2
	9	9.43	24.19	47.30	83.49	21	9
	9 1/8	8.67	22.33	43.85	77.76	22	5
	9 1/4	7.91	20.45	40.32	71.82	23	2
	9 3/8	7.14	18.53	36.70	65.68	24	0
	9 1/2	6.37	16.59	33.00	59.33	24	11
	9 3/4	4.81	12.62	25.32	45.95	27	3
	10	3.23	8.54	17.27	31.64	30	7
	7	23.86	57.69			14	6
	7 1/4	22.52	54.84			14	11
	7 1/2	21.15	51.90	96.57		15	4
	7 5/8	20.46	50.39	94.15		15	7
	7 3/4	19.77	48.86	91.67		15	10
	7 7/8	19.07	47.31	89.12		16	1
	8	18.37	45.74	86.51		16	4
	8 1/8	17.66	44.14	83.83		16	7
	8 1/4	16.95	42.51	81.08		16	11
	8 3/8	16.23	40.87	78.26		17	3
11%	8 1/2	15.51	39.20	75.37		17	6
	8 5/8	14.78	37.50	72.41		17	11
	8 3/4	14.05	35.78	69.37		18	3
	8 7/8	13.31	34.03	66.26		18	8
	9	12.57	32.25	63.07		19	1
	9 1/8	11.82	30.45	59.80		19	6
	9 1/4	11.07	28.62	56.45		20	0
	9 3/8	10.31	26.77	53.01	94.87	20	6
	9 1/2	9.55	24.89	49.49	88.99	21	1
	9 5/8	8.79	22.97	45.89	82.90	21	9
	9 3/4	8.01	21.04	42.20	76.58	22	5
	9 7/8	7.24	19.07	38.41	70.05	23	3
	10	6.45	17.07	34.54	63.28	24	1
	10 1/4	4.87	12.99	26.51	49.03	26	4
	10 1/2	3.27	8.78	18.08	33.77	29	7

EVEN TOTAL CONSTANT PERCENT

TOTAL CONSTANT RATE	INT- EREST RATE	PERCENT PAID OFF IN 5YR	10YR	15YR	20YR	FULL TERM YRS	MOS
	7	26.85	64.91			13	6
	7 1/4	25.52	62.15			13	10
	7 1/2	24.18	59.31			14	2
	7 3/4	22.81	56.38			14	7
	8	21.43	53.36			15	0
	8 1/8	20.73	51.81	98.41		15	2
	8 1/4	20.03	50.24	95.82		15	5
	8 3/8	19.32	48.65	93.17		15	8
	8 1/2	18.61	47.03	90.45		15	11
	8 5/8	17.89	45.39	87.65		16	2
11½%	8 3/4	17.17	43.73	84.79		16	5
	8 7/8	16.45	42.03	81.85		16	9
	9	15.71	40.32	78.83		17	1
	9 1/8	14.98	38.57	75.74		17	5
	9 1/4	14.24	36.80	72.57		17	9
	9 3/8	13.49	35.00	69.32		18	1
	9 1/2	12.74	33.18	65.99		18	6
	9 5/8	11.98	31.33	62.58		19	0
	9 3/4	11.22	29.45	59.07		19	5
	9 7/8	10.45	27.54	55.49		19	11
	10	9.68	25.61	51.81	94.92	20	6
	10 1/4	8.12	21.65	44.18	81.71	21	9
	10 1/2	6.54	17.57	36.17	67.54	23	5
	10 3/4	4.94	13.37	27.76	52.35	25	7
	11	3.31	9.04	18.95	36.07	28	8
	7	29.83	72.12			12	7
	7 1/4	28.52	69.46			12	10
	7 1/2	27.20	66.72			13	2
	7 3/4	25.85	63.90			13	6
	8	24.49	60.98			13	10
	8 1/8	23.80	59.49			14	0
	8 1/4	23.11	57.97			14	2
	8 3/8	22.41	56.44			14	5
	8 1/2	21.71	54.87			14	7
	8 5/8	21.01	53.29			14	10
12%	8 3/4	20.29	51.68			15	0
	8 7/8	19.58	50.04	97.44		15	3
	9	18.86	48.38	94.60		15	6
	9 1/8	18.13	46.69	91.69		15	9
	9 1/4	17.40	44.98	88.70		16	0
	9 3/8	16.66	43.24	85.63		16	4
	9 1/2	15.92	41.48	82.49		16	7
	9 5/8	15.18	39.68	79.26		16	11
	9 3/4	14.42	37.86	75.95		17	3
	9 7/8	13.67	36.02	72.56		17	8
	10	12.91	34.14	69.08		18	0
	10 1/4	11.37	30.30	61.85		18	11
	10 1/2	9.81	26.35	54.25		19	11
	10 3/4	8.23	22.28	46.27	87.24	21	2
	11	6.63	18.08	37.89	72.14	22	9

EVEN TOTAL CONSTANT PERCENTAGE

Select an interest rate and the total constant payment, and read the term and the percent paid off along the way.

EVEN TOTAL CONSTANT PERCENT

TOTAL CONSTANT RATE	INT-EREST RATE	5YR	10YR	15YR	20YR	YRS	MOS
12½%	7	32.81	79.33			11	10
	7 1/4	31.53	76.78			12	1
	7 1/2	30.22	74.14			12	4
	7 3/4	28.90	71.41			12	7
	8	27.55	68.60			12	10
	8 1/8	26.88	67.17			13	0
	8 1/4	26.19	65.70			13	2
	8 3/8	25.51	64.22			13	4
	8 1/2	24.81	62.71			13	6
	8 5/8	24.12	61.18			13	8
	8 3/4	23.42	59.63			13	10
	8 7/8	22.71	58.05			14	0
	9	22.00	56.44			14	3
	9 1/8	21.28	54.81			14	5
	9 1/4	20.56	53.16			14	8
	9 3/8	19.84	51.48			14	11
	9 1/2	19.11	49.77	98.99		15	1
	9 5/8	18.37	48.04	95.95		15	4
	9 3/4	17.63	46.28	92.83		15	8
	9 7/8	16.88	44.49	89.63		15	11
	10	16.13	42.68	86.35		16	2
	10 1/4	14.62	38.96	79.52		16	10
	10 1/2	13.08	35.14	72.34		17	7
	10 3/4	11.52	31.19	64.78		18	5
	11	9.94	27.12	56.84		19	5
13%	7	35.80	86.54			11	1
	7 1/4	34.53	84.09			11	4
	7 1/2	33.24	81.55			11	7
	7 3/4	31.94	78.93			11	9
	8	30.62	76.23			12	0
	8 1/8	29.95	74.84			12	2
	8 1/4	29.27	73.43			12	3
	8 3/8	28.60	72.00			12	5
	8 1/2	27.92	70.55			12	7
	8 5/8	27.23	69.08			12	9
	8 3/4	26.54	67.58			12	10
	8 7/8	25.84	66.05			13	0
	9	25.14	64.50			13	2
	9 1/8	24.44	62.93			13	4
	9 1/4	23.73	61.34			13	6
	9 3/8	23.01	59.71			13	9
	9 1/2	22.29	58.07			13	11
	9 5/8	21.56	56.39			14	1
	9 3/4	20.83	54.69			14	4
	9 7/8	20.10	52.96			14	6
	10	19.36	51.21			14	9
	10 1/4	17.86	47.62	97.19		15	3
	10 1/2	16.35	43.92	90.42		15	10
	10 3/4	14.81	40.10	83.29		16	5
	11	13.25	36.17	75.78		17	2

EVEN TOTAL CONSTANT PERCENT

TOTAL CONSTANT RATE	INT-EREST RATE	5YR	10YR	15YR	20YR	YRS	MOS
13½%	7	38.78	93.75			10	6
	7 1/4	37.53	91.40			10	8
	7 1/2	36.26	88.97			10	11
	7 3/4	34.98	86.45			11	1
	8	33.68	83.85			11	4
	8 1/8	33.02	82.52			11	5
	8 1/4	32.36	81.16			11	6
	8 3/8	31.69	79.79			11	8
	8 1/2	31.02	78.39			11	9
	8 5/8	30.34	76.97			11	11
	8 3/4	29.66	75.53			12	0
	8 7/8	28.97	74.06			12	2
	9	28.28	72.57			12	4
	9 1/8	27.59	71.05			12	5
	9 1/4	26.89	69.51			12	7
	9 3/8	26.18	67.95			12	9
	9 1/2	25.47	66.36			12	11
	9 5/8	24.76	64.75			13	1
	9 3/4	24.04	63.11			13	3
	9 7/8	23.32	61.44			13	5
	10	22.59	59.75			13	7
	10 1/4	21.11	56.28			14	0
	10 1/2	19.62	52.70			14	5
	10 3/4	18.10	49.01			14	11
	11	16.57	45.21	94.73		15	5
14%	7	41.76				10	0
	7 1/4	40.53	98.71			10	2
	7 1/2	39.29	96.38			10	4
	7 3/4	38.02	93.97			10	6
	8	36.74	91.47			10	8
	8 1/8	36.09	90.19			10	9
	8 1/4	35.44	88.89			10	10
	8 3/8	34.78	87.57			11	0
	8 1/2	34.12	86.23			11	1
	8 5/8	33.45	84.86			11	2
	8 3/4	32.78	83.48			11	4
	8 7/8	32.11	82.07			11	5
	9	31.43	80.63			11	6
	9 1/8	30.74	79.17			11	8
	9 1/4	30.05	77.69			11	9
	9 3/8	29.36	76.19			11	11
	9 1/2	28.66	74.66			12	0
	9 5/8	27.95	73.10			12	2
	9 3/4	27.25	71.52			12	4
	9 7/8	26.53	69.91			12	6
	10	25.81	68.28			12	7
	10 1/4	24.36	64.94			12	11
	10 1/2	22.89	61.49			13	4
	10 3/4	21.39	57.93			13	8
	11	19.88	54.25			14	1

THE PRESENT VALUE OF $1.00 DUE AT VARIOUS TIMES
IN THE FUTURE AND AT VARIOUS RATES OF INTEREST

Year	5%	6%	7%	8%	9%	10%
1	.952	.943	.935	.926	.917	.909
2	.907	.890	.873	.857	.842	.826
3	.864	.840	.816	.794	.772	.751
4	.823	.792	.763	.735	.708	.683
5	.784	.747	.713	.681	.650	.621
6	.746	.705	.666	.630	.596	.564
7	.711	.665	.623	.583	.547	.513
8	.677	.627	.582	.540	.502	.467
9	.645	.592	.544	.500	.460	.424
10	.614	.558	.508	.463	.422	.386
11	.585	.527	.475	.429	.388	.350
12	.557	.497	.444	.397	.356	.319
13	.530	.469	.415	.368	.326	.290
14	.505	.442	.388	.340	.299	.263
15	.481	.417	.362	.315	.275	.239
16	.458	.394	.339	.292	.252	.218
17	.436	.371	.317	.270	.231	.198
18	.416	.350	.296	.250	.211	.180
19	.396	.331	.277	.232	.194	.164
20	.377	.312	.258	.215	.178	.149
21	.359	.294	.242	.199	.164	.135
22	.342	.278	.226	.184	.150	.123
23	.326	.262	.211	.170	.138	.112
24	.310	.247	.197	.158	.126	.102
25	.295	.233	.184	.146	.116	.092
26	.281	.220	.172	.135	.106	.084
27	.268	.207	.161	.125	.098	.076
28	.255	.196	.150	.116	.090	.069
29	.243	.185	.141	.107	.082	.063
30	.231	.174	.131	.099	.075	.057
31	.220	.164	.123	.092	.069	.052
32	.210	.155	.115	.085	.063	.047
33	.200	.146	.107	.079	.058	.043
34	.190	.138	.100	.073	.053	.039
35	.181	.130	.094	.068	.049	.036
36	.173	.123	.088	.063	.045	.032
37	.164	.116	.082	.058	.041	.029
38	.157	.109	.076	.054	.038	.027
39	.149	.103	.071	.050	.035	.024
40	.142	.097	.067	.046	.032	.022

PERCENTAGE OF PRINCIPAL UNPAID
AT END OF 5-10-15 YEARS
BY INTEREST RATE

LOAN TERM	5 YEARS									
	6%	6½%	6.9%	7%	7.2%	7½%	7⅜%	8%	9%	10%
10 Years	57	58	59	59	59	59	59	60	61	62
15 Years	76	77	77	77	78	78	78	79	80	81
20 Years	85	86	86	86	86	87	87	88	89	90
25 Years	90	91	91	91	91	92	92	92	93	94
30 Years	93	94	94	94	94	95	95	95	96	97

LOAN TERM	10 YEARS									
	6%	6½%	6.9%	7%	7.2%	7½%	7⅜%	8%	9%	10%
15 Years	44	44	45	45	46	46	46	47	49	50
20 Years	64	66	66	67	67	68	68	69	71	73
25 Years	76	77	78	79	79	80	80	81	83	84
30 Years	84	85	86	86	86	87	87	88	89	91

LOAN TERM	15 YEARS									
	6%	6½%	6.9%	7%	7.2%	7½%	7⅝%	8%	9%	10%
20 Years	37	38	39	39	39	40	40	41	43	45
25 Years	58	59	60	61	61	62	62	64	66	69
30 Years	71	72	74	74	75	75	76	77	79	81

Appendix III

Code of Ethics

REALTOR®

NATIONAL ASSOCIATION OF REALTORS®

As Approved by the
DELEGATE BODY OF THE ASSOCIATION
at its 67th Annual Convention
NOVEMBER 14, 1974

* * * * *

Preamble . . .

Under all is the land. Upon its wise utilization and widely allocated ownership depend the survival and growth of free institutions and of our civilization. The REALTOR® should recognize that the interests of the nation and its citizens require the highest and best use of the land and the widest distribution of land ownership. They require the creation of adequate housing, the building of functioning cities, the development of productive industries and farms, and the preservation of a healthful environment.

Such interests impose obligations beyond those of ordinary commerce. They impose grave social responsibility and a patriotic duty to which the REALTOR® should dedicate himself, and for which he should be diligent in preparing himself. The REALTOR®, therefore, is zealous to maintain and improve the standards of his calling and shares with his fellow-REALTORS® a common responsibility for its integrity and honor. The term REALTOR® has come to connote competency, fairness, and high integrity resulting from adherence to a lofty ideal of moral conduct in business relations. No inducement of profit and no instruction from clients ever can justify departure from this ideal.

In the interpretation of his obligation, a REALTOR® can take no safer guide than that which has been handed down through the centuries, embodied in the Golden Rule, "Whatsoever ye would that men should do to you, do ye even so to them."

Accepting this standard as his own, every REALTOR® pledges himself to observe its spirit in all of his activities and to conduct his business in accordance with the tenets set forth below.

ARTICLE 1

The REALTOR® should keep himself informed on matters affecting real estate in his community, the state, and nation so that he may be able to contribute responsibly to public thinking on such matters.

ARTICLE 2

In justice to those who place their interests in his care, the REALTOR® should endeavor always to be informed regarding laws, proposed legislation, governmental regulations, public policies, and current market conditions in order to be in a position to advise his clients properly.

ARTICLE 3

It is the duty of the REALTOR® to protect the public against fraud, misrepresentation, and unethical practices in real estate transactions. He should endeavor to eliminate in his community any practices which could be damaging to the public or bring discredit to the real estate profession. The REALTOR® should assist the governmental agency charged with regulating the practices of brokers and salesmen in his state.

ARTICLE 4

The REALTOR® should seek no unfair advantage over other REALTORS® and should conduct his business so as to avoid controversies with other REALTORS®.

ARTICLE 5

In the best interests of society, of his associates, and his own business, the REALTOR® should willingly share with other REALTORS® the lessons of his experience and study for the benefit of the public, and should be loyal to the Board of REALTORS® of his community and active in its work.

ARTICLE 6

To prevent dissension and misunderstanding and to assure better service to the owner, the REALTOR® should urge the exclusive listing of property unless contrary to the best interest of the owner.

ARTICLE 7

In accepting employment as an agent, the REALTOR® pledges himself to protect and promote the interests of the client. This obligation of absolute fidelity to the client's interests is primary, but it does not relieve the REALTOR® of the obligation to treat fairly all parties to the transaction.

ARTICLE 8

The REALTOR® shall not accept compensation from more than one party, even if permitted by law, without the full knowledge of all parties to the transaction.

ARTICLE 9

The REALTOR® shall avoid exaggeration, misrepresentation, or concealment of pertinent facts. He has an affirmative obligation to discover adverse factors that a reasonably competent and diligent investigation would disclose.

ARTICLE 10

The REALTOR® shall not deny equal professional services to any person for reasons of race, creed, sex, or country of national origin. The REALTOR® shall not be a party to any plan or agreement to discriminate against a person or persons on the basis of race, creed, sex, or country of national origin.

ARTICLE 11

A REALTOR® is expected to provide a level of competent service in keeping with the Standards of Practice in those fields in which the REALTOR® customarily engages.

The REALTOR® shall not undertake to provide specialized professional services concerning a type of property or service that is outside his field of competence unless he engages the assistance of one who is competent on such types of property or service, or unless the facts are fully disclosed to the client. Any person engaged to provide such assistance shall be so identified to the client and his contribution to the assignment should be set forth.

The REALTOR® shall refer to the Standards of Practice of the National Association as to the degree of competence that a client has a right to expect the REALTOR® to possess, taking into consideration the complexity of the problem, the availability of expert assistance, and the opportunities for experience available to the REALTOR®.

ARTICLE 12

The REALTOR® shall not undertake to provide professional services concerning a property or its value where he has a present or contemplated interest unless such interest is specifically disclosed to all affected parties.

ARTICLE 13

The REALTOR® shall not acquire an interest in or buy for himself, any member of his immediate family, his firm or any member thereof, or any entity in which he has a substantial ownership interest, property listed with him, without making the true position known to the listing owner. In selling property owned by himself, or in which he has any interest, the REALTOR® shall reveal the facts of his ownership or interest to the purchaser.

ARTICLE 14

In the event of a controversy between REALTORS® associated with different firms, arising out of their relationship as REALTORS®, the REALTORS® shall submit the dispute to arbitration in accordance with the regulations of their board or boards rather than litigate the matter.

ARTICLE 15

If a REALTOR® is charged with unethical practice or is asked to present evidence in any disciplinary proceeding or investigation, he shall place all pertinent facts before the proper tribunal of the member board or affiliated institute, society, or council of which he is a member.

ARTICLE 16

When acting as agent, the REALTOR® shall not accept any commission, rebate, or profit on expenditures made for his principal-owner, without the principal's knowledge and consent.

ARTICLE 17

The REALTOR® shall not engage in activities that constitute the unauthorized practice of law and shall recommend that legal counsel be obtained when the interest of any party to the transaction requires it.

ARTICLE 18

The REALTOR® shall keep in a special account in an appropriate financial institution, separated from his own funds, monies coming into his possession in trust for other persons, such as escrows, trust funds, clients' monies, and other like items.

ARTICLE 19

The REALTOR® shall be careful at all times to present a true picture in his advertising and representations to the public. He shall neither advertise without disclosing his name nor permit any person associated with him to use individual names or telephone numbers, unless such person's connection with the REALTOR® is obvious in the advertisement.

ARTICLE 20

The REALTOR®, for the protection of all parties, shall see that financial obligations and commitments regarding real estate transactions are in writing, expressing the exact agreement of the parties. A copy of each agreement shall be furnished to each party upon his signing such agreement.

ARTICLE 21

The REALTOR® shall not engage in any practice or take any action inconsistent with the agency of another REALTOR®.

ARTICLE 22

In the sale of property which is exclusively listed with a REALTOR®, the REALTOR® shall utilize the services of other brokers upon mutually agreed upon terms when it is in the best interests of the client.

Negotiations concerning property which is listed exclusively shall be carried on with the listing broker, not with the owner, except with the consent of the listing broker.

ARTICLE 23

The REALTOR® shall not publicly disparage the business practice of a competitor nor volunteer an opinion of a competitor's transaction. If his opinion is sought and if the REALTOR® deems it appropriate to respond, such opinion shall be rendered with strict professional integrity and courtesy.

ARTICLE 24

The REALTOR® shall not directly or indirectly solicit the services or affiliation of an employee or independent contractor in the organization of another REALTOR® without prior notice to said REALTOR®.

NOTE: Where the word REALTOR® is used in this Code and Preamble, it shall be deemed to include REALTOR®-ASSOCIATE. Pronouns shall be considered to include REALTORS® and REALTOR®-ASSOCIATES of both genders.

The Code of Ethics was adopted in 1913. Amended at the Annual Convention in 1924, 1928, 1950, 1951, 1952, 1955, 1956, 1961, 1962, and 1974.

Index

A

B

293